Montgano

THE AMERICAN G. I. FORUM:
ORIGINS AND EVOLUTION

MONOGRAPH NUMBER 6
CENTER FOR MEXICAN AMERICAN STUDIES
THE UNIVERSITY OF TEXAS AT AUSTIN

The American G. I. Forum: Origins and Evolution

By

CARL ALLSUP

CENTER FOR MEXICAN AMERICAN STUDIES
THE UNIVERSITY OF TEXAS AT AUSTIN

The Mexican American Monograph Series is published by the Center for Mexican American Studies of The University of Texas at Austin.

International Standard Book Number 0-292-70362-7
Library of Congress Catalog Card Number 82-72812

The Mexican American Monograph Series is distributed for the
Center for Mexican American Studies by
> University of Texas Press
> P.O. Box 7819
> Austin, Texas 78712

FOR ANNA

Contents

Preface

The presence of Chicano people is now a documented fact. NBC recently produced a two-hour special, "We're Moving Up". Demographic experts and politicans have projected Hispanic folks as the most populous minority in the United States by the latter 1980's. Paul Ehrlich applies his considerable talents to an analysis of Mexican immigration to the United States and mentions the presence of Chicanos as an important factor. All sorts of revelations will now illuminate this "new reality". Perhaps American history textbooks will eventually include a chapter on Chicanos instead of a few sentences. Enlightenment is just around the corner.

If anyone desires facts instead of media fantasy and WASP "discoveries", a considerable body of literature is available. Pioneers and recent scholars have produced many accounts of the Chicano experience; everything from polemical diatribes to narrative and analysis of the highest quality is available. The major publishers, both academic and commercial, have been somewhat reluctant to accept these materials. Fortunately, Latino presses have filled the vacuum; Chicano and Mexican American studies centers are "establishing" themselves with major presses; occasionally a well-known publisher takes a chance.

The historical component of this literature includes studies on the more obvious areas of importance. Immigration, agriculture and the radicalization of the 1960's have received major emphasis. One particular gap is the organizational activities of Chicanos. Many theories have been proposed on the nature of such development, but nothing in the manner of specific organizational history is available to buttress or challenge those theories. Hopefully this work will contribute to that need.

This study was made possible by a remarkable man. As a graduate student at the University of Texas, and searching for a dissertation topic in Chicano history, I learned of an organization called the American G.I. Forum. My wife's uncle, Ignacio Moreno, was a charter member of the Jr. G.I. Forum in Lamesa, Texas. This small West Texas town contained all the typical Anglo Texas prejudices against Mexican Americans, an attitude exacerbated by the presence of many migrant workers. I became fascinated by Nacho's descriptions of the Forum's activities during the 1950's in the midst of the hostile atmosphere of Lamesa. Nacho told me about Dr. Hector Garcia, the founder of the G.I. Forum, and suggested a history of the organization as a potentially valuable contribution to Chicano scholarship.

When I met Dr. Garcia in Corpus Christi, Texas, he agreed to open his files to me without any qualifications. In his office was the accumulated raw data of the Forum since its inception in 1948. Every conceivable type of primary material could be found in over seventy file cabinet drawers.

The basis of this study is the archives of the G.I. Forum, maintained by Dr. Hector Garcia of Corpus Christi, Texas. If I am a prisoner of the material, so be it. However, a historian is assumed to have a fair, if not objective, perspective of the process of history. If the theme or the presentation of a certain view is unduly biased, then the always present critics will rightfully denounce that bias. But if the research, data, or "primary sources" have an important story, then it must be told. The theme of this research is clear: the Mexican American people did not suddenly become aware of the problems confronting them in the turbulent decade of the sixties. Nor did an "awakened minority" flounder among an Anglo-manipulated society until rescued by proponents of *La Raza.* Americans of Mexican origin have fought for their place in American society throughout the twentieth century. One of the most important periods of this struggle began in the immediate years after World War II. Returning veterans did not accept the subordinate status that Anglo America felt was a proper and traditional "place" for these people. The cutting edge of this movement was the American G.I. Forum. Beginning in Texas and spreading throughout the United States, Mexican American Forumeers established the "identity" of *Mexicanos,* pursued policies and programs beneficial to all minorities, and represented *la gente* most ably. As the more militant and young Chicanos of the 1960's demanded the rights of Americans, the G.I. Forum continued its opposition to prejudice and its advocacy for Mexican Americans. Indeed, I contend that the Chicano movement was a natural transition of the 1950's; the groundwork was laid by people like the members of the American G.I. Forum.

Some of the terms or labels used in this project require some explanation. Latin American, Spanish-speaking, Spanish-surname, *la gente* (the people), and Chicano mean Mexican Americans. (The first three can also apply to any Spanish-oriented ethnic group, such as *puerto riqueños.)* I have attempted to use the term Latin American sparingly and only in its chronological period, 1945 to the late 1950's. "Spanish-speaking" and "Spanish-surname" are used when they are part of statistical data or study (most often, demographical investigation has employed those terms for Mexican American, a questionable practice at best) or are present in quotations or titles. Mexican American is probably the most inclusive name and is used more than the other descriptive nouns. "Chicano", an important political term, does not appear as much as "Mexican American" because of my intention to describe the activists of the Forum as they saw themselves. While many Forumeers now call themselves "Chicanos", my decision to emphasize "Mexican American" represents the dominant term used by members of the American G.I. Forum at various periods. I have frequently employed *Mexicano* in describing Mexican Americans. It is the most common word in the vernacular of the Southwest.

Many individuals were prominent in their support of my endeavor. Dr. Hector Pérez Garcia is a central figure of this history, and is also a passionate, caring individual who is deeply committed to the progress of his people. Because he had the rare quality of historical perspective, this project is a reality. Clarence "Bud" Lasby of the University of Texas served as the official advisor for my dissertation. While encouraging me to formulate my own analysis and conclusion, Dr. Lasby also demanded rigid scholarly presentation. If the historical process in this study and the validity of its theme is clear, Bud Lasby deserves much of the credit; if it is not obvious, one can only say that the lack occurs despite his efforts, not because of them. Leodoro Hernandez of Stanislaus State College has provided constant suggestions as to the climate of the 1950's for Mexican Americans; his own experiences have provided valuable guideposts. Barry Johnston of Indiana University Northwest was instrumental in the fellowship and course reduction given me by IUN for this project. Jack Bloom, also of Indiana University Northwest, took the time to critically assess the conclusion—as his research deals with the civil rights movement of the post-war period, his assistance was welcomed.

Lastly, I must thank a very important person in my life. Anna Marie Zamarripa Allsup contributed more to this thesis than even she knows. Not because she typed and edited numerous revisions, or because of her constant support—after all, I expected that. More importantly, Anna Marie's life is a testament to that quality called "human dignity" and self-awareness. She has never felt "subordinate" or "underprivileged" or "culturally deprived". She and her family, have struggled and succeeded against many obstacles—her sense of that experience is a vital part of whatever worth this book may have.

Dr. Hector Perez Garcia, founder of the American G.I. Forum and first Mexican American appointed to the U.S. Commission on Civil Rights, delivers a speech in support of the farmworkers cause at the state capitol, Austin, Texas, 1979.

(photo by Allen Pogue)

THE AMERICAN G. I. FORUM:
ORIGINS AND EVOLUTION

CHAPTER I

Land of the Free, Home of the Brave

The relationship between Spain and the United States had been tenuous at best. The Spanish leaders did not enjoy the "spectre of colonies in revolt" and did not endorse the American Revolution. Although France, the major ally of the thirteen colonies, did convince Spain to declare war against Great Britain in a secret alliance, the United States was not recognized as an independent nation. The Spanish goal of retaking Gibraltar from Great Britain failed miserably: Spain never accepted American ambassadors, and became the first of the major nations to seek peace with Great Britain, thus undermining the designs of the United States in the negotiations.

The United States did not exactly display warmth and friendship toward Spain. After the revolution, one of the most difficult problems was the matter of expansion. Manifest Destiny did not suddenly appear in the 1840's; the idea and its implementation are constant in American history. The first European nation to confront that reality after 1783 was Spain. American settlers needed the Mississippi River; Spain did not appreciate the constant expansionist movement and closed it down. Twelve years of procrastination, futility, intrigue, and comedy ended with the Treaty of San Lorenzo (in American textbook lexicon, Pinckney's Treaty). Spain surrendered to the pressures and potential unleashed by the French Revolution. Reflecting on a possible alliance between the United States and Great Britain and recognizing the reality of American population growth in the area, Spain agreed to all American demands, the most important being full use of the Mississippi.[1]

The nineteenth century only increased the difficulties encountered by Spanish officials in protecting its holdings in North America. Congress staked out the Floridas as an area of imminent U.S. ownership. American leaders expressed their delight with the revolt of the Spanish Americas. Although no substantive aid was ever dispatched to the revolutionaries, the United States did recognize the independence of the new nations before any European state. After 1823, Spain did not worry

1

about its borderlands because the republic of Mexico assumed that burden. A portent of the new relationship occurred in 1825 when Secretary of State Henry Clay announced, "This country prefers that Cuba and Puerto Rico should remain dependent on Spain. This government desires no political change in that condition".[2] Those islands remained under Spanish control and American opinion designated those colonies as eventual American territories. So much for revolutionary sentiment.

The province of Tejas now received the focus of the Manifest Destiny religion. Americans viewed Texas as a natural addition to the dominions of the United States. In 1819, the Adams-Onis Treaty between Spain and the United States seemed to surrender all claims on Texas in return for annexation of the Floridas and a new boundary agreement in North America. Many Americans protested this "give-away", citing natural right and God-awarded title to this land.[3] However, John Quincy Adams felt the United States would acquire Texas as, Spain, and later Mexico, would be too weak to protect it. His position proved quite correct, as evidenced by the Texas Revolution of 1836. Much more will be said about Texas, but at this point, it is sufficient to state that the Alamo syndrome that developed out of the Texas Revolution accurately represented the popular attitude toward Mexico and Mexicans.

The next great event involving Mexico and the United States was the worst and most abusive reality of Manifest Destiny. By the Mexican War, the United States achieved its design for the Southwest of North America. A presidential conspiracy by James K. Polk, which contrived a war as the solution to American needs, incorporated half of Mexico into the United States. Although many American people came to oppose this aggression after Mexico did not willingly or quickly give in to American expansion, most people were quite eager to teach Mexicans "their place". As Walt Whitman said,

> We are justified in the face of the world, in having treated Mexico with more forbearance than we have ever yet treated an enemy-for Mexico, though contemptible in many respects, is an enemy deserving a vigorous lesson. We have coaxed, excused, listened with deaf ears to the insolent gasconnade of her government, submitted thus far to a most offensive rejection of an Ambassador personifying the American nation, and waited for years without payment of the claims of our injured merchants. We have sought peace through every avenue and shut our eyes to many things, which had they come from England or France, the president would not have dared to pass over without stern and speedy resentment.We have damned up our memory of what has passed in the South years ago—of the devilish massacres of some of our bravest and noblest sons, the children not of the South alone, but of the North and West—massacres not only in defiance of ordinary humanity, but in violation of all the rules of war. Who has read the sickening story of those brutal wholesale murders, so

useless for any purpose except gratifying the cowardly appetite of a nation of braves, willing to shoot down men by the hundred in cold blood—without panting for the day when the prayer of the blood should be listened to—when the vengeance of a retributive God should be metered out to those who so ruthlessly and needlessly slaughtered his image?

That day has arrived, we think there can be no doubt of the truth of yesterday's news; and we are sure the people here, ten to one, are for prompt and effectual hostilities. Tame newspaper comments, such as appear in the leading Democratic print of today, in New York, and the contemptible anti-patriotic criticisms of its contemporary Whig organ, do not express the sentiments and wishes of the people. Let our arms now be carried with a spirit which shall teach the world that, while we are not forward for a quarrel, America knows how to crush, as well as how to expand![4]

Whitman, most Americans, and too many historians easily accepted the facile explanations constantly offered by those justifying power and the accumulation of such. What was viewed by Whitman as "offensive rejection of an Ambassador personifying the American nation" was realistically perceived by Mexicans as an attempt to coerce and extort Mexican land by avaricious *norte americanos*; the ridiculous reference to England and France is belied by England's constant presence in Latin America contrary to the dictates of the Monroe Doctrine. The "massacres" and "wholesale murders" could easily be ascribed by Mexican observers to the Texas Rangers of the 19th Century.[5] The criticism of the critics is typical and very familiar to Americans of the Vietnam era. Just as familiar is the notion that President James K. Polk would indeed lead the United States to war for certain objectives; those objectives would also be cloaked in the most stirring democratic and republican rationales. (More recent historical inquiry and analysis still has difficulty in forming a balanced depiction of the Mexican War.)

No account would deny the outcome. Mexico lost, and the United States won. The spoils included California, New Mexico, Arizona, Nevada, Utah, Colorado, and South Texas. The "conquered subjects" would now reap a legacy of oppression and colonialism.

The Treaty of Guadalupe Hidalgo ended the Mexican War. Despite compromises and weakened versions of the original draft, the articles pertaining to the Mexican inhabitants of the new American territories were clear. Deeds and titles obtained under Spanish law remained valid under American law; rights granted by the Constitution applied to the new population.[6] Mexican people in the annexed territories now enjoyed the freedoms inherent in the greatest republic on earth. This flight of fantasy quickly yielded to reality.

The Anglo invasion of the Southwest began in earnest. Texas had already been settled and more will be said later about the process. New Mexico and California became other areas of occupation and coloniza-

3

tion. In 1890, Mexican Americans comprised only ten percent of California's population. By varying methods, Mexican landholders were dispossessed, political rights dissembled, and economic opportunity destroyed. However, the official textbook history, the "stars and stripes" school, describes Anglo heroes and heroic institutions. The great cattle barons and railroad entrepreneurs brought "civilization". Corporate money and individual initiative made a desert into a garden. Settlers from the east established communities and stability. As described in the rhetoric of Manifest Destiny, the land was "regenerated". Superior values and culture replaced the primitives.[7]

Depending on the locale, the superior values included conspiracy and calculated, whether legal or illegal, processes whose inevitable result meant Anglo control. In New Mexico, courts and banks worked together with landowners to possess Mexican land. High taxes, loopholes, syndicate activity, and financial power eventually removed the Mexicans from their land. In California, both state and federal laws shifted the burden of proof from those challenging Mexican ownership to the owner. Expansion of American farming and the changing nature of agricultural enterprise to a corporate entity supported and even demanded such activity. The all-encompassing racism of the colonizer justified the retention of Mexican labor without the "onerous" spectacle of Mexican land control.[8]

The stars and stripes version does not resemble reality. Contrary to the popular Anglo conceptions of the Spanish land grant, it was a total system responsible for whole communities. Evolved from different land management entities in the seventeenth and eighteenth centuries, it came to be a combination of livestock, produce, and mining activities. One person might be accorded the title to the grant, but just as often, the community land grant was used by Spain and Mexico to provide incentive for settlement and a means of regulation. The land was divided into housing and farming lots with the remainder held in common for open grazing, water, and building resources. Several villages could develop on one grant; governmental structure was an important provision of the grant itself. Indeed, one could easily understand the communal grant as an Hispanic parallel to the Jeffersonian agrarian.[9]

There were opportunities that established a ruling class within the grant. Rich and powerful families could assume control of neighboring lands; individual or private grants often subsumed large areas. But the *rico* (rich one) would still be responsible for workers and other people. Conflicts and feuds were also common occurrences but, the very nature of the Spanish land system allowed resolution or at least coexistence. The lack of specified rights and exact policies compelled a leadership or authority based on tradition, power, and personal force. That power and force depended on abilities at persuasion, economic sanctions, and the provision of tangible benefits. The workers were as much a part of this relationship as the owners.

Anglo-Americans could not understand this (to them) casual attitude. Psychologically, they would not tolerate it. Their own system demanded and required precise rules and regulations. A deed specified and re-specified. Public land, in Anglo tradition, became private land. Unfortunately, many of the *ricos* attempted to survive by playing the Anglo game. They either failed and lost their position or became dismally co-opted.

In addition to the loss of land, and thereby the elimination of economic power, the history of the Southwest became a blend of distortion, myth, and fabrication. By the turn of the century, the history text described a curious and even nonsensical sequence of events and results. The dogma and rationales inherent in the concept of Manifest Destiny have already been mentioned, but another body of "information" was just as extreme. The Southwest was a vast wasteland of ignorant Mexicans and vicious Indians. As the so-called frontier became pacified, Anglo ingenuity and inventiveness brought new techniques and abundant resources that transformed the region; the most vital ingredient was the dynamic, progressive vision and lifestyle of the white race as contrasted to the passive, stagnant culture of Mexican society.

Again, the reality merits description, besides the basically corrupt processes used in dispossession and takeover. Livestock industries were pioneered by Mexican hacendados; cattle and sheep manipulation did not arrive with the cattle kings. Irrigation was a Spanish device adapted by Spanish and Mexican landowners. The mining industry was totally a Mexican system; the popular scene that depicts the California miner and his washpan activity is an excellent example of facts stood on their head because Mexican and South American miners taught Anglos how to search for gold. The system devised by miners in California to bring order and stability was a Mexican practice *completely adopted* by Anglos; in the textbooks, it is described as a classic demonstration of Anglo ingenuity. This type of mythogenesis goes on and on. Perhaps the most ridiculous is the legend of the American cowboy, the most well-known American figure to the world. Tex learned everything from Juan and then Juan was removed from his own history by the official storyteller.[10]

The cultural robbery culminates with twentieth-century entertainment. Movies and TV reflected and continued the ethnocentrism and racist myopia of the nineteenth century. The contrast between an American

5

(white) lawman or cowboy and the sneering bandido or Mexican general said it all.

As the twentieth century began, Mexican Americans were landless, powerless, and invisible. While Mexican Americans were invisible, the corporate growth of the United States triumphantly heralded new characteristics and values for the American Southwest. Between 1870 and 1900, total farm acreage in the West tripled; irrigated landholding doubled; federal legislation provided major capital incentives for large-scale farm investment. Railroad expansion provided transportation routes; refrigerated cars and new canning processes kept the food fresh for Eastern mouths. One other commodity became integral for the golden harvest—cheap labor. The Mexican "joined" black Southerners in the fields.[11]

The economic conditions in Mexico aided American agribusiness in its exploitation of Mexican labor. By 1900, the Mexican economy was in shambles; while foreign investment and development had been very successful for the foreigner, the Mexican people were in a desperate situation. Inflation and unemployment ravished the countryside. Rural workers could not feed their families. Many immigrated to the United States, with the encouragement and recruitment of American agribusiness agents. The Mexican Revolution of 1910 only added to the economic factors that resulted in the large-scale immigration.[12]

World War I institutionalized Mexican immigration as a "special" necessity for American agriculture. As the war effort intensified in Europe, the United States became the source of supply for the Allies. Although new legislation restricted European immigration, Mexico received exemption. The growers convinced Department of Labor officials of the "need" for farmworkers, consequently the entry fee or head tax and literacy requirements were suspended in regard to Mexicans. Anti-immigration groups, especially union leaders and nativists, were outraged, but, after all, patriotism demanded sacrifice, and American agribusiness could now "sacrifice" by acquiring millions in profit.[13]

This noble effort continued after the war. Growers (led by the Arizona Cotton Growers) were joined by Midwestern industrialists in their determination to maximize their new-found resource. Agricultural lobbyists persuaded the Labor Department that any sudden withdrawal of Mexican labor would result in massive crop ruin (this particular argument would become a cliché and a very successful one for the next fifty years). Midwestern industries (especially steel) began importing Mexican workers as strikebreakers and found that they could be exploited as well as other immigrant groups because of their lack of political power and their severe economic needs. However, one event did interfere with this

6

bonanza. A recession temporarily halted the economic growth fostered by the war. As quickly as Mexican labor had been exhalted, it now became a millstone. Workers imported from Mexico found themselves without employment and without aid. They were simply left to fend for themselves. Many cases of extreme malnutrition and starvation were reported in the winter of 1920-1921. But employers did not care—after all, America was for Americans. This irresponsible and immoral response to a condition created by the entrepreneur class would occur time and time again in the twentieth century.[14]

The recession ended in 1921, and the 1920's proceeded into, as contemporaries saw it, the New Era. The consumer goods revolution transformed American life; the automobile became the new symbol of American progress and ingenuity. The basic industries prospered and new, subsidiary industries appeared. Life had never been better, and Americans reveled as the conspicuous consumers. Not surprisingly, the value, need, and integral role of Mexican labor was extolled. Immigration totals reached all-time highs, and Mexican workers traveled and lived in all parts of the United States. The auto industry, meatpacking industry, coal mines, and steel mills recruited Mexicans and Mexican Americans for work in Pennsylvania, Ohio, Indiana, Michigan, Missouri, Nebraska and Illinois. Gary, Chicago, Detroit, St. Louis, Kansas City, Omaha and many other cities and towns east of the Mississippi received Mexican residents.

Mexican American society and Mexican immigration now coalesced to represent new reality. In 1900 the approximate census data "found" 100,000 people of Mexican and Latin descent in the Southwest. In 1930 the number was about 1.3 million.[15] Workers of Mexican origin were employed in all of the basic industries; most of the jobs were the lowest paying, dirtiest, and most dangerous. The last-hired, first-fired condition constituted the basics of economic life. There were actually many subgroups within the Mexican community, such as the Mexican contract worker, the illegal alien, the migrant worker, the factory worker, the urban resident, the rural dweller, the barrio population. But these people shared certain characteristics.

For the agricultural and industrial workers, union protection did not exist. Farmworkers were not even considered as a legitimate part of union activity, except by union organizers separate from the mainstream of organized labor. For example, the American Federation of Labor would not seek inclusion of farmworkers until after World War II. More radical groups such as the Southern Tenant Farmers League wanted such inclusion, but they did not and could not secure the traditional support of other unions; socialists attempting more basic change were considered

7

pariahs. Coupled with the weakness of the union movement in general and the lack of political rights by the illegal workers, the potential for union organization was limited at best. Mexican groups formed their own labor unions but did not make long-term inroads.[16] Industrial workers fared somewhat better, but they were a part of unions such as coal steel. Their activities had more "visibility" in American society, but the economic and social climate of the 1920s prevented gains.

Farmworkers were the most vulnerable to the economic power of the employer. The seasonal nature of agriculture left the farmworker with two or three options: stay and find work in the local area; follow the migrant trail; if from Mexico, go back home. All of these "options" required money which was not available. The wage policy of the grower was no policy at all or the least amount possible for the greatest amount of work. Employers did not maintain records or any type of accountability procedure that might have protected workers. Minimum wage did not exist, nor would later minimum wage legislation cover the farmworker. The migrant worker was "fortunate" to participate in the American system and have the opportunity for and access to honest labor for fair pay. This nonsensical litany permeated the rhetoric and dogma of the employers. However, they were not so foolish as to depend on it.

Agribusiness executives, i.e., growers, had a common denominator; they received all laborers with scorn, contempt, and derision. The growers also felt that destabilization of the work force was essential and employed a number of methods to assure that circumstance. Citizens associations comprised of growers and their allies (merchants, bankers, etc.) carried the banner of capitalism, the open marketplace and 100 percent Americanism. Their public relations campaigns touted the critical nature of their work, their struggles to achieve success by the traditional American standards of hard work, and their fierce determination to maintain those standards. The last part, translated, means they would never recognize unions or workers' rights. This message was very receptive in the 1920's as socialism, communism and unionism were linked together in the public mind. Throw in the anti-foreign vote, and the growers were definitely strong in the saddle. Of course, one might mention the inconsistency of using anti-foreign feeling when many of the workers were from other countries (besides Mexicans, many Chinese, Japanese, and Filipinos worked in the fields), but foolish consistency and hobgoblins should be avoided.

However, as mentioned, these fearless standard-bearers did not depend on their speeches. The economic sectors in the agricultural regions were united by sentiment, ideology, and the profit motive. Merchants, bankers, and other groups considered the growers as the elite class in their cities and towns. Support of workers was tantamount to treason. Local courts, police and state officers cooperated and even followed the dictates of the agribusiness sector. Goons could be employed as strikebreakers or for "simple" harassment, and the Mexican would be arrested for disturbing the peace while defending himself. Violence against the labor camps was simply an exercise of patriotism against radicalism.[17]

The effects of this system never ended. In addition to the environment created by the employer class, a new group of workers appeared. When huge numbers of Mexican workers were imported, many Mexican Americans were displaced and sought jobs on the migrant trail. After the land dispossession of the nineteenth century, many did not have the economic strength to hang on. This exodus became another part of the ongoing migration, and many *colonias* appeared as Mexicans and Mexican Americans decided to locate as near as possible to their seasonal work. The barrio expanded and incorporated the contract laborer, undocumented worker, migrant farm worker, industrial laborer, Mexican and Mexican American.

The barrio of the Southwest, Midwest, or any other region became the center of Mexican American society. As with other immigrant people, their locale was determined by the value of the land, the proximity to the industrial areas and the caprice of the white landlords. Politicians and landlords conspired to reap the largest profits for the least service; city administrations pretended that they could not deliver the basic services and were primarily concerned with tax collections.

Consequently, health and sanitation conditions became abysmal. Social agencies, including health care administrators, blamed the barrio residents, citing lack of intelligence, unclear cultural traits, and a general disposition toward dysfunction. If infant diarrhea, tuberculosis, and infant mortality were high, then it was the fault of the poor because these diseases were poverty problems, and the Mexicans were poor. Hospital and physician care did not reach out to the community and placed numerous obstacles in front of those in need. These conditions existed in most immigrant, black, and poor neighborhoods, but the Mexican had the additional difficulty of language. Most attendants in the various health institutions did not speak Spanish and wondered why the "dummies" did not learn English.[18]

They tried. Education administrators did not display much concern for the schooling of Mexican and Mexican American children. Numerous difficulties were cited. The families moved too much to establish residence; a child could not benefit from three weeks in one school, four weeks in another, etc; the children suffered from inadequate preparation and entered school too far behind; the parents did not support education, LANGUAGE.[19]

Except for the mobility factor involving migrant workers, these complaints reveal more about the complainers than the complainee. WASP-oriented educators in the public schools simply did not understand or care to understand the needs of bilingual peoples, particularly the Spanish-speaking. English was the language of heaven, and other tongues were foreign and un-American. To entertain the notion that all languages and cultures are valid on their own terms would undermine the belief, even religion, of one America. Expanding an educational system to include all classes might also challenge the dominance of certain groups over others. The Supreme Court had formalized and legalized the separation of Blacks and Whites with the 1896 *Plessy v. Ferguson* decision; segregation was a legal doctrine. The inclusion or exclusion of brown children did not require a large leap of imagination. In many regions triple school systems developed: black, white, and Mexican. The distrust that Mexican parents logically felt toward people embodying these attitudes added to the situation, but did not create it. In fact, Mexican and Mexican American parents endorsed and supported education as a priority for the betterment of their children. But they could do little with a system that permitted physical punishment for children who "insisted" on speaking Spanish. (It should be noted that some administrators did recruit Spanish-speaking children when they discovered that appropriations correlated to enrollment could be manipulated. In other words, as long as these pupils showed up the first day, everything was fine.)[20]

The political power or process that might have alleviated or at least addressed some of these issues was not accessible. That is not to say that Mexicans and Mexican Americans were not concerned. Mexican Americans particularly agreed to the need for political power. But they also understood the realism of their position. The economic base was non-existent, the social experience limited, and the willingness of Anglo dominated politicians to *practice* democracy absent. Even in the states of large Mexican American population there were few Mexican American representatives in the state legislatures of the pre-World War II twentieth century (The one exception was New Mexico, where machine politics had to incorporate Mexican Americans as they made up the great majority of the state. Consequently, the 1910 state constitution included a strong guarantee of Mexican American civil and political rights. However, machine politics concentrated on Anglo and upper-class Hispanic interest, the New Mexican term for Mexican Americans.) Most grassroot Mexican Americans had no voice in official places.

One of the more inhibiting factors limiting Mexican American political power was the lack of voters. Many individuals chose not to be involved.

After participating in a system that did not meet, reach out, or even attempt to understand the basic issues, voting seemed a wasted effort. There was also the matter of residency, registration, and poll taxes. This process was designed to eliminate black voters in the South; its effect on Mexican Americans in the Southwest was much the same, particularly in Texas. The difficulty for migrant workers in establishing residency and the financial burden of the poll tax did not rouse the sympathy of many Anglo politicians. However, many "disinterested" observers ignored these realities and often commented on the reluctance of Mexican immigrants to take advantage of naturalization, become voters, and participate in the democratic process. Indeed, very few Mexicans chose naturalization. Most, at first, felt that their presence in the United States would be temporary. The vast majority did not leave Mexico to "seek a better life", but to find work. When they made the decision to stay, for reasons already enumerated, they did not feel particularly wanted and felt no urge to go through the motions of becoming "second-class" citizens. At the same time, many understood that their best legal protection came from the Mexican consul. As American citizens, they would lose that without any compensating support from American institutions.[21] These reasons and attitudes account for the reluctance of Mexican Americans and legal Mexican immigrants to participate in politics. Obviously the largest group of immigrants, the illegal aliens, were not going to undergo a legal process from an illegal position.

A series of events in the 1920's and 1930's confirmed the mistrust that Mexican immigrants felt toward the American system. The nativist and organized labor campaign against immigration centered on the Mexican due to the virtual elimination of European entry by the 1924 Immigration Act. In 1924 the Border Patrol was established. In 1925, Congressmen William Harris and John Box introduced a bill enacting a quota system for countries in the Western Hemisphere. In 1925 the first serious debate on the implications of Mexican immigration produced "scientific" evidence that Mexican natives were inferior and a significant detriment to American culture. The bill roused opposition from railroad and agriculture lobbyists, cattlemen, and sugar manufacturers. Southwest money overcame Southwest restrictionists. In 1928 the same battle ensued. The American Legion, public health and social services agencies, teacher organizations, and the American Federation of Labor confronted industry and agriculture plus the State Department which, did not want an adverse effect on Latin American economic programs. Although this bill was also defeated, a tacit agreement was reached with Mexican government officials in 1929 to restrict visas in return for the cessation of restrictive legislation attempts.[22] However, the Great Depression resolved the "problem", at least from the United States position.

11

Border and immigration restrictions tightened; illegal entry became a crime. Visas had already been denied to illiterates, contract laborers and LPC's (those "liable to become public charges"); those prohibitions were more stringently enforced. The Secretary of Labor, William Doak, suggested that the removal of alien labor would solve unemployment, and the Bureau of Immigration moved to implement that solution. In Los Angeles, a city committee linked unemployment with the illegals; raids and propaganda began and continued despite the objections of the Mexican consul and Mexican community. The process developed into three methods: deportation, "voluntary" self-removal, and repatriation by harassment and intimidation. Besides the raids, which violated every tenant of due process, social agencies informed Mexican families that they would not be welcome on the relief rolls, nor would they be easily included in support services. The replies of the supporters of this campaign emphasized the voluntary aspect. Most of those who did leave in the first stages of the repatriation possessed the economic means to relocate in Mexico, but that group was a small percentage of the total. They could also see what was coming. The numbers involved were staggering. Approximately 500,000 people of Mexican origin left; about 250,000 were Mexican Americans, that is, citizens of the United States. Only 82,400 were legally deported, as that process was too slow. In the Midwest, many *Mexicano* communities were reduced by as much as 50 percent of the original population. Mexico created relocation centers and programs designed to ease the burden of resettlement, but simply could not cope with the economic needs of so many people. The culture shock for children born in the United States and the psychological impact from the disruption of so many lives was incalculable. Repatriation tapered off by 1937, but the trauma of the experience would remain with the Mexican and Mexican American communities for many years. Many, if not most, of the American citizens would return to the United States but not without undue harassment regarding their legal status.[23] Even the slightest mention of this sordid episode is difficult to find in any American history textbook.

Meanwhile, the New Deal of Franklin Roosevelt created relief programs for the millions of people suffering in the depression. While some in the Mexican/Mexican American *colonias* obtained aid, most did not and could not. Local residency requirements prevented many from receiving aid; agricultural workers were exempted from the Social Security Act of 1937; most did not trust the federal government. Their experiences with repatriation and the threat of it "discouraged" any belief in government largesse. Finally, local politicians administered federal programs in their areas, and they were not sympathetic.

The institutional attitudes, values and perceptions evident by the described conditions were matched by the so-called common man, especially when that commoner was a White Anglo Saxon Protestant. However, others of the "white is right" persuasion also shared similar beliefs. Mexicans and Mexican Americans were inherrently inferior, whether by cultural dysfunction or genetic influence—these people simply were not capable of initiative, logical analysis, or plain common sense. In the southern and southwestern parts of the United States, the racial prejudice of whites toward blacks was easily transferred to Mexicans; particularly in the Southwest was the stigma of "Indian" identified with "Mexican". Peculiar ideas developed to justify or explain the nature of the Mexican.

They loved bright colors and music—in other words, they were children; a Mexican could grow anything and was talented at farmwork; they did not know how to save money, so higher wages were impractical and wasteful; they were hard workers, so maximum hours were unnecessary for fieldworkers; they were short and built close to the ground, so stoop work with the short hoe was ideally suited. (Mexicans also had the "mental ability" for stoop work.) These stereotypes and rationales permeated the Anglo concept of Mexicans.[24]

Another pervasive notion was the idea that the Mexican worker was only a temporary resident of the United States. If they were not permanent, then who needed to worry about social services, protracted employment, schooling, and other basic needs? While the contractor and employer especially pushed this characteristic of Mexican labor, most Anglos accepted it. However, there were some indications that it was not entirely believed. For instance, laws were passed in various states to prohibit non-citizens from employment as lawyers, accountants or public employees; only citizens could obtain hunting and fishing licenses; and in Pennsylvania, a person could not own a dog if he or she was not an American citizen.[25] Mexican Americans felt the overall effect of this type of discrimination. Many did not have birth records and/or their parents were illegal entrants who did not seek such artifacts at the risk of revealing their "crime".

Institutions such as the Catholic church did not offer support for their own Mexican congregations. On the contrary, the Catholic hierarchy viewed the Mexican segment with some hostility. Officials complained that Mexican Catholics were a burden on the charity obligations of the church; too many were in jail; Mexicans or Mexican practices adversely affected the health of the overall community; they presented too many problems in schools because of their low mentality; their tendency toward or even the possibility of miscegenation corrupted the "morality" of Catholic populations; horror of horrors—they (Mexicans) remained foreign in their culture. The very real problems encountered by all

13

Catholics in the United States and the historical differences between European and Latin American Catholicism created enough conflict without the additional burden of white ethnocentrism. But many in the American Catholic church were all too willing to join with their Anglo brothers in the stereotypical exercise of prejudiced rationalization. One consequence of this attitude was the encroachment of Protestant missionary work among Mexican communities. The Catholic church did not hesitate to condemn the treachery of these Protestant Mexicans while refusing to appoint Mexican priests and recognizing Mexican parishes.[26]

This description, depiction, and analysis of Mexican and Mexican American society is admittedly grim and negative. If these realities were the only operative conditions, then one could have expected to encounter a rather depressed, even dysfunctional people living on the edge of psychological morbidity. But the individuals who had to face and exist within the confinements of Anglo-manipulated parameters did not surrender to the desired ends of such restrictions. Mexicans, Mexican Americans, people of Latin origin, Spanish-surnamed, Spanish-speaking, by whatever label, survived. They maintained their own dignity and self-respect by refusing to accept the stereotypes and roles defined by those who, for different reasons, did not wish the benefits of American society to extend past a select group. Responses varied from region to region, and success or failure evolved to more substantive initiative and action. The impact of World War II would have enormous consequences for the post-war Mexican American generation. Contrary to a popular analysis among many scholars and/or Chicano activists, those individuals would introduce a new positive and achieving phase of the Chicano history and experience. The next chapter will examine the dynamics of the war's effects and the birthplace of the most important new organization to emerge among the participants of that time.

CHAPTER II

World War, Texas

The United States had already committed itself to the defeat of Germany and Japan long before its entry into the conflict. The reorientation of the American economy to a wartime stance had largely eliminated the disasters of the Great Depression. Expansion in agriculture and industry created new jobs; the federal government opened its coffers; deficit financing and the military-industrial complex asserted its dominance in American society, a dominance that would remain to the present. Migration and mobilization became a daily reality—people moved to work; communities absorbed persons of varying cultural, ethnic, and social background. After Pearl Harbor, military bases expanded and appeared to provide the training for new personnel; these centers reinforced the upheaval and change in the country. They would also remain as mainstays of the new economy. As with World War I, the impetus of war left the U.S. as the preeminent economic power in the world.[1]

The rationale for American participation in the war did not, of course, include economic self-interest. The attack by Japan on Pearl Harbor and the subsequent declaration of war by Germany confirmed the consensus of most Americans. The barbarian at the gates would now receive justified retribution. The well-publicized actions of Japan in China, and the rather aggressive attitudes and policies of Germany had not received favorable press. The United States of America, acting with other liberty-loving allies, would now crush tyranny and "restore" democracy and freedom to the world—at least most of it.[2]

Unfortunately, white America did not question the systematic "tyranny" that governed the lives of many "other" Americans. Blacks obtained new employment opportunities in the defense plants but had to threaten Roosevelt with mass protest in 1940 to secure those positions. In the armed services, particularly in the army training camps, discrimination and racism continued to govern the social environment; most whites did not appreciate black men with guns. Many, if not most, Japanese Americans lived out the war in internment camps, courtesy of the federal government—after all, the U.S. could not risk treachery and subversion; the Supreme Court ruled the action constitutional in 1944. Several race riots occurred during the war years involving minority people. Clearly, the war against totalitarian rule and the struggle for freedom, liberty and democracy was for other folks. The changes caused by the war effort on the domestic front only exacerbated the prevailing social and economic realities in the United States.[3]

For Mexican Americans, those prevailing conditions were joined by an interesting fact of war—the draft. Agricultural workers did not receive deferments (as did their industrial counterparts). The local draft boards controlled the allotments and were inclined to provide exemption for sons of Anglo farmers, but rarely extended the same privilege to non-whites. Most Mexican American males were eligible for conscription and approximately 500,000 Spanish-surnamed persons served in the armed forces. This disproportionately large number was manifested in the combat divisions where Mexican Americans had the highest ethnic group representation in the country.[4] For most of these individuals the war experience marked their first time away from the standard patterns of American society. The economic, political, and social relationships of New Mexico and Texas did not have the same meaning or influence in a European or Pacific war zone.

The Mexicans in World War II performed well and even heroically. At Bataan, about 25 percent of the defenders were Mexican American; many died in the infamous and legendary Death March. In all theaters of war, Mexican Americans served with great credit; seventeen won the Congressional Medal of Honor, again the highest ethnic group representation during the war. These successes contributed to a growing awareness among *Mexicanos* of their won abilities. The drama of war destroyed any credibility of the Anglo created rationalizations regarding their lives. This confidence and self-improvement also influenced some Anglo soldiers' attitudes toward Mexican Americans: "No longer were we cheated and shunted by other GIs and Army officers. Where we had been held in contempt by others who disliked us because of our constant Spanish chatter or our laxity in military discipline, we were now admired, respected, and approved by all those around us, including most of our commanding officers."[5]

Unfortunately and unsurprisingly, this record of achievement was not publicized, and the home front did not appreciably reflect the more egalitarian nature of the foxhole. In 1942 the United States and Mexico signed an agreement that provided contract laborers for agribusiness "needs" (a repeat of the 1917 situation, except that the U.S. had to guarantee several protections for those workers). In that same year, the

Fair Employment Practices Committee scheduled hearings on discrimination against Mexican Americans in Southwest copper mines, shipyards, and oil refineries. President Franklin Roosevelt cancelled the public investigation after his advisors warned of the possible negative impact such revelations might produce in Latin America.[6] In 1943, one of the most violent race riots in American history took place in Los Angeles. Anglo servicemen invaded the barrio and attacked pachucos indiscriminately with police approval.[7] Around the same period, the Office of Coordinator of Inter-American Affairs, in its analysis of the Southwest, concluded that Mexican Americans were the most submerged and destitute people in the United States.[8]

The contrast between these two experiences, environments, and realities would produce important and substantive change in the methods, or more significant, the attitudes by which Mexican Americans attempted to deal with their needs. A hero in Europe should have been a hero in New Mexico. A Chicano fighting against oppression in Germany should not have to fight for his people in Texas. In facing the political, economic, and social inequities of American society, many individuals faced themselves and their own concept of what their country could be or wanted to be. The American G.I. Forum emerged from this examination and originated in possibly the worst place for Mexican people—the Great State of Texas.

"Texas, Our Texas"

Texas was one of the borderlands of New Spain. Explorations in the sixteenth century only peripherally included the area, but the missionary impulse of Spanish colonization brought mission development in the seventeenth century. However, not until French penetration into the Mississippi Valley did Spain consider the region an important territory. Even then, more permanent settlement did not appear until 1717. The War of the Spanish Secession reinforced the Bourbon strategy that the province of Texas must be defended. The remainder of the century included some efforts at expansion, but the mission and presidio did not succeed, at least past the central area of the territory. Policies after 1763 focused on retrenchment with San Antonio as the center of activity.

That activity suffered from the general liabilities of borderland development. With the economic and political power remaining in the more densely populated areas such as Mexico City and surrounding provinces, incentive for immigration was almost nil. The Indian populations did not easily surrender their land or independence, and the lack of resources for garrison and outward expansion only intensified the initial problem of defense. Grandiose schemes in the eighteenth century designed to link the military posts of northern Mexico never received a total commitment from the crown, which concentrated on improving the more lucrative capital return from the interior. The fact that Spain managed to hold Texas until the Mexican Revolution of 1821 did not change the reality of Texas as an isolated outpost now confronted with a new aggressor—the United States of America.[9]

A few Americans had crossed the Sabine River between 1800 and 1820 and the colonial government of New Spain allowed them to stay. As only three Spanish outposts "protected" the province, there was very little that the authorities could do. Spain did not want Americans in Texas; the outcry of Henry Clay and others after the Adams-Onis Treaty of 1819 that the United States had surrendered Texas confirmed the expansionist nature of the Yankee. (John Quincy Adams did not fear Spain but realized the annexation of Texas would contribute to the debate over the territorial limits of slavery.)[10] However, with the liberal takeover in Spain in 1820, immigration policy changed and Texas was opened for settlement.[11]

Moses Austin of Connecticut became the first *empresario* and received a grant for 300 settlers but died before he could begin his colony. His son, Stephen Austin, continued the operation but could not implement the plan until 1823, after the Mexican Revolution and the approval of the Republic of Mexico. The government of Mexico then enacted a very generous colonization law that allowed individual states the right to distribute unoccupied land. Consequently the state of Coahuila -Texas drew its own law in 1825, which encouraged more immigration. The laws required allegiance to Mexico, provided tax exemptions for ten years, including the suspension of customs duties, permitted importation of slaves, and formalized the *empresario* system; land fees were exceedingly cheap. Immigrants had to be Catholic, but this requirement was not enforced.[12]

As incentives for immigration, the Mexican plan was very successful. Land prices in the United States were high and the Panic of 1819 had a depressing effect on land sale. By 1830, 8,000 Americans had taken advantage of the colonization opportunity. Unfortunately these people brought their own cultural chauvinism with them. Most came from the "Old South" and shared that region's racial views; most Americans also accepted the Black Legend stereotype of anything Spanish, adding the pervasive notion of Indian people as savage, ignorant, and any other pejorative adjective. The idea that North Americans and Mexicans could co-exist smacks of highly developed fantasy. Conflict between cultures and "races" was immediate in Texas. Other customs and laws had little meaning for the Yankee "pioneers", and they made no effort to mask their feeling that their own values, abilities, and racial character were infinitely superior to those of the host country.[13] An incident of 1826 in which Texan Haden Edwards declared a Republic of Fredonia confirmed the distrust and suspicion. Mexican suppression of the revolt only made Edwards a martyr. When Mexico abolished slavery in 1829, Anglo Texan anger forced exemption for them but heightened the mutual dislike. The unsuccessful attempts by the Adams and Jackson administrations to purchase Texas, which included attempted bribery of Mexican officials, seemed to Mexican officials a typical play of the unscrupulous American drive for territory.[14] In January 1830, an official investigation and report by Mexican authorities warned of imminent aggression from the United States. Mexico closed the border, and immigration to Texas was suspended but that decree was unenforceable. After three years of tension and protest the anti-immigration law was repealed and the atmosphere appeared calm. New Americans in Texas brought the Anglo population to 30,000 versus 3,000 Mexicans.[15]

When Antonio Lopez de Santa Anna continued the internal political wars by declaring himself dictator, the Texas colonists responded with revolution. Certainly, they were afraid of Santa Anna policies, but there had already been considerable movement toward independence. On March 2, 1836, the Republic of Texas came into being, a birth that surprised no one.

The battles of the Texas Revolution included the world-famous Battle of the Alamo, where 185 men held out thirteen days in an old mission against the army of Santa Anna. The defeat of the garrison and the death of its defenders made the Alamo a rallying cry for Anglo Texans. But, it became much more. The defeat was turned into a glorious victory by the forces of freedom, liberty, and democracy. The attacking Mexicans were depicted as savage murderers. Disregard of the nature of revolution, the vanity and pride of Santa Anna which compelled him to use the Alamo as an act of terror, and the very real courage involved on both sides, produced the Alamo syndrome. The enmity and bigotry which characterized Anglo feeling toward Mexicans had found a symbol. That symbol was in evidence at the Battle of San Jacinto. A surprise attack by the Texas army killed 630 Mexicans in thirty minutes—that took some effort. The republic was now a firm reality.[16]

That reality eliminated viable Mexican influence on Texas society. Although many Mexican citizens participated in the revolution and held important political office, Anglo dominance became more and more evident. Border conflicts, particularly in the Rio Grande Valley, always seemed to be the fault of Mexican lawlessness. The Texas Rangers, created to stabilize and pacify areas for economic development, acquired mythical status as the legendary Anglo lawman. The myth served to

19

cover the truth that the Rangers were little more than thugs hired to convert "bad" Indians and Mexicans into "good" ones. Texas volunteers in the Mexican War performed atrocities so repugnant to regular army officers that they were kicked out.

After annexation in 1845, migration increased to such an extent that by 1850, Anglos outnumbered Mexican Americans fifty to one.[17] Agriculture remained the chief mainstay of the Texas economy until 1850, when livestock enterprises became more profitable.[18] A tremendous cattle boom occurred from 1870 to 1890 due to increased world demand and improvement in transportation, particularly the railroad.[19] Extensive use of barbed wire prompted a vast enclosure process that quickly subsumed small Mexican ranches and farms which depended on livestock ownership rather than land possession. Many Spanish grant claims had already been invalidated during the Republic of Texas period; these losses were accelerated by the cattle boom, often for nonpayment of taxes. Other factors contributing to the economic decline of the *tejano* were the growth of the sheep industry, which ironically expanded because of Mexican expertise and labor, and an increase in cotton production.[20] The development of Southwest agribusiness attracted a steady flow of migrants and immigrants, and coupled with the increase in Anglo migration to Texas, the already developed racial and cultural prejudices intensified, Anglo economic and political dominance asserted itself, and Texas society established itself on a have/have-not basis. By 1910, the typical Mexican immigrant and *tejano*—Mexican American could be labeled as a landless and dependent wage-laborer subject to Anglo economic design.[21] The Mexican Revolution and its effect were most obvious in Texas and firmly fixed the despondent condition of the Texas Mexican.

Texas became one of the two major recipients of the immigration boom of 1910-1930, California being the other. Texas had already more Mexican population than any other state, with approximately 71,000 in 1900; by 1930, census data showed 684,000 persons of Mexican descent in Texas, both native and foreign-born.[22] The majority of these people lived in the southern part of Texas; Laredo, El Paso, and San Antonio became the three major centers for Mexican immigrants. By 1949, 1,033,768 Mexican Americans lived in Texas as compared with 3,389,550 in the entire Southwest.[23]

Problems

If Anglo Texans ever complained that Mexicans in Texas were aliens, and they did in 1948, that criticism had no validity. By the late 1940's, 46.5 percent of Spanish-surnamed persons were of native parentage, that is of people born in the United States (Texas), and 35.3 percent were American citizens of foreign-born parentage.[24] In other words, 81.8 percent of Spanish-surnamed individuals in Texas were United States citizens in a full constitutional sense. But "constitutional sense" does not always equate with reality, and Mexican Americans hardly pursued "life, liberty, and happiness" with the same opportunities enjoyed by Anglo America.

The employment and income statistics for Mexican Americans in Texas during the post-war 1940's portray a group with little hope for improvement. The median income for the Spanish-speaking was $980 per year as contrasted to $1,925 per year for Anglo Americans.[25] Urban Mexican Americans, at $1,134 per year, enjoyed a minor increase in income but hardly enough to engender prosperity.[26] A breakdown in specific employment categories is even more revealing. Whereas 8.2 percent of the Anglo male work force engaged in professional and technical categories, only 1.7 percent of the Mexican American male labor force were so employed. As to the lowest paid category, farm laborers, 26.8 percent of the Mexican American male labor force were so occupied, compared to only 4.2 percent of Anglo males.[27] Between 1930 and 1950, the percentage of Mexican American males employed in Texas agriculture had decreased from 51 percent to 32 percent. However, Anglo decline went from 47 percent to 17 percent. These changes caused Mexican Americans to occupy 40 percent of farm labor jobs in 1950 as compared to 25 percent in 1930.[28] Many of these people worked the cotton fields of South Texas where most families were earning less than $400 per year.[29]

The conditions described by these income and employment statistics are obviously those of a poverty-burdened people. A contributing factor was the general lack of labor rights and power that had been won by the Anglo unions in the 1930's. With the approval and cooperation of the federal government, organized labor had made tremendous strides in securing the rights of collective bargaining, majority-elected unions, and effective economic benefits such as social security and workers compensation. As mentioned in Chapter I, these gains simply did not cover the vast number of Americans of Mexican descent. While some unions did allow *Mexicanos* to join, they relegated them to laborer work without an opportunity to progress; and many unions even forbade Mexican Americans from holding office in the union.[30]

In Texas, most Mexican American agricultural workers were not represented by major unions because of the nature of their work. The major labor organizations that attempted to incorporate farm workers failed because of the growers' ability to control wages and the amount of work available to the employees. The presence of *mojados* or undocumented workers who could always be used as strikebreakers and the cooperation of law officials assured that control.

The best example of these conditions occurred in 1938 in the pecan-shelling industry in San Antonio, Texas, a city which had been the center of that enterprise for over fifty years. Due to the large numbers of Mexican American migratory workers and immigrants, the San Antonio operation had resisted the trend toward mechanization evident in other areas of pecan-shelling. The work was exclusively manual, and a corollary to the manual aspect was the contracting system by which the nuts bought from farmers by the factory were transferred to "independent contractors" who hired pickers and crackers. The major pecan-shelling operators actually contracted these "independents", which resulted in rigid price-fixing, including wages.[31]

The *Mexicanos* employed in this industry performed in small rooms (100 people in 25' x 40' area) with poor lighting and inadequate ventilation which did not eliminate the harmful pecan dust.[32] Wage income at the pecan factory ranged from five to eight cents per hour and $2.75 per week; at one point the average "reached" $1.29 per week.[33] Although the work was of a seasonal nature, most of the 10,000 workers lived on the west side of San Antonio in overcrowded, dilapidated housing (median average was two persons per room, while 5 percent had five or more) with poor sanitation (12 percent had running water, nine percent had indoor plumbing). The rent paid for these "living quarters" was often over $4.00 per month. Efforts at union organization for the improvement of these conditions brought attempts by the owners to form a company union led by a "*vendido*" that opposed the NRA wage of fifteen cents per hour. On February 1, 1938, thousands of workers went on strike in support of the first union and for better wages.[34]

The mayor, police commissioner, and chief of police of San Antonio opposed the strike and helped the owners of the factory with every legal foul blow in the book. Many strikers were arrested and held in overcrowded jail cells for days because of failure to obtain approval for posters. Although the National Labor Relations Board disapproved of these actions, the tactics continued. Tear gas became a standard weapon against strikers, and soup kitchens were ordered closed for the duration. Strikers remained peaceful despite excessive police force. (A decision by the 45th District Court judge against an injunction on police interference stated that any strike gathering produced tension and disorder and any injunction would strain the minds of police.) The strike ended with a minute wage increase but did not provide for rehiring the thousands of workers fired during the incident. Thousands of other workers lost their jobs in the 1940's. By 1948 only a few hundred employees remained because of conversion to mechanization.[35]

Discrimination

Discrimination by employers also played a vital role in job opportunity. Texas State Employment records showed an overwhelming percentage of agricultural workers to be Spanish-named, not a very shocking revelation; after all, these people had very little education and hence no skills. But what of those Spanish-named individuals who, in fact, had equivalent education to their white counterparts? Did they benefit from that education or did social attitudes substantially reduce the benefits of that education? In the case of equal education for an Anglo and Spanish-speaker, the Mexican male had a much better chance of getting a job as a busboy and a female as a dime-store sales clerk than a clerical job. For the job classification which depended on past experience, those Spanish-named persons with equal amounts of training and / or education as their white competition rarely had the same amounts of job experience. Furthermore, many interviewers responsible for determining job classification were most influenced by the code "Spanish or White". The classification seemed arbitrary at best and often reflected the interviewers' prejudices. Some interviewers even admitted that many Mexican American applicants were automatically displaced from certain availability lists or referrals because of previous refusals by employers to accept persons with Spanish names.[36]

Education

Education levels were equally depressing for the Mexican American in Texas in the 1940's. An early indicator of educational difficulties pointed out that the illiteracy rate for Texas counties with large Mexican populations was 15.5 percent as compared to 6.8 percent for the whole state and 1.4 percent illiteracy rate for the Anglo population.[37] Although somewhat lacking in precision, these figures were not encouraging. A more intensive study in 1944 pointed out that 47 perent of a total Mexican American scholastic population of 206,759 children received no education. Of those in school, 72 percent were in the first three grades; or 52 percent of all Mexican American children were in grades one through three.[38] The number graduating from high school could be called infinitesimal, as illustrated by an Austin, Texas, study that showed 79 Mexican American high school graduates from 1937-1947 out of a total of 6,511.[39] This record continued into higher education during the 1940's, where approximate college and university enrollment records

1.6 percent Spanish-surnamed individuals.[40] These figures translate into a median figure of 3.5 years of schooling for Mexican Americans in 1949 with approximately 27 percent of the Mexican American population receiving no school at all. Anglo Americans by 1949 received a median level of 10.3 years of education.[41] When coupled with the income level and job discrimination, it appears doubtful that Mexican Americans of this period were talking of a post-war boom.

Health

A glance at health statistics does not change the image already portrayed. Particularly illuminating are the records dealing with tuberculosis and infant diarrhea, two prime indicators of the problems of low-income families. According to the Texas State Department of Health in 1944, an average of 209 "Latin Americans" out of 100,000 died of tuberculosis in contrast to 31 out of 100,000 for Anglos.[42] The Mexican American infant death rate in Texas was even more appalling at 65.1 per 1,000.[43] In San Antonio, a city with a large Mexican American population, an average of 459 Mexican American infant deaths out of 4,287 live births occurred from 1940 through 1944; for Anglos the figures were 156/4311. Infant diarrhea accounted for 37 percent of those deaths for Mexican Americans, 7 percent for Anglos.[44] Other studies showed 35.2 percent of Mexican Americans in Texas living in "dilapidated" housing, 47.9 percent living in houses without piped running water inside the unit, and 67.2 percent living in dwelling units without inside flush toilets.[45]

Public Concern

The Mexican American position in Texas society of the 1940's was clearly substandard when compared to dominant Anglo American group. As much as these conditions and facts were economically oriented (if incomes were higher, discrimination might have had less impact, and more money might have improved health factors), prejudice and bigotry on the part of Anglo Texas were a vital part of the environment for Mexican Americans. A favorite cliché of many Americans is that every ethnic group or "new" group of Americans must go through the same hardship experiences on their way "up". Unfortunately, when social attitudes of the dominant population toward Mexican Americans are revealed, the path "up" becomes littered with many obstacles. Mexican Americans, Latin Americans, Spanish-surname or Spanish-speaking persons, whatever name or label used, were not particularly liked in white America. This statement is reinforced by some interesting research.

A 1950 study dealt with the views of 1,672 white college students in

Arkansas, Louisiana, Oklahoma, and Texas. The students were presented with a series of positive and negative statements and then asked to check the statements that applied to various racial and ethnic groups. Such terms as native-born white, foreign-born white, Chinese, Indian, Jew, Filipino, Japanese, Negro, and Mexican were employed in the "check-off". The "native-born white" category received the highest "positive" rating with 86.7 percent of the statements checked being positive and only 13.3 percent negative. In contrast, the "Mexican" drew the highest percentage of negative statements, 61.4 percent.[46] If more education per se for the dominant group produced more tolerance, as many sociologists would have it, then "Mexicans" were in trouble.

The ugly manifestation of these beliefs, discrimination, existed in the social and public attitudes of Anglo Texas. Many "warnings", such as *"Se sirve solamente a raza blanca"* (Only whites are served) and *"Este baño solamente para Americanos"* (This restroom for Americans only), occupied prominent positions in and on many public places.[47] Restaurants, barber shops, movie theaters, hotels, nightclubs and swimming pools were judged as improper settings for the mingling of "whites" and "Mexicanos". Many who explained this arrangement hastened to point out that only "low-class" Mexicans were inadmissible to these monuments of free enterprise, but that "fact" probably irritated the Mexican consul when he too became "low-class".[48] Returning servicemen, including Medal of Honor winners, also suddenly became "low- class" when in the presence of the Anglo owners and managers of the aforementioned establishments. Real estate agents refused to sell to Mexican Americans or charged inflated prices when they did sell. (One real estate agent would not wear ties when he dealt with *Mexicanos* because he "understood" their uneasiness about well-dressed people). Mexican American babies could not be baptized in uptown Anglo churches.[49]

Anglo discrimination played a major role in the educational status of Mexican Americans. The low education levels did not particularly disturb Anglo educators. Indeed, Spanish-surnamed individuals did not enter the schools in some districts until late in the nineteenth century. Segregation had become official policy after the 1876 Texas Constitution permitted racial separation using the terms "white" and "colored" to connote the separate races.[50] When *Mexicano* children did not enter these schools, no one became excited.

However, when Mexican American children did take advantage of the educational opportunities, local school systems initiated the policy of the "Mexican school" and eventually a tri-ethnic program of Black, Chicano, and Anglo schools developed throughout the state. During the decade before World War II, this system became entrenched wherever

Mexican American children made up a part of the scholastic population. By 1943, the "Mexican school" existed in 122 school districts in fifty-nine counties. Spanish-surnamed children were usually "expected" to attend the Mexican school regardless of where they lived.[51]

Those who might have prevented or ameliorated this situation actually contributed to its development. Anglo officials were quite aware of segregation and were equally unwilling to change it. Local authorities often requested and received additional state funds to accommodate the "separate but equal" Mexican American schools, and then used those monies for the Anglo schools. This blatant misallocation had the tacit approval of state officials. Even after a 1930 state court decision ruled against the arbitrary nature of most Chicano segregation (while permitting the continued use of pedagogical segregation), school officials across the state promoted the same policies, including the funding of injustices.[52]

Many Anglo educators did adopt the rationale of language and "cultural" deficiencies as the sole justification for separation, but pointed out that this segregation occurred only in elementary levels. (However, it must be noted that most Mexican American children never made it through elementary school.) When more *Mexicano* students began attending high school during and after World War II, the Anglo educators took steps. Segregated high schools quickly became a part of the school systems throughout Texas.[53]

A policy of official school segregation for Americans of Mexican descent by Texas education authorities after 1945 was not easy to prove; ignorance and disavowal were effective excuses. But the intent of school officials and the results of their system were open secrets. Those that desired change or reform were powerless to accomplish that goal because most Anglo administrators did not care.

Political Response

Public discrimination and school segregation did not prevent Anglos from enacting another deprivation of fundamental rights. Jury duty did not occupy the time of most Mexican Americans because Anglo-dominated courts did not bother to call them for service, much less selection. Even in the counties that had large numbers of *Mexicano* citizens, a "jury of his peers" was an extremely rare occasion for Chicano defendants. Regarding this elemental constitutional right, Americans of Mexican descent were simply disregarded.[54]

A particularly destructive aspect of Anglo discrimination and bigotry concerned law enforcement. The relationship between police officials and Mexican Americans was mostly one-sided. Law officers consistently arrested *Mexicanos* for "offenses" and "crimes" that most Anglos rarely "committed". Such "crimes" as vagrancy, drunkenness, and the ubiquitous "resisting arrest" were constantly used as excuses to incarcerate individuals. A readiness to convict *Mexicanos* and impose higher sentences was prevalent among judges and justices of the peace. Complaints of brutality and abuse toward Latin Americans were a common part of the *barrio*. Especially in small Texas towns, Spanish-speaking persons were subject to the moods and whims of Anglo policemen. Newspapers played their part by frequently referring to "Mexican" juvenile delinquents and "Mexican" arrests, a stereotyping that would be laughable if applied to Anglos. The most brutal part of this relationship had to be the special forces known as the Texas Rangers, who considered Latin Americans as little more than human animals to be chastized by their "betters". Equal application of law was a joke for Americans of Mexican descent, but not a funny joke.[55]

The political power that might have alleviated some of these problems did not exist in Texas. Very few Mexican Americans had ever served in the state legislature. When *Mexicanos* were elected in the twentieth century, they could do little without the cooperation of Anglo representatives, a cooperation that existed only in the rarest of times and generally not at all. This is not to say that all Anglo legislators refused to work with or even for Mexican Americans, but those who did so constituted a small minority within their own ranks. In addition, the Texas Legislature was controlled by disproportionate rural elective power, and, indeed, few of these men (or in some cases, women) were sympathetic to Latin American interests.[56] Except in South Texas and Laredo, *Mexicanos* were not represented even on local governing bodies. In San Antonio, no Mexican American had served on the school board up through 1948.[57]

Attempts to organize the Mexican American vote for *Mexicano* issues often aroused the opposition of Texas politicians. "Bloc" voting when employed by the Spanish-speaking was considered unethical or un-American. But if Anglo politicians sought the Latin vote, suddenly these people became "honest Americans" exercising a constitutional privilege.[58]

Many Mexican organizations attempted to alleviate some of these problems. In the 1920's some sixteen organizations in Texas developed in response to the new increase in Mexican immigration. Most of them tried to ease the transition between the "new" *Mexicano* and the "old", and others attempted political action aimed at improving the prevalent conditions.[59] The most successful of the organizations involved a merger in 1929 in various Texas communities, particularly Somerset, San Antonio, Pearsall, Corpus Christi, Harlingen, Brownsville, Laredo, McAllen, La

Grulla, and Encino, of the *Orden de Hijos de America*, the League of Latin Americans, and the Knights of Columbus. The new group called itself the League of United Latin American Citizens (LULAC) and hoped to penetrate the apathy of the new immigrants, educate the citizenry, and develop the potential voting strength in heavily Latin-populated areas.[60]

This strength had already manifested itself to some extent in Corpus Christi, where Mexicans, because of their numbers, could determine the political balance of power, yet were controlled by Anglo politicians.[61] However, a strong paternalism within the organization manifested itself in the desire of LULAC to accept only the most advanced elements of the Spanish-speaking population in order to "guide" the lower classes.[62] But the few middle-class Mexican Americans often lost identity with the lower-income class and became more concerned with assimilation, thereby ignoring those conditions which required more drastic solutions or actions that might upset Anglo elements. LULAC, for instance, did not support the pecan-shellers' strike in San Antonio.[63]

LULAC did achieve some success in improving education and eliminating some discrimination practices in South Texas, but by and large, very little changed for Mexican Americans, particularly for the most disadvantaged.[64] Very few held any effective political office, nor did any white institutions or individuals seek to accomplish anything other than win votes.

Conclusion

Texas became a unique place for Mexican people, whether they were immigrants or citizens. Other regions displayed the basic antipathy toward *Mexicanos*; all contained the general institutional and social restrictions. However, no other area had an Alamo, San Jacinto, or Texas Ranger in their histories. While Mexican immigrants and Mexican Americans shared the same experiences, Texas was a "special" society for them. After World War II Mexican American *tejanos* would seek to make it less so.

CHAPTER III

Welcome Home

Millions of American soldiers returned after World War II eager to immerse themselves in "the good life". They had defeated the threat to democracy and freedom, and their country had once more proven itself to be the beacon of liberty for free men everywhere. Contrary to previous post war experience, the national government seemed determined to make the transition from military to civilian life as smooth as possible. By 1947, benefits for ex-servicemen in the form of federal programs depicted an unprecedented concern for veterans. As one historian has put it, "From subsidized education to privileged ocean travel for their war brides, World War II veterans received a rich bounty."[1] The anticipation by the Roosevelt and Truman administrations of these needs undermined any significant impact that veterans organizations might have had as a self-interest group. While these groups did contribute to the least controversial aspects of the new policies, they were essentially coopted by the agreeable benefit standards established and maintained by the politicians in Washington. Consequently no new organizations appeared to represent neglected veterans.[2]

Unfortunately, but not surprisingly, this analysis provides only an incomplete view of the total situation. Without contradicting the thesis of the exceptional provisions delivered to returning servicemen, one must point out that they applied only to those groups *already* organized. Hundreds of thousands of these individuals were Americans of Mexican descent, whose "good life" would not be considered on a par with their Anglo counterparts. The American Legion, and Veteran of Foreign Wars *did not* represent these people and the beacon shone dimly for these modern Ulysseses.

One of these veterans was a young doctor named Hector Perez Garcia in Corpus Christi, Texas. In 1945, Dr. Garcia began a struggle to improve the standard of life for Mexican American people. At first his efforts were focused only on Corpus Christi and other parts of Texas where Mexicans did not share in the so-called American dream of upward mobility in the economic and social sectors. With the formation of the American G.I. Forum, Hector Garcia and others were able to expand their energies to encompass a more widescale effort for *Mexicanos*. In 1948 and 1949, the G.I. Forum established their viability and vitality as an active and dynamic Mexican American organization.

Hector Perez Garcia

Hector Garcia was born in Mexico, January 17, 1914, the oldest son of Señor Jose Garcia and Señora Faustina Perez Garcia.[3] At the age of three he accompanied his family to Mercedes, Texas, a small town in the Lower Rio Grande Valley,[4] the largest geographical area of Mexican American population in the Southwest. Because of its proximity to the border, the presence of large agricultural enterprises, and the ongoing Mexican Revolution, many Mexican nationals were migrating to this region.[5] Although Señor Garcia acquired a general store, Hector and his *hermanos y hermanas* participated in the most "popular" labor activity, picking cotton. The Garcia family's economic status was such that this money was not an absolutely integral part of their family income, but it was welcome. The experience also provided young Hector contact with the extremely poor Mexicans and Mexican Americans who worked in the fields. He also noticed the constant turnover of workers as the migrant labor stream continued year after year and the relatively wealthy status of the Anglo rancher and farmer employers.[6]

In Mercedes, the young Hector attended the common *"solamente Mexicano"* schools, and would remember this experience and its effect on his classmates, deprived of the opportunity to "mix" with their Anglo counterparts and a different culture.[7] Racial segregation had been expressly forbidden in 1930 because Mexicans were considered "white" and did not fall into the racial segregation system permitted by the United States. Therefore, the usual practice in Texas was segregation based upon "language" difficulties and other pedagogical arguments.[8]

In 1929, at the age of fifteen, Garcia joined the Citizens Military Training Corps. This peacetime branch of the United States Army held a military camp one month a year in San Antonio, one of the largest urban locations for Mexican Americans in the United States. In 1932 he received a commission equivalent to second lieutenant in the U.S. Infantry, and also benefited by venturing out of the Valley and encountering other people and societies in urban America.[9]

In 1933, Edinburg Junior College received a new student. In high school, Hector Garcia had encountered a teacher who made it clear that "no Mexican will ever make an A in my class." After this verbal putdown, Garcia worked so hard and achieved such an exceptional record that such teachers could not ignore him. Indeed, educators became some of his strongest supporters. In later years, Dr. Garcia remembered this. "I really owe that teacher a lot . . . she taught me that respect and dignity can be acquired with knowledge and skill." In 1934, he entered the University of Texas and finished in the top ten of his class.[10] After two years he graduated with a Bachelor of Arts degree and entered the University of Texas School of Medicine, graduating in 1940 as a doctor of medicine.[11]

Dr. Garcia interned at St. Joseph's Hospital of Creighton University in Omaha, Nebraska from 1940 to 1941 and performed his surgical internship from 1941 to 1942. Upon completion, he immediately volunteered for combat and was placed in command of a company of infantry and then combat engineers; seven months later he was transferred to the medical corps. In the years 1942-1945, 1st Lt., Captain, and finally Major Garcia participated in the European theater of operations, earning the Bronze Star and six Battle Stars (awarded for each geographical area of combat). During that time he trained and commanded men of all ethnic and racial backgrounds. In 1945, while serving in Italy, the doctor met, courted, and married Wanda Fusillo. The next year he and his wife returned to civilian life in Corpus Christi, a city on the east coast of Texas, only a few miles from the Rio Grande Valley. Like any ambitious young man, Dr. Hector Garcia anticipated a bright and prosperous future.[12]

But this particular doctor did not have the normal attributes of "bright young men". Dr. Garcia was an American of Mexican descent, who had escaped the emasculating and devastating poverty of most of his people, and had managed to educate himself far beyond the average level of the Mexican American (3.5 years).[13] He saw the immense problems of *La Raza*, and most importantly, he cared. In 1947, while recuperating from a serious kidney ailment, he happened to hear a radio broadcast in Texas which told of the rather blatant admission by the Beeville and Sinton (small towns surrounding Corpus Christi) school superintendents that children of Mexican descent were segregated in school through the eighth grade. The doctor took a private oath to himself that if he fully recovered his health, he would spend the rest of his life working on behalf of his people.[14] He did recover, and began channeling his energies to projects that would at least publicize the plight of the Mexican Americans. The first issue the doctor took up was social discrimination. Numerous, if not most, public establishments in Texas displayed the sign "No Mexicans Served Here" *(Se sirve solamente a raza blanca")*.[15] As Mrs. Garcia recalled, "In Italy and in many European countries that I have visited, the word America is always associated with liberty, equality, and the freedom of opportunity. . . I was dumbfounded at the attitudes displayed toward Mexican people." Dr. Garcia visited Central and West Texas, talking with Mexican Americans and taking photographs to provide evidence of the prejudice. The doctor then presented his pictorial exhibitions to various groups, mostly in Corpus Christi, trying to encourage some type of interest in confronting obvious social inequities. Some people exhibited concern and some did not, including many *Mexicanos* who seemed quite complacent about their second-class status. The League of United Latin American Citizens (LULAC) seemed more interested than most, and Dr. Garcia joined the group.[16] However, he mainly pursued individual activities and rapidly became involved in the specific problems of Mexican Americans in the Corpus Christi area.

An urgent difficulty for Mexican Americans in Corpus Christi concerned health and sanitation. The poverty diseases of tuberculosis, infant diarrhea, and pneumonia were particularly prevalent in Mexican American areas. In Corpus Christi, approximately 34 percent of all family dwelling units were classified as substandard by the city-county health unit. The death rate because of tuberculosis was 51.7 per 100,000, as compared to 38.5 statewide; that of dysentery (including infant diarrhea) was 27.5 per 1,000 as compared with 3.9 statewide, and that of pneumonia stood at 45.5 compared to 35.6.[17] Appalling as these figures were, an even more distressing condition existed in the knowledge that with sufficient information, particularly on the signs and emergency treatment for infant diarrhea, the mortality rates could be reduced. Beginning in late 1946, Dr. Garcia provided this communication through weekly Spanish-language radio broadcasts. He extended his efforts with lectures to PTA groups and any others who wanted to help in the battle against the disgusting "statistics". In addition, the doctor's efforts reduced the "open pit privies" so prevalent in poor neighborhoods and a major cause of diarrhea.[18]

Dr. Garcia also became more involved in the representation, or lack of such, of Mexican Americans in education, politics, and organizations that affected their daily conditions and standards. More important, he began advocating more participation and influence in area affairs. One excellent example of his advocation appeared in his report on the migrant labor camps in Mathis, Texas. The sanitary conditions of this particular camp established as the living quarters for *braceros* and migrant workers in the area, were outrageously below the minimum standards required for any human beings or the requirements of law. These facts and recommendations were delivered in a detailed and documented report to the Texas Health Department. The doctor believed that because Mexican Americans were the principal individuals inhabiting these camps, they should be more concerned about their condition; he also concluded that because the migrant worker often had no opportunity to speak, other individuals had to assume responsibility.[19]

In 1948, Dr. Garcia became more active in LULAC when that local organization became involved in fund raising for the state LULAC school segregation case concerning the Bastrop Independent School District.[20] This participation offered an opportunity for him to meet other individuals, who also felt that Mexican Americans needed to protest the conditions forced on them by the Anglo power structure and to organize to change those conditions. When the opportunity came for a more intense program to fulfill these desires, acquaintance of these individuals would be vital.

The American G.I. Forum

Despite these various activities, Dr. Garcia did not hesitate to assume other responsibilities that might improve conditions for Americans of Mexican descent. Among his patients were a substantial number of World War II veterans. The doctor held a contract with the local Veterans Administration office by which he would treat veterans with service-connected illnesses and send the bills to the Veterans Administration office. In treating these men, he encountered difficulty from the Corpus Christi Naval (Base) Hospital in securing beds for the patients. The general excuses given centered around the "fact" that this particular facility was a naval hospital, not a veterans hospital, and thus was available only for emergencies. While trying to acquire additional beds and secure medical benefits, the doctor became aware of problems concerning other types of veterans benefits.[21]

These problems existed long before 1948. The Washington, D.C. administration had attempted to expedite the delivery of such benefits[22], but the Veterans Administration of Texas had been uncooperative with the doctor's patients, most of whom were Mexican Americans. Applications for formal schooling were not being processed in time to allow the veteran to attend school; compensation checks were often six to eight months overdue. Even the distribution of disability checks was inefficient, with some reduced or totally eliminated without the due process of review. Because most of these men were Mexican American, the local American Legion and Veterans of Foreign Wars groups would not represent them.[23] Anglo organizations ostensibly welcomed "all" veterans, but most Mexican Americans chose not to join, primarily because of the prevalent cultural and ethnic prejudices in those groups, and their lack of concern for Mexican Americans.[24]

When informed of the situation, Dr. Garcia and others decided to conduct a meeting of all disgruntled veterans in the area. They publicized their intentions in local newspapers, including the "Mexican" paper, and scheduled the meeting for March 26, 1948, at Lamar School, Corpus Christi. Approximately 700 men attended the affair; Dr. Garcia chaired the meeting and led the discussion of various issues, the first of which concerned the lack of "Latin Americans" on draft boards and the need for such "political" representation. But financial benefits and medical care quickly became the main topic of discussion.[25]

The Veterans Administration had notified veterans that pensions would be reduced unless data justifying current levels could be submitted within two months. Dr. Garcia pointed out that the adjudication boards in San Antonio were not capable of fairly deciding the pension status of the men involving education benefits and medical checks and presented many documented cases to prove his claim.

> BENITO PADILLA of 748 Cheyenne St. One day Mr. Padilla brought his sick wife to the doctor and begged him to take care of her until his check arrived. He had not received a check since six months ago, and he had his wife and child to support, the Red Cross had been helping him out. He had receipts from the Red Cross that he received money from them on the following dates: Feb. 12—$13.00, Feb. 26—$13.00, Mar. 5—$13.00, Mar. 12—$13.00, Mar. 19—$13.00. He has been to the Veterans Administration fourteen times and yet nothing has been done.

> MARTIN MARTINEZ of 1417 Sabinas St. He goes to training school at Northside Jr. High; his check has been delayed five months. He has been to the Veterans Administration four times, has a wife to support and is taking money from his father.

> ANDRES RAMIREZ of 1930 Jasmine Cts. Mr. Ramirez's wife has bled a lot, so Mr. Ramirez brought her to the doctor; the doctor in treating her, can see very clearly that Mr. Ramirez is sicker than his wife. Mr. Ramirez has lost 30 lbs. in one year and has malaria. His pension had been reduced from $69.00 to $41.00 on Dec. 1947. Statements were submitted by his doctor as should be done but yet the pension was reduced.

> JESUS RAMOS of 905 Duncan St. One day Mr. Ramos came to see the doctor because of his painful stomach. The doctor's diagnosis was possible appendicitis. The doctor sent him to the Veterans Administration with a note, and from there he was sent to the Base Hospital, where the doctor just felt his stomach and told him to come back. He came to see his doctor again and was sent to the VA and from there to the hospital, and at the hospital they told him he had to get a letter from San Antonio. In the meantime, Mr. Ramos is suffering from pain; had it been appendicitis, he would not be living now.[26]

The city-county sevice officer presented further corroboration of these serious dilemmas when he stated that 300 veterans had enrolled in school under the G.I. Bill of Rights in September of 1947 and did not receive their checks until January, 1948.[27] Additional testimony added evidence

34

of the desperate situation for many individuals and their families. The men decided to form a permanent organization, elected Dr. Hector Garcia president, and named their group the American G.I. Forum.[28]

In the following weeks the Forum contacted various officials in the Veterans Administration and the political representatives of the Corpus Christi area. The initial reaction from the VA did not offer encouragement. The local VA officer pointed out that "the number of delayed checks as compared to the number of checks issued on time is pretty small," and that the matter of presenting evidence of inequities "is primarily the responsibility of the individual veteran." As to the matter of hospital facilities, the navy had been "lenient and friendly" in its treatment and had "contributed immeasurably to the success of the veterans' medical program in South Texas."[29] While the concern of the VA office might have been sincere, the lack of understanding was apparent to the Forum.

The organization did not relax its efforts. Because documentation did exist, and because the Forum could present that evidence in an organized manner, corrections were obtained. While some of the inefficiencies and hardships had existed as long as two years, within six weeks delayed benefits were delivered and school applications returned.[30] The initial attempts by the American G.I. Forum had been at least partially successful. (Such matters as hospital facilities would require years of effort.) This raised the hopes of many Mexican American veterans that conditions could change. The Corpus Christi American G.I. Forum formed several committees to study various issues and initiate programs to enlarge Mexican American influence in those areas. They included organization, housing, education, political education, child welfare, hospitalization, poll taxes, legislative policies and employment.[31] Veterans affairs still held top priority, but the Forum became more and more aware that to improve the standard conditions of the veteran would require more than compensation checks and pensions. If the Mexican American veteran was to have just treatment in Texas, all facets of the Mexican American lifestyle would have to be improved. Back-to-school and pay-your-poll-tax drives, largely replicas of the LULAC programs, rapidly became part of the Corpus Christi Forum movement.[32]

Precisely because of veteran-connected issues, the leaders of the new Forum envisioned a much stronger and more organized group than previous Mexican American organizations. Dr. Garcia particularly believed that veterans had considerable potential for cohesive, ongoing programs because of the nature of their military life. Their ability to be "soldiers", to persevere, and to follow orders when they perceived such orders as correct might sustain their organization against any opposition or frustration.[33] The doctor hoped that after the initial success of the "soldiers", to persevere, and to follow orders when they perceived such orders as correct, might sustain their organization against any opposition or frustration.[33] The doctor hoped that after the initial success of the Corpus Christi Forum, Mexican American veterans would form G.I. Forum units in other areas of Texas. By July 1948, G.I. Forum groups existed in eleven towns surrounding Corpus Christi and in the Rio Grande Valley; by December of 1948, forty Texas communities had an American G.I. Forum.[34]

The efforts behind the organization drives usually consisted of simple communication and not so simple travel. Dr. Garcia and other leaders of the Corpus Christi chapter traveled to virtually every area that expressed a sincere desire for a G.I. Forum unit. Quite often the doctor received letters or telephone inquiries about the American G.I. Forum which culminated in a visit from the doctor or another official of the Forum. If the veterans expressed a serious interest in joining the Forum, membership cards and a copy of the Corpus Christi unit's constitution were distributed, officers elected, and general strategies discussed. (Twenty memberships became the minimum number required for the acceptance of a new unit. Dues of twenty-five cents per member constituted the only initial cash outlay.)[35] Clearly, the American G.I. Forum was being established as a grassroots organization.

The issues most discussed at these meetings concerned veterans problems and needs. Quite often the first activity consisted of requests from a particular unit to local educational institutions and VA offices for schooling, such as a vocational and educational school; the individual Forums were quite successful in starting such schools. The VA had demonstrated its "ability" to deliver veterans financial aid under the G.I. Bill of Rights, and schools such as Texas A & I University welcomed the additional money provided by the program; a few local high schools also provided classroom facilities.[36] While many veterans did not remain in the classes, often because of language difficulties, many Mexican Americans received valuable aid in "breaking through" their otherwise "segregated" educational background. Indeed, many received their first schooling since their elementary years.[37]

Obviously this type of endeavor would have to be pursued if the Mexican American position was to be effected. But acquisition of vocational and educational schools required little political strength in that the funds were already allocated; taking advantages of the opportunity was the more difficult step. If the Forum was content to simply acquire the materials and provide the schooling as its main group function, then the G.I. Forum would last as long as their schools did, but without making sufficient inroads in other areas of concern to Mexican Americans. Dr. Garcia felt that the Forum needed to participate in more complex areas.

36

For Mexican American veterans, the doctor believed the initial issue should be the lack of Americans of Mexican descent on the Texas Selective Service Board.[38]

In Texas, no "Spanish-speaking" individuals served on the various draft boards in different cities and regions. Despite the large percentage of "Spanish-surnamed" persons in the state (18 to 22 percent depending on the various population data), and the very large percentage of Mexican American volunteers and draftees in World War II (the Army kept no records of this ethnic group; analysis of numbers comes from draft lists and casualty figures), no representatives spoke for the interest of these men. To Dr. Garcia, the issue seemed clear and precise—individuals of an ethnic group that served and died for their country could not participate in the process that to a large extent determined their fate. With the rapidly increasing G.I Forum membership, the doctor wanted to mount an extensive and intensive campaign to pressure the governor of Texas to name "Latin Americans" to draft boards.[39]

The president of the Corpus Christi Forum proceeded to notify all units of this campaign. Various chapter presidents were asked to form draft committees to coordinate all draft-related communications and to write local draft officials for information regarding "Latin Americans" being placed on the boards. Local city leaders and state legislators received thousands of letters. Emphasizing the patriotic nature of the Forum's request, focusing on the majority population percentage of "Latin Americans" in much of Texas and asking for cooperation, the American G.I. Forum demanded that membership of the draft boards reflect the facts.[40]

But the Forum did not limit its activities to local regions. Communication to national leaders became an important part of the programs; letters and telegrams went to Texas congressmen and senators. One recipient of these demands and requests was President Harry Truman, who concurred in a telegram with the G.I. Forum's belief that Mexican Americans had earned the right of representation with their blood and courage. The attitude of the president of the United States differed somewhat from that of local Texas VA officials who pointed out that qualified individuals of Mexican origin were difficult to find, even though the Texas Selective Service would try.[41]

The Governor of Texas, Beauford Jester, began receiving not only the letters from the American G.I. Forum, but also requests from many of the state and national legislators who had been bombarded with information and demands. Perhaps the "revelation" of thousands of potential votes on veterans issues stirred the sincere desire for fairness that so many politicians can suddenly "reveal" at certain times. Whatever the reason, the state Selective Service director asked the G.I. Forum for a list of Latin Americans to serve on the boards, and the Governor named a minimal number to various local draft boards, including Corpus Christi.[42]

When analyzing this act by the Anglo power structure, in this case the governor, a term that comes to mind is tokenism. But in 1948, this view must be qualified. The very real success of placing *Mexicanos* on an otherwise totally Anglo-led institution represented a major victory for a Mexican American organization, expecially after the years of disregard for such efforts. Other "Latin American" groups certainly joined in the struggle, contributing valuable assistance, but the initiative and hard work of the American G.I. Forum must be credited for the advance by Mexican Americans in this area.

After this success, the American G.I. Forum became increasingly active in ethnic affairs and additional problems of the Mexican American community began assuming more importance.[43] School segregation, illegal alien labor, real estate discrimination toward *Mexicanos,* public discrimination and political representation received more attention. As the Forum began investigating the needs and difficulties of Mexican Americans, its various activities assumed a broader and more representative nature. Any progress for the American G.I. Forum would mean progress for all Mexican Americans.

CHAPTER IV

The Felix Longoria Affair

"The Buck Stops Here?"

The Federal Government was not a part of this early attempt to improve the status of Mexican Americans. As mentioned, in 1942, President Roosevelt aborted the Fair Employment Practices Committee attempt to investigate discrimination against Mexican Americans in the Southwest. They were cancelled by President Roosevelt to avoid the harmful effect they might have on relations with Latin American countries. In 1946, Harry Truman made racism a national issue. Subsequent to the Democratic Party's defeat in the congressional elections, the president appointed a civil rights committee and authorized that group to investigate the status of civil rights in the United States. He also requested in a final report "more adequate and effective means and procedures for the protection of civil rights." The fifteen members of the committee represented industry, labor, higher education, the legal profession, the South, various religious denominations and black Americans; *no* Mexican American names appeared among this prestigious group.[1]

The report produced by these individuals was called "To Secure These Rights". A remarkable document in its frank account of the problems faced by many minority groups, its focus was Black America. Nonetheless, the report contained references concerning Mexican Americans on housing and job discrimination, school segregation, public prejudice, the high rate of tuberculosis deaths and the infant mortality. The report included a statement that "the wartime gains of Negroes, Mexican Americans, and Jewish workers are being lost through an unchecked revival of discriminatory practices."[2]

Truman's reaction to "To Secure These Rights" seemed promising. The federal government increased its concern for the civil rights but concentrated on the problems of black Americans. No direction or even support for Mexican Americans emanated from federal officials. The initial success of Dr. Garcia in the Texas veterans' difficulties did not totally disrupt the traditional attitudes of Anglos toward Mexican Americans in the state. But from December 1948 through April 1949, the American G.I. Forum would have its baptism of fire.

A Hero's Burial

In December 1948, the Live Oak County service officer of George West, Texas, wrote the Fort Worth quartermaster of the American Graves Registration of the Department of the Army in reference to a deceased soldier, Private Felix Z. Longoria. He informed the department he was writing on behave of Beatrice Longoria of Corpus Christi, and named the Rice Funeral Home under the ownership of Mannor-Rice as the funeral establishment undertaking the burial of her husband, Pvt. Longoria, who had been killed in 1945 on a volunteer mission in Luzon, Philippines. His remains had finally been recovered and sent to the United States in 1948. His final destination would be Three Rivers, Texas, the residence of his parents.[3]

On January 10, 1949, Miss Sara Moreno, the sister of Beatrice Longoria, telephoned Dr. Hector Garcia. Miss Moreno explained the circumstances of Felix Longoria's death and impending burial but added a new factor. On January 8, 1949, Mr. Tom Kennedy, the new owner of the Rice Funeral Home (but the manager for the preceding fifteen months), had informed Mrs. Longoria that he would handle the arrangements for burial (in the *segregated* "Mexican" cemetery separated by a barbed wire), but would not allow the use of the chapel for the wake because "the whites would not like it." The widow did not expect this denial (no such qualifier had been issued in December), but accepted the "suggestion" to have the body lie in state in her home.[4] Mrs. Longoria returned to Corpus Christi and discussed the conversation with her sister. Miss Moreno at that time worked with a G.I. Forum-sponsored girls' club. She met Dr. Garcia when the club encountered discrimination at Mathis State Park in the form of a refusal by one of the park workers to allow the girls to use the facilities. (Miss Moreno had contacted the doctor, who obtained an apology and a promise from Texas park officials that such action would not be permitted.) When her sister informed Miss Moreno of the denial of the chapel, she suggested talking with the president of the Forum.[5]

Dr. Garcia expressed sympathy and asked to talk with Mrs. Longoria. The widow confirmed everything Miss Moreno had related, and told the doctor that she would authorize him to contact Kennedy and ask for the use of the chapel; if he still denied its use, Mrs. Longoria hoped Dr. Garcia would help her arrange the burial in Corpus Christi. The doctor expressed his regrets and agreed to do what he could.[6]

Dr. Garcia immediately telephoned the Rice Funeral Home in Three Rivers and asked to speak to the owner. Tom Kennedy informed him that he was the manager/owner and had the responsibility for all business. The doctor introduced himself and explained that he had the authority of Mrs. Longoria to request use of the chapel for the burial. Kennedy explained that all arrangements had already been made to the satisfaction of "Beatrice". When Dr. Garcia replied that she had changed her mind and was not satisfied, the conversation became interesting. Kennedy said that the chapel would not be used:

> *Dr. Garcia*: But why Mr. Kennedy?
>
> *Mr. Kennedy*: Well, you see it's this way—this is a small town and you know how it is. I'm sure you understand. I am the only funeral home here, and I have to do what the white people want. The white people just don't like it.
>
> *Dr. Garcia*: Yes, but Mr. Kennedy, this man is a veteran, I mean, soldier who was killed in action and he is worthy of all our efforts and our greatest honors. Doesn't that make (a) difference?
>
> *Mr. Kennedy*: No that doesn't make any difference. You know how the Latin people get drunk and lay around all the time. The last time the Latin Americans used the home they had fights and got drunk and raised lots of noise and it didn't look so good. I—we have not let them use it and we don't intend to let them start now. . . . I don't dislike the Mexican people but I have to run my business so I can't do that. You understand the whites here won't like it.
>
> *Dr. Garcia*: Yes, I understand Mr. Kennedy, thank you.[7]

This particular doctor understood all too well. He proceeded to do two things, both of which would have a critical effect on the events of the next few months. First, after his conversation with Kennedy, Dr. Garcia called George Groh, a reporter for the *Corpus Christi Caller-Times* who had been covering the activities of the local American G.I. Forum chapter. He told Groh of the Longoria matter and his own conversation with Kennedy; he informed Groh that the Forum would have a protest meeting the next evening, January 11. The reporter called Kennedy for verification. Warning him that anything he said was for publication, he asked if he had denied chapel services to Beatrice Longoria. Kennedy answered in the affirmative. Groh then asked if refusal had been based on Longoria's race. Kennedy replied, "We never made a practice of letting Mexicans use the chapel and we don't want to start now."[8]

Dr. Garcia's second action entailed a telegram to Senator Lyndon Baines Johnson. The two men had never met, but the doctor had learned about Johnson through Texas Congressman John Lyle, a mutual friend of both Dr. Garcia and Senator Johnson.[9] In his telegram, the doctor called Kennedy's action " . . . a direct contradiction of those same principles for which this American soldier made the supreme sacrifice in giving his life for his country and for the same people who now deny him the last funeral rites deserving of any American hero regardless of his origin."[10]

On the morning of January 11, Dr. Garcia began issuing announcements of a protest meeting of all area G.I. Forums with circulars explaining the Longoria incident, and George Groh wrote an article in the morning edition of the *Caller-Times*. Groh had called Kennedy that morning for double confirmation. Kennedy qualified his previous statement of denial by saying he would "discourage" the chapel service for Longoria, but would not refuse service. However, he did not deny nor retract his statements of the previous night, and Groh duly noted this in his article.[11] Events began to assume their own momentum.

The mayor of Three Rivers, probably alerted by the newspaper article and/or Tom Kennedy, sent a telegram to the American G.I. Forum that must stand as a monument to desperation.

> I have just interviewed T. W. Kennedy of Rice Funeral Home Stop Some mistake Stop Kennedy did not refuse use of his facilities and does not refuse Stop Arrangements can be made for use if desired by Longoria Family Stop American Legion has arranged full military honors also offers use of American Legion Hall Stop Mayor's home offered if necessary.
>
> J. K. Montgomery, Mayor[12]

Obviously some mistake had been made somewhere by somebody. Other wires came to Dr. Garcia from all over the state, both in reply to messages sent by the Forum and in response to this obscene affront to human dignity. The attorney general of Texas expressed his deep regrets and promised cooperation with the Good Neighbor Commission. (This organization was created to improve and expand relations between Mexico and the United States and among Texas citizens.) Congressman John Lyle promised action as did Congressman Lloyd M. Bentsen, who advocated "everything possible to remedy this deplorable situation."[13] Texas state senator Rogers Kelley condemned the "un-American conduct and reprehensible conduct on the part of the Three Rivers Funeral Home."[14] Late that afternoon a wire arrived from Texas governor Beauford Jester. He regretted the incident and gave assurances that the funeral could be held as requested by the family and as promised by Kennedy to the governor.[15] National news commentators Drew Pearson, Walter Winchell, and Westbrook Pegler also commented on the affair. As Walter Winchell put it, "The state of Texas, which looms so large on the map, looks mighty small tonight. . . ."[16] And indeed it did.

In Corpus Christi, Dr. Garcia conducted an understandably emotional meeting of more than 1,000 people. Mrs. Beatrice Longoria and the Forum president related the events, and others were discussing possible avenues of action when the meeting was interrupted by a message. It was a telegram from Senator Lyndon Johnson.

> I deeply regret to learn that the prejudice of some individuals extends even beyond this life. I have no authority over civilian funeral homes. Nor does the federal government. However, I have today made arrangements to have Felix Longoria buried with full military honors in Arlington National Cemetery here at Washington where, the honored dead of our nation's war rest. Or, if his family prefers to have his body interred nearer his home, he can be reburied at Fort Sam Houston National Military Cemetery at San Antonio. There will be no cost. If his widow desires to have reburial in either cemetery, she should send me a collect telegram before his body is unloaded from an army transport at San Francisco, Jan. 13th. This injustice and prejudice is deplorable. I am happy to have a part seeing that this Texas hero is laid to rest with the honor and dignity his service deserves.
>
> Lyndon B. Johnson, USS[17]

To comprehend the feelings of the people gathered at that meeting would require an understanding of what it meant to live under the shadow of bigotry and hate. Suffice it to say, they were moved. Dr. Garcia promptly requested funds for the Longoria family to make the trip to Washington, D.C. Nine hundred dollars were received that night, and a compaign began to gather sufficient funds.[18]

By this time, the Anglo community of Three Rivers realized that this would be no simple or temporary protest by a few "radicals." Kennedy sent letters to Dr. Garcia and Mrs. Longoria denying that he had refused the chapel, arguing that he had only discouraged its use because of *his* belief that trouble existed between Mrs. Longoria and Pvt. Longoria's parents. This excuse became Kennedy's standard reason for his action. The Three Rivers Chamber of Commerce supported the statement and lambasted the "bad publicity" of the entire affair.[19] Dr. Garcia, realizing the importance of *la familia* in the culture of *Mexicanos,* had worked closely with the family since that first night when he became involved. The doctor felt confident that this would be one fight where the time-worn "divide and conquer" strategy would not succeed.[20] But that did not keep certain individuals from trying.

The Good Neighbor Commission also had involved itself and the nature of that involvement bears scrutiny. The commission had been created to improve relations among Texas citizens, specifically to augment the opportunity for Texas to participate in the Mexico-U.S. contract labor agreements. Texas was blacklisted in 1942 because of discrimination and only in 1947 had received another chance. But a

43

serious controversy surrounded the commission. Many people considered it ineffective and more of a public relations gimmick than a sincere effort at improving Mexican-Anglo relations. A substantial number of Texans considered it a worthless and unnecessary interference in state affairs.[21] The GNC managed to antagonize both sides in the Felix Longoria case. Its representatives desperately wanted the burial to be in Texas. They seemed more concerned about the image of Texas than with the essence of the incident. As a member of the Commission wrote to Dr. Garcia:

> We all agree that the happening at Three Rivers is to be regretted, and we must bear in mind that the reputation of Texas will be at stake in history's recording of our handling of this very delicate matter. . . . Bear the thought in mind that Texas and all Texans and the children of Texas now living will feel the effect of the criticism, and *we all know that none of them has anything to do with it* (emphasis mine) . . . the future (of the Good Neighbor Commission) will be greatly handicapped unless this is satisfactorily handled . . . she (Beatrice Longoria) has an opportunity to contribute one of the *finest acts* toward this better understanding—and she is the only one who can do it.[22]

Neither the American G.I. Forum nor Beatrice Longoria yielded to this appeal.

The Longoria family had decided to have the funeral at Arlington National Cemetery, but there were further activities by the Three Rivers power structure that solidified their decision. The Longorias had committed themselves to the Johnson proposal the night of January 11, but had remained open to a funeral in Three Rivers, mostly because they had lived there most of their lives. Senator Johnson and the Forum completely agreed to that alternative, but the attitude of certain Three Rivers citizens prevented any possibility of such an option. The proverbial straw came on January 20, 1949, when the *Three Rivers News* issued a massive condemnation of Senator Johnson and defense of Three Rivers.[23]

This article pointed out that "no town in South Texas has better relations with Americans of Mexican descent . . . ", and that the "hasty action of Senator Johnson was largely responsible for unfavorable publicity." The news of the proposed Arlington ceremony "stunned" the people of Three Rivers because they "were prepared to bury their deceased brother and had even arranged the firing squad". There had never been any strife in Three Rivers; the town had even cared for a poor, crippled Mexican American boy named Juan. Tom Kennedy acted improperly, but only out of concern for "Beatrice", who was disliked by the Longoria family. He had "lost his head" but was "misquoted and misjudged."[24] Obviously the entire matter was a conspiracy of the press and a political ploy by LBJ.

As Dr. Garcia pointed out, the Longoria family simply would not tolerate this idiocy, including the abuse of Senator Johnson. The funeral took place on February 16, 1949. Besides the Longoria family, Senator Johnson and Major General Harry Vaughn, the personal representative of the President of the United States, were present to honor this Mexican American soldier.[25]

In fairness, it must be stated that many Anglos in Texas and the U.S. supported the Longorias and the G.I. Forum in their struggle with Three Rivers. Many viewed the issue as a clear-cut case of discrimination against a "Latin American comrade (who) had made the supreme sacrifice of giving his life honorably on the battlefield."[26] Some, however, viewed the incident as much more reflective of a deep and pervasive attitude of Anglos; people who felt that ". . . an American of Mexican extraction is (not) entitled to the privileges of United States citizenship in life or in death."[27]

On the other hand, a significant number of Texans felt that the people of Three Rivers were misunderstood or misjudged. These individuals accepted the weak rationalizations of the *Three Rivers News*, Tom Kennedy, and others. Officials in the governor's office became excited with the "facts" of that January 20 edition, believing that it contained an answer to the troublemakers of the Forum.[28] The San Antonio American Legion passed a resolution on January 27, 1949, emphasizing the "careless and immature actions by people in high and honorable places (that brought) harmful humiliation and embarassment . . . to the Kennedy family. . . the good people of the City of Three Rivers and the State of Texas." The people of Three Rivers had enjoyed "at all times" peaceful, orderly and most pleasant relations among the races.[29]

The best expression of this attitude came in Texas state representative J. F. Gray's proposal for a bill to eliminate the Texas Good Neighbor Commission because of incidents like the Longoria affair. (Some opposition to this attempt pointed out the responsible behavior of the commission but with the inevitable disclaimer that "there is less racial discrimination among Americans today than ever before.")[30] The act did not pass, but Congressman Gray did not give up. On the day *after* the Longoria funeral, he called for a House investigation of the controversy surrounding the reburial of Pvt. Felix Longoria; the membership authorized a committee for said purposes by a vote of 104—20.[31]

The reaction of the American G.I. Forum left no margin for misunderstanding. Dr. Garcia welcomed the investigation and demanded an open hearing for all of the people. The chairman of the Good Neighbor Commission offered to resign if the investigation found duplicity in the commission's action. The committee decided to hold the open hearing in the Chamber of Commerce building at Three Rivers. The Forum prepared

45

its case but faced many "man-made" obstacles.[32]

The chairman and a majority of the committee imposed restrictions on evidence introduced at the hearing. Only testimony directly linked to the specific Felix Longoria/Funeral Home incident was allowed; remarks or testimony concerning prejudice and discrimination in Texas had no bearing on the case, according to a majority of the body. Few Mexican Americans attended the sessions, but many of the Anglo citizens of Three Rivers did. A final exquisite touch was the continued presence of the sheriff of Bee County with his loaded pistols.[33]

The supporters of Kennedy and Three Rivers (the town certainly considered itself on trial) emphasized the "lack" of prejudice in the city and their "esteem" for the Longoria family. Investigations by other parties showing no discrimination in the incident were presented as evidence for the innocence of Kennedy and others; the letters by Kennedy to Mrs. Longoria denying any refusal became a part of that evidence. The most extreme attempt to discredit Dr. Garcia and the Forum was the "accusation that Guadalupe Longoria wanted the burial at Three Rivers, disliked the doctor, and felt insulted by the collections gathered for the journey to Washington, D.C." Consistent with this presentation, Johnson and the American G.I. Forum (not to mention the GNC) were denounced as troublemakers and political opportunists.[34]

Hector Garcia and Gus Garcia, an attorney with considerable experience in combating Anglo institutions, had effective evidence of their own. Thomas Sutherland, chairman of the GNC, testified that the manager of the funeral home had told him that he could not allow Mexicans to use the chapel. Notarized statements of Sara Moreno, Beatrice Longoria, Gladys Bucher (the doctor's nurse who had listened to the first conversation between Kennedy and Dr. Garcia) and other individuals completely supported the fact of discrimination. Two pariculalry critical statements came from George Groh, the *Caller-Times* reporter and Señor Guadalupe Longoria.[35]

Groh's statement confirmed that Kennedy had indeed denied service on the basis of "the whites would object." Kennedy's excuse that he had used those words to Dr. Garcia in anger does not bear up in his conversation with Groh. Furthermore, Groh's testimony proved that in fact discrimination did exist; he cited Kennedy as stating, "We have never made a practice of letting Mexicans use the chapel, and we don't want to start now."[36]

Guadalupe Longoria's statement completely contradicted Kennedy and those who tried to convince the committee that a feud existed between the widow and the inlaws. He pointed out that the Longoria family had supported and cooperated with Beatrice and Dr. Garcia since the first night of the incident. In addition, Señor Longoria stated he had requested financial assistance from the Forum and other Mexicanos. Most significantly, the father described the attempts of the president of the Three Rivers Chamber of Commerce, the mayor, and city secretary to obtain his signature on a statement of repudiation of the Forum. In fact, as he emphasized, he never signed such a document. Finally, the father of Felix Longoria stated:

> I want it clearly understood that I am very grateful to Dr. Garcia and the American G.I. Forum for their efforts in our behalf . . . to other organizations . . . , and particularly to Senator Johnson.
>
> If any embarrassment has been caused by this case to anyone, I am sorry, but after all, I did not create a feeling of prejudice which seems to exist in many places in Texas against people of my national origin. Other people are responsible for that. I think that we would only be fooling ourselves to try to leave the impression that people of Mexican descent are treated the same as anyone else through the State of Texas.[37]

Evidence not allowed at the hearing including a report proving that segregation (which had been ruled illegal in 1948) existed in Three Rivers elementary schools through the fifth grade. The separate, barbed wire "Mexican" cemetery was already a well-known fact. An incredible incident occurred *during* the hearing when a young Mexican American was denied service in a barbershop *next door* to the chamber of commerce because ". . . we don't serve Latin Americans."[38]

Despite this overwhelming evidence to the contrary, the committee issued a majority report on April 7 that concluded "there was not discrimination on the part of the undertaker of Three Rivers, relative to the proposed burial of the body of the deceased Felix Longoria." In a literal "whitewash" the report accepted the dubious contentions of the undertaker that "strained relations" existed between Beatrice Longoria and other members of the family. The committee excused Kennedy's actions with the notion that he had acted only in the best interests of the widow. He had the impression there would not be any reason for chapel services because the "deceased veteran was supposed to be a Catholic and would want interment in accordance with the rules and regulations of the church of his faith."[39] Dr. Garcia was branded, by implication, as the instigator of subsequent actions. The previously quoted telegram by the mayor of Three Rivers and Kennedy's letter denying any refusal were accepted as absolute fact and proof of good intentions. As for the "unfortunate expressions" of Kennedy, the committee concluded that upon reflection, he had displayed anger but had apologized. Four of the five committeemen signed the majority report.[40]

47

The fifth member of the Committee, Frank Oltorf, filed a minority report in which he stated he "could not concur in their majority report without violating both my sense of justice and my intellectual honesty."[41] The substance of his report concerned Kennedy's actions from January 8 through January 11, 1949. Employing the evidence of his conversations with Dr. Hector Garcia, George Groh, and Tom Sutherland, Congressman Oltorf concluded that indisputable and undeniable statements, particularly of reporter Groh, had clearly established discrimination. As Oltorf said, "I cannot look into the heart of Mr. Kennedy to ascertain his true intent but can only accept his oral words which appear to me discriminatory."[42]

While Three Rivers citizens celebrated the majority report, Texas senator Rogers Kelley called it "a tragic blot on the democracy of Texas and the United States." Criticizing the obvious selectivity of the evidence incorporated in the majority statement, Kelley called for a more complete account.[43] The next day a member of the House Committee essentially agreed with Senator Kelley. Although he had signed the majority report, Bryon Tinsley asked that his name be withdrawn. Citing hasty action and new evidence, Tinsley requested additional study; otherwise he would have to withdraw his signature and make his own report. In fact Congressman Tinsley did file his own account admitting Kennedy's actions may have been on the "fine line of discrimination", although not "absolute and deep-seated."[44]

What had begun as a whitewash of the Felix Longoria case ended as an emasculated and repudiated collection of excuses. The courage of Frank Oltorf and the following action of Bryon Tinsley (although an inconclusive statement) destroyed the credibility of the majority report. The document was never incorporated into the legislative record. Dr. Hector Garcia and the American G.I. Forum had won their vindication.

The Felix Longoria case produced important results for the civil rights movement of Mexican Americans in Texas and the southwestern United States. For at least a brief time, Americans of Mexican descent were united in a single effort to fight Anglo prejudice and discrimination. Letters of support and financial donations to the Longoria family came from all areas of the nation.[45] A strength developed by unity and endurance would be a lesson not lost on many of these people. Obviously this concept played a major role in the determination of the G.I. Forum to persevere in "la lucha".

But more important than any single victory, the Felix Longoria case demonstrated a number of realities. Democratic ideals as they applied to Mexican American people were acts of hypocrisy. Prejudice and bigotry in Texas was a genuine force that had to be confronted.[46] The national media coverage of the incident demonstrated to many otherwise unconvinced or unknowing persons that being a Mexican American was a different experience than being an Anglo American, not only regarding the obvious dissimilarity of culture but of attitude. For the leaders of Three Rivers, a "Latin American" did not merit the same respect as "white people". All "races" lived together in harmony, a harmony defined by Tom Kennedy and J.F. Gray. When Hector Garcia's concept of harmony, which meant equality, disrupted the Anglo precepts, other people were forced to listen and the G.I. Forum firmly established its credibility, both to Mexican Americans and Anglos, as a state organization that could and would fight for *Mexicanos*. They heard a new voice, a man and an organization that would seek "to secure these rights."

CHAPTER V

Texas and Beyond

Befor the Felix Longoria case, the G.I. Forum operated as an association of individual chapters which recognized the Corpus Christi unit as the titular head. However, with the success of the Longoria affair and the subsequent acquisition of new groups, leaders of the Forum saw a need to develop a more cohesive organization. Consequently, the first state convention of the various units developed a constitution which officially established the American G.I. Forum of Texas. From this base, policies were formed regarding membership, direction, and methodology producing a system by which programs and activities could be more firmly and effectively managed.

The immediate concerns remained veteran-oriented, but gradually evolved to more than pension checks and vocational schools; the first success after state organization was a challenge of the Veterans Administration to prevent the loss of the benefits won before the Longoria case. Assistance to individuals also retained the attention of Forumeers, but better hospital care and political representation in the nature of draft board participation attracted their active efforts to make Anglo officials more aware of Mexican American needs. Finally, the first years (1949—1952) witnessed the expansion of the Forum into New Mexico and Colorado; these organizational efforts became precedents for a growth that would eventually encompass national development.

Part 1 - A Framework

The efforts of the Forum during the critical period of January through April 1949 established the group as a viable representative of Mexican Americans in Texas. But to continue and maintain the momentum of the preceding thirteen months, and to incorporate the expanding membership into an efficient unit, a framework had to be developed. From that first group established in March 1948, the Forum would grow to 100 chapters in 1950. The need for a flexible yet consistent set of guidelines to accommodate that growth was obvious to the leaders even before the Felix Longoria affair. The rapid formation of new groups immediately after the so-called "investigation" confirmed their belief. In September 1949, the American G.I. Forum of Texas became a state organization. The first state convention took place in Corpus Christi and the first elected state president was Dr. Hector P. Garcia.[1]

The state constitution developed by the convention based many of its tenets on the Corpus Christi constitution. The basic purpose of the Forum was "to strive for the procurement of all veterans and their families, regardless of race, color or creed, the equal privileges to which they are entitled under the laws of our country" and for the "preservation of the democratic ideals for which this country has fought in all wars." Stressing the right of all citizens to equality in social and economic opportunities, the constitution emphasized improved understanding between all nationalities.[2]

Rules for membership were simple enough. All persons, male or female, who had served honorably in the armed services were eligible to join. In addition, all women over 21 and related through marriage or in the third degree to a veteran could be active in the American G.I. Forum Auxiliary. Furthermore, all young people between 14 and 21 years of age related through marriage or in the third degree to a veteran were eligible to become members of the Junior G.I. Forum; these persons had to be citizens of the United States.[3] The constitution of 1949 also permitted a non-veteran adult male of "high moral character and of good reputation in the community" to be a regular member with limited privileges, excluding voting or holding office. Such individuals had to have the sponsorship of a veteran and majority approval of the membership. And to prevent coopting of the original goals of the Forum, the number of non-veterans could not exceed 25 percent of the total membership (although the percentage would not require a decrease if the number of veterans decreased). To retain their charter, each chapter had to have ten active veterans. Finally, "no person, veteran or not, who is member of a Communist, Fascist, or other conspiracy that advocates the overthrow by force of the government of the United States shall be eligible to membership in any G.I. Forum, or Junior Forum."[4]

The organizational structure consisted of four major bodies: the state convention, the state board of directors, the district organization, and local chapters. Each had its own independent function and a dependence on each other for final action.

The state convention became the chief and supreme legislative and judicial body of the G.I. Forum, meeting once a year and/or at the call of the state chairman at a designated location. Attending the convention were state officers, representatives of the districts and delegates from each chapter (four for the first twenty members and one of each additional ten). In each debate on the convention floor only the delegates had the right to participate and vote, and the state officers could vote only if they were duly-elected chapter representatives. All resolutions and actions of the state convention were binding on all officers and units of each gradation. In addition, the convention body would elect a state chairman and three vice-chairmen from the G.I. Forum, Auxiliary, and Junior Forums. The state convention would have the authority to pass its own rules of procedure insofar as they did not conflict with the constitution.[5]

When the state convention was not in session, the governing body of the Texas G.I. Forum would be the Board of Directors.* Other officers selected by the state convention could attend the Board of Director meetings, but the aforementioned persons were the chief governing officers of the Texas Forum.[6]

Executive, administrative, legislative, and judicial functions were carried on by these people. All resolutions and actions of the Board of Directors were binding on the officers and members of local chapters; any failure to abide by their actions would subject the offender to impeachment or charter removal. However, due process, including notification of alleged charges and opportunities to present rebuttive evidence, was an inviolate procedure of any such punitive action.[7]

The third organization within the structural hierarchy of the G.I. Forum was the district unit. The state was divided into geographical county regions by the Board of Directors. The local G.I. Forums, Auxiliaries. and Junior Forums fell under their particular district and were allowed four representatives at each district meeting. Besides these local representatives, the district gatherings included the district chairman and district representatives (elected to attend meetings of the Board of Directors), a vice-chairman, secretary, treasurer, chaplain, reporter and other designated officials. The primary function of the district officers was the implementation of the policies of the state convention and Board of Directors. At these meetings, policies and programs of the local chapters could be initiated and modified if they did not conflict with actions and policies established by the Board of Directors and the state convention. A final important duty of the district body concerned the organization of additional groups in each district.[8]

The heart of the G.I. Forum remained the individual chapters that had carried the organization in 1948 and through the Longoria case. The Texas Constitution of 1949 designated those units as "local groups". Any Forum officer or member could, with permission of the Board of

*Composed of the State Chairman, the Chairman of the Board, the three State Vice-Chairmen, the State Secretary, Treasurer, Legal Advisor, Chaplain, Executive Secretary, the immediate past State Auxiliary Chairman, State Auxiliary Vice-Chairman, State Auxiliary Recording Secretary, State Auxiliary Treasurer, and State Veterans Affairs Officers, District Chairmen and District Representatives.

Directors, state chairman, or district chairman, organize a G.I. Forum group. When ten members joined the chapter, a charter would be issued by the state chairman subject to the approval of the Board. Local Forums could legislate and administer any local program not in conflict with the constitution or structural hierarchy. Auxiliary groups were required in every community that had a G.I. Forum. It was hoped that Junior Forums would be organized in such communities, but they were not required; however, Junior units were allowed in any community regardless of the presence of the G.I. Forum. Auxiliary and Junior units were expected to conform with the constitution and leadership of the state structure. All of these groups had a chairman, vice-chairman, secretary, treasurer, chaplain, reporter and other officers if so desired. The only other "requirement" of the local groups was the monetary dues of members and groups. These were determined by the state convention to be twenty-five cents per year. Failure to pay constituted an offense punishable by revocation of the individual local charter; a sixty-day grace period was granted to allow reactivation without a penalty fee.[9]

The state convention of 1949 also formally defined the functions and duties of the state officers, at that time the highest-ranking leaders of the G.I. Forum. The state chairman, elected to a one-year term by a majority of the convention, was designated as the presiding officer at the state convention and Board of Directors meetings. Other duties were the appointments of all committees and officers occupied by such manner and the role of official G.I. Forum representatives at all social, civic, and other functions. Other officers created were the vice-chairman, state secretary, state treasurer, legal advisor, state chaplain, and executive secretary. All were one-year elective offices except the Legal Advisor and secretary, which were appointed by the state chairman and the Board of Directors, respectively. Tenure for the latter was left to the discretion of the appointee and the demonstrated ability of the officer holder; the chairman and Board supervised these two positions.[10]

Other provisions of the 1949 constitution included impeachment or removal of officers and members, with appeal provisions, a nepotism clause and rules of procedure (Robert's Rules of Order). A final paragraph outlined the political role of the American G.I. Forum.

> While this organization seeks the participation of all citizens as individuals in political affairs, it is forbidden to all officers and members (sic) of this organization use the name "The American G.I. Forum of Texas or G.I. Forum" or any other derivative of any political party. Letterheads, emblems, and other insignia or material identified with this organization shall not be used for such a purpose either, and all officers and members are urged, when participating in political affairs as individuals to do their utmost not to be iden-

tified publicly as officers and members of this organization when involved in such activity.[11]

This section as well as other provisions of this constitution served the G.I. Forum well in its first years. As the organization expanded into other states (as well as Texas) the guidelines formulated in 1949 became the basis for development and implementation of the new chapters and state units through 1955. While some states modified the structure (New Mexico used "regions" in place of "districts"; Colorado eliminated the district concept), the functions, duties, and procedural methods outlined in the Texas convention of 1949 did act as the general precedent for organization, with the Convention/Board of Directors-District/Local structure adopted by the new states. New chapters also adopted the political proviso; Dr. Garcia and other leaders were concerned that political associations would subject the Forum to criticism of "political" self-interest that could interfere with development. These individuals realized the necessity of political strength for the improvement of Mexican American life, but to seek entrance to the strongest Anglo institution with an obviously disorganized interest group with meager economic, social or political power seemed self-destructive.[12] Hostile Anglo politicians could easily destroy a Spanish-speaking "political" group, but a family-oriented veterans organization (hence, the name American G.I. Forum) was the proverbial "horse" of a different color. "Forumeers" wanted the opportunity to succeed; they did not contemplate suicide.

Part 2 - Veterans Needs

Representation of the veteran and his needs continued to be of critical priority to the Texas G.I. Forum. In fact, an important issue discussed at the 1949 Texas convention concerned a directive by the National Veterans Administration that reinterpreted the education benefits section of P.L. 266. According to this order by the Washington, D.C., office, thousands of veterans were ineligible to receive monetary aid because of a distinction between vocational and educational schools. After deliberating methods of changing this policy, State Chairman Garcia, representing the unanimous will of the G.I. Forum, immediately notified the Texas congressional representatives of the American G.I. Forum's opposition to the new restrictions. Emphasizing the original intent of the G.I. Bill to reward the American veteran for his services, Dr. Garcia accused the Veterans Administration of violating the promise and spirit of that legislation. He argued that if Congress sustained the new directive, thousands of Mexican Americans would have to change classes to accommodate and retain their benefits; many would automatically lose the financial help. (A difficulty for many *Mexicanos* was the basic problem of securing the facilities and instructor for the courses, whether "educational or vocational"; while federal money financed many of the classes, bureaucratic disruption could have been a detrimental influence on continued educational opportunities.) The doctor did not spell out these concerns in official communiqués, realizing that patriotism tended to be a more compelling reason for cooperation of federal officials than the eradiction of discrimination. The doctor asked Congress to support a Senate bill to supercede Directive 1-A and restore the eliminated benefit. The Forumeers' standard procedure of sending telegrams and letters to their political representatives went into effect. Congress agreed with the Forum, and many Anglo as well as Mexican American veterans did not lose valuable and well-earned benefits.[13]

Dealing with these institutions reinforced the Forum's belief in 1948 that "political" representation in the sense of *Mexicano* office holders had to become a reality. The appointment of Mexican Americans to Texas draft boards in 1948 acquired new significance in 1949. When the Korean police action began in the summer of 1950, the draft laws were revived, reactivating old boards of World War II and creating new ones. The Board of Directors of the G.I. Forum called on all local chapters to notify mayors and those citizens who usually recommended men to the State Selective Service for draft boards of their intentions to have a Mexican American on those bodies. Citing the daily casualty lists of the war and the presence of a large number of Spanish names, and pointing out the over-representation of Spanish-surnamed persons in the armed forces, Forumeers demanded representation for Latin Americans. The governor of Texas was especially singled out for attention, because he received the lists of suggested names at the end of the nominating process, and had the most influence on the new appointments. Apparently not willing to create another confrontation with the Forum (a la Felix Longoria), Governor Allan Shivers did approve a few *Mexicanos* for draft board membership. After all, when South Texas counties with 40 to 70 percent Mexican population lacked even one Spanish surname among the draft board names, and when thousands of letters informed politicians of that fact, and finally when that practice took place during a war, recognition of a few people did not require great humanitarian concern. But it did call for massive action by many people —which the Forumeers provided.[14]

The Forum also remained attentive to individuals and their difficulties. Men who were not paid pension and benefit checks on time, men who never received entitled aid, Mexican Americans who often

55

lacked the necessary abilities (writing a coherent letter or presenting an organized, documented case) to deal with bureaucracy—these were the people the Forum represented so well. Often the Forum service amounted to nothing more than writing a letter to a veterans official, or filling out required documents to enable a widow to receive compensation. If a *Mexicano* veteran needed help with interviews, Dr. Garcia and others were there. But just as often the problems demanded a more abrasive approach; why was this person denied services, why did this individual lose a job or why was he denied disability? Hard questions were asked and evasive answers not accepted. The batter of red tape with triplicate copies and detailed demographics did not defeat those who understood the game. The Forum did not always win these individual struggles, but the reality of its attitude and endurance increased the self-respect and dignity for Mexican Americans so assaulted by years of prejudice and bigotry. Prolific correspondence between Dr. Garcia and politicians, and between Forum leaders and "administrators", testifies to the fact that at least a dent was made in the massive indifference usually displayed by Anglo institutions, in this instance, the Veterans Administration, toward Mexican Americans.[15]

Another issue connected with veteran facilities, but actually much broader in its impact, concerned health care, specifically hospital availability for Mexican Americans. Sixty South Texas counties were served in 1948 by one veterans hospital in San Antonio, which could not fulfill the needs of that vicinity, much less all of the Rio Grande Valley. Persons requiring immediate treatment were often placed on long waiting lists; many applicants with terminal illnesses did not receive any hospitalization. These crowded conditions "forced" most hospitals with veteran contracts to a policy of emergency treatment only. Inefficient medical programs had plagued the Veterans Administration for many years; in 1945 President Truman fired the Administrator of Veteran Affairs after numerous complaints. The problems did not clear up and were a concern of the Forum's first organizational efforts in Corpus Christi.[16]

The situation did not improve by 1950; if anything, it worsened. The Forum inundated Texas congressmen with demands for improving existing facilities and creating additional structures; a bill introduced in Congress proposing a new hospital garnered little support. The matter became more acute with actual proposals to *reduce* the ability of the U.S. Naval Hospital in Corpus Christi to administer minimal emergency care. An order in February 1950 from the Veterans Administration terminating its contract with the hospital brought angry protests from the Texas G.I. Forum and other veteran groups affected by the plan. The opposition carried enough strength to produce a Special House Armed Services Committee investigation. The formal request came from Texas Congressmen John Lyle and Lloyd Bentsen. Along with other interested participants, the committee asked Dr. Garcia to testify.[17]

The founder of the G.I. Forum pointed out that more than 60 percent of 150,000 to 200,000 veterans in South Texas were Americans of Mexican origin. Most lived in the worst slums of Texas cities, where the virulent diseases of poverty, including tuberculosis, pneumonia, and dysentery were prevalent. The limited resources in South Texas forced these individuals to travel over 400 miles for desperately needed and usually prolonged treatment. Besides the intolerable loss of income forced on the traveler, the journey decreased the already poor health of the patient. The doctor presented documented cases from his own practice in which people, who did not fall into the "emergency" category, died because of the lack of immediate treatment. The committee must have been impressed with the evidence of the doctor and other witnesses, for a total of fifty beds were allocated to the Corpus Christi Naval Hospital (after the VA decreased allocations elsewhere). It might be added that Senator Lyndon Johnson obtained fifty additional beds after weeks of working with the Department of Defense and the Veterans Administration.[18] The efforts expended for results gained may seem disproportionate, but "ropes for drowning men" must not be discounted.

In 1952, it appeared that another such "rope" would be severed when the Department of Defense decided to reactivate an air force base in South Texas. The problem concerned the adaption of the hospital on the base for tuberculosis patients; reactivation meant displacement of those people, most of whom were *Mexicanos*. For years the G.I. Forum had fought for a new TB hospital but had been unsuccessful;[19] now it appeared as if the old treatment areas were to be subjected to the same disinterest. (TB beds at veterans hospitals had been decreased in 1950-1951 despite all that the Forum and its political supporters such as Bentsen, Lyle, and Johnson could do.)[20] This time, South Texas legislators appealed to the Forum for its support in assuring the residents of South Texas continued facilities. Forumeers were urged to contact Tom Connally, Johnson, Lyle and others to demand support and put pressure on Governor Shivers and the VA for substitute treatment centers. The G.I. Forum did not have to be asked; indeed, it remained in the forefront of the campaign to secure surrogate care. Influential persons indicated agreement with the position of the concerned parties, but unfortunately, temporary hardships were imposed.[21]

The paradoxical and frustrating dilemma of securing adequate health care for those who most needed it, yet were the most likely not to receive any, remained a vital issue for the G.I. Forum. Continually during the Eisenhower administration veterans hospitals decreased their capacity to provide services for veterans. Economizing usually meant reducing beds, clerical help, and other such aids that *Mexicanos* so obviously needed. However, the Texas G.I. Forum never allowed such deprivation to happen unnoticed; the attitude of the federal government did not totally yield to this pressure, but clearly the Anglo leaders were increasingly aware of a new voice in Texas,[22] and that voice did not remain a provincial shout.

Part 3 - People Contribute

As more Mexican Americans learned about the G.I. Forum, particularly the dynamic success of the Longoria affair, the founder and leaders of the first chapters were asked to meet with groups of *Mexicano* veterans and other interested people. Dr. Garcia personally logged thousands of miles in Texas spreading the news about the organization, distributing information, organizing material, and actively participating in the formation of many of these groups. But this effort did not end with the acceptance of a charter by the Board of Directors; Dr. Garcia spent countless hours following up on the initial work. Constant communication, frequent speeches, and numerous Board and District meetings filled his daily schedule as well as those of his colleagues. One fact must be emphasized. These men were working at their vocation while participating in the Forum's development; sixteen or eighteen hour "days" were the rule, not the exception. By March of 1950, the American G.I. Forum represented approximately 10,000 people and it was only the beginning.[23] Quite fortunately for its ultimate success, very talented individuals became involved in its growth.

Ed Idar

In June of 1950, such a person joined the G.I. Forum. Born in South Texas in 1921, Ed Idar, Jr., grew up in a family that actively participated in LULAC and other Mexican American political organizations before World War II. After serving in the Indochina theater during the war, Idar attended the University of Texas on the G.I. Bill and graduated in 1949 with a degree in journalism. He then served on the American Council of Spanish-Speaking People under Dr. George I. Sanchez, one of the most noted historians and spokesmen for the Mexican American people of the Southwest. When foundation funding ended for the ACSSP, Idar chose the American G.I. Forum as a focus for his abilities and desire to improve conditions for his people.[24]

Ed Idar rapidly became involved in the expansion of the organization.

His background furnished him with excellent abilities for the growth and development of this movement. His own dynamic personality manifested itself in the tedious activities needed for a growing Forum. Traveling throughout Texas, usually alone, Idar proved a valuable ally with Dr. Garcia in sustaining the rapid expansion of the state organization. In 1951, he was elected as state chairman of the Texas G.I. Forum, succeeding Hector Garcia. Rather than reducing his organizational efforts, he increased them. A particularly noteworthy accomplishment was the creation of a monthly news bulletin in 1952 that became the central method of dispatching information to Forum members; Idar was the editor and the primary force behind this valuable tool for years.[25] Such people as Ed Idar accounted for the amazing evolution of this organization; however, his early work, as well as that of Hector Garcia, was confined mostly to Texas. A pivotal moment for national expansion of the Forum occurred in the summer of 1950 because of a fishing trip.

Vicente Ximenes

During that summer Vicente Ximenes, a Garcia family friend, stopped by to pay his respects on his way to a fishing expedition on the Gulf Coast. Ximenes was born in Floresville, Texas, in 1919 and graduated from Floresville High School. During World War II, he flew fifty missions as a bombardier, received the Distinguished Flying Cross, and left the service after seven years as a major. Ximenes then moved to Albuquerque, New Mexico, with his wife and children to enroll in the University of New Mexico, eventually receiving a Master of Arts degree in economics and graduating Phi Kappa Phi.[26] But that summer he anticipated only a pleasant visit with Dr. Garcia.

Ximenes knew of the Longoria incident and the role of Dr. Garcia in the Texas movement, but when presented with the actual facts and figures detailing the status of life for *Mexicanos*, he became more interested in the G.I. Forum. As a veteran, he also appreciated the hypocrisy implicit in the reluctance of Anglo institutions to improve the lot of the Mexican American veteran. Even more important, Vicente Ximenes knew Dr. Garcia and perceived the dedication of the doctor to changing these conditions. Inspiration is often a nebulous concept to describe, but it is a viable factor inherent in some people. Ximenes was moved by that quality of the Corpus Christi physician; he cancelled his fishing trip and immediately went back to New Mexico to begin organizing a new American G.I. Forum. Employing the same procedures developed by the Texas organizers, Ximenes started a chapter in Albuquerque. By 1951, New Mexico officially became the second American

G.I. Forum state with a constitution, charter, and state officers.[27] It would not be the last.

Before the success of the New Mexico organization, Dr. Garcia had not really considered national expansion as a viable possibility. However, with the enthusiasm displayed by Ximenes and the obvious desire of *Mexicanos* in New Mexico to have a G.I. Forum, the Texas leadership began formulating goals for an eventual national Forum. Because Hector Garcia was the most well-known of the Forum leaders, and had acquired experience and abilities for organization, the major task for transferring the Forum from state to national status became a natural obligation.[28] (This is not to imply that he was the only person responsible for this development; indeed many persons worked together in this endeavor. However, the successful transition of this local group to a national organization is difficult to conceive of without Dr. Garcia.)

Chris Aldrete

In August 1952, Hector Garcia and Chris Aldrete, an attorney from Del Rio, Texas, and a member of the Texas Forum set out on a two-week journey for the purpose of national development. Aldrete had founded the Alba Club of the University of Texas in 1946 to provide focus for young *Mexicano* students in studying the problems of the Spanish-speaking. (Dr. Garcia was named Latin of the Year by the Alba Club in 1949). Alderete shared a major responsibility for ending segregation in the Del Rio schools in 1949, and in 1952 became city commissioner of Del Rio.[29] Like Ed Idar and Vicente Ximenes, Chris Aldrete proved very adept at organizing new chapters, and like these men, Aldrete had another necessary virtue for this work, exceptional energy. In the two weeks Garcia and Aldrete traveled to nineteen cities in four states. Included in this exhausting journey were visits to San Angelo, Sweetwater, Big Spring, Lamesa, Lubbock, and El Paso, Texas; Albuquerque and Alamagordo, New Mexico; Pueblo and Denver, Colorado; and Tucson, Arizona. The immediate result of this trip was organization of a third American G.I. Forum state, Colorado; in 1953, the first convention of the American G.I. Forum of Colorado took place in Pueblo.[30] National status was fast becoming a reality.

Growth

The methods developed by Garcia, Idar, Aldrete and many other *Mexicanos* did not differ much from any other organization, but two important factors explain why the G.I. Forum was able to sustain a dynamic expansion rather than a piecemeal, stuttering type of growth. First,

Forum workers did not automatically assume that all Mexican Americans understood or even realized the depth of prejudice on the part of Anglo institutions. Indeed, Dr. Garcia noticed the rather common "phenomena" that middle-class *Mexicanos* often opposed initial Forum activities with the rationalization that Anglos were not that bad. The evidence was their own elevation into a better economic position. For these persons, abilities could overcome any minor obstacles such as bigotry, and the essential basis for any "American" had to be a willingness to work within the system. Rather than waste time and effort in trying to dispel these naive beliefs, the doctor and other leaders concentrated their work in the poorer sectors of the Mexican community without worrying about "appealing to the better class of the Spanish people".[31]

It was this second "tactic" that became the bulwark of the G.I. Forum's growth. While even the *pobre Mexicano* did not always accept the reality of prejudice, the G.I. Forum did not give up its goal to provide a cohesive voice for Mexican American people. Time and time again, Forum organizers patiently explored areas that did not welcome "radical Latin Americans" who wished to "disrupt the racial harmony" of that particular place. Often the other half of that team (Anglos) supplied the evidence that there was trouble in a given location. Perhaps *Mexicanos* were turned away from high school dances[32] or the "Latin Americans" suddenly discovered that a qualified individual did not have the same opportunity as a less-qualified Anglo (once a janitor, always a janitor). When these occurrences upset the rose-colored view of a *barrio*, the Forum was readily available to take advantage of the circumstances. The attempt to change those conditions focused on the people within the community. The structure of the organization proved readily adaptable to practically any region. Hector Garcia, Vicente Ximenes, and others provided the experience and training needed by people to confront a system comfortable with the status quo. If any "magic secret" is needed to account for those first years it was the cliché of "dedication, belief, faith, and patience." A setback was never accepted as anything other than a reaffirmation of the need to continue the work, a success was never equated with victory.

Patriotism

The discovery of immediate issues was easy enough and movement toward resolution provided motivation and impetus for the participants. Expansion of the Forum, therefore, quite naturally depended upon issues. The structure of the organization proved adaptable and flexible enough to accommodate different regions. *La familia* (the family concept) involved cultural characteristics that made the Forum's growth different, as Mexican culture differs from Anglo culture. The additional factors of oppression, prejudice, discrimination, and Anglo resistance also qualified the Forum's expansion as more than just another organized group seeking entrance and access to the benefits and opportunities of American society. The nature of the struggle helps explain another aspect of Forum development.

In the post-war era, and well into the 1960's, the Cold War provided considerable tension and fear for most Americans. Emotions were often manifested in unreasoned and irrational defense of the "American Way." Those who implied or otherwise indicated that the status quo left much to be desired asked for trouble—the easiest rebuttal was to simplistically stigmatize critics as communists! The most extreme and yet best example of this "disease" was McCarthyism. Patriotism was a valuable tool in undermining this type of criticism. By manipulating patriotic symbols and slogans, Forumeers eliminated or at least diffused this potent weapon. If veterans who have fought for their country were not pro-American, then who was? Mexican Americans had earned the right to question their society. Their record in the war proved their loyalty.

Unfortunately, many in the Forum were as strident in their own attitude toward communism and accepted the popular rhetoric which condemned dissent. A tenuous balance between manipulating and being manipulated characterized the employment of the patriotic game. While effectively reducing the knee-jerk reaction of their opponents, most of the Forum leaders did not question the use of such tactics against other groups. In the directives and correspondence between chapters, there is constant admonition to be on guard against those who might attempt to infiltrate the organization for subversive ends. The attorney general's list of subversive organizations was continuously circulated as a guide on communist and/or un-American groups. Some Mexican American activists were members of those groups and were uncategorically condemned by most Forumeers. Red-baiting was not an exclusive exercise of right-wing fanatics. As the Vietnam debacle eventually engendered different responses toward dissent, the G.I. Forum rightfully questioned previous reaction. But during the Holy Crusade of Democracy against Communism, Mexican Americans were as likely to engage in the name-calling as any other American.[33]

Stability

Incorporating and improving the trial and error techniques of expansion, the American G.I. Forum had to deal with many issues and many obstacles. The stability earned by the Longoria case, the hospital and health affair, and the successful growth of the period would be tested. The next chapter deals with some of those moments.

CHAPTER VI

Many Fronts

Forum programs in these formative years began representing more wide-ranging interests. As the organization moved into new states, and the number of chapters increased, so did the concern of Mexican American veterans for the welfare of *toda la gente*. The American G.I. Forum had successfully fought the ugly spectre of discrimination in the Felix Longoria affair; the momentum of that victory would not be blunted nor eroded by self-satisfaction. Operating with only their own resources, and often at great personal risk, Forum activists fought for their constitutional rights. Police brutality, public discrimination, voting rights, and organized labor representation became an ongoing part of the activities of the Texas, New Mexico, and Colorado G.I. Forums as well as those in other regions.Culminating with the Hernandez case of 1954, in which the Supreme Court declared that Mexican Americans were subjected to discrimination as a separate class, the struggle for civil rights established important precedents for the more minority-oriented federal programs of the Kennedy and Johnson administrations. These efforts also added impetus to the already rapid expansion of the G.I. Forum into other states.

Edna Ferber

A most rewarding episode during these years of struggle occurred when Edna Ferber contacted Dr. Garcia to gather information for a book she was writing about Texas. Miss Ferber wanted to portray all aspects of the state, including such sordid parts as the bigotry of most Anglos toward "Latin Americans". Ferber had learned of the American G.I. Forum and wanted first hand information from the founder. She visited Corpus Christi for three weeks, accompanied Dr. Garcia on his rounds in the *barrio*, attended Forum meetings, and traveled with Forum members in South Texas; Ferber also met with other Forums in different cities. Her book became a bestseller from which Hollywood made the epic movie, *Giant*. In the book and movie, some expecially moving moments describe the plight of Mexican Americans in Texas: a young Latin doctor escorting the wealthy Yankee mistress of the Riata Ranch through the brutally poor living quarters of the Mexican workers, the *Mexicana* wife of the son of the Riata owner being refused service in a beauty parlor, and the poignant funeral of the son of Segundo, a hero of World War II who died in action.[1] Critics panned much of the acting in *Giant*, but praised the movie as a courageous portrayal of discrimination and its effect on human beings. This national attention to the problems of Mexican Americans in Texas in no way affected the attitude of state officials.

Good Neighbors

A vehicle for resolving some of these problems supposedly existed in Texas in the form of the Texas Good Neighbor Commission which ostensibly acted to improve the relations between Anglos and *Mexicanos*.[2] But any substantive effort by the GNC always produced outrageous denunciations from the Anglo sector that had created the GNC as a token to "do-gooders" and more importantly, for the sake of Mexico, which refused to send contract workers to a bigot-filled state like Texas. If the GNC attempted conscientiously to fulfill its stated obligation, people like Rep. J.F. Gray of Three Rivers, business leaders, and farm growers used their political power to undermine the commission.[3] The Forum constantly urged Texas government to make the agency more effective but with meager success. Even those in the GNC who supported the Forum had to appease the governor and legislature to maintain what minimal influence they had. An excellent example of this dilemma happened in November of 1949 when a Beeville Mexican American was refused service at a cafe in Edna, Texas. Governor Allan Shivers' secretary reported to his superiors that Tom Sutherland of the GNC would take the usual steps to investigate, but something had to be done to mollify the "always excited Dr. Garcia who started the Three Rivers business". Since the governor had pledged in Mexico City to "make war" on discrimination, it was suggested by his staff to write "a carefully couched statement, probably not referring to the specific incident, reflecting thoughts that such treatment of *educated, presentable* (emphasis mine), ex-G.I. Texans of Latin American descent (was) out of style."[4] One must wonder if uneducated, unpresentable Anglos ever encountered such prejudice or if discrimination against uneducated, unpresentable Mexicans was permissible. Dr. Garcia was not deceived. He told Sutherland that the only way of eliminating discrimination would include a change of attitude on the part of the governor and more intense efforts by the commission to enforce its duty. When Dr. Garcia's wife and daughter, in the company of the Diaz family, were refused service at the Manhattan Cafe in Gonzalez, Texas, the governor did nothing. Sutherland sadly explained that the GNC was helpless; the mayor of Gonzalez failed to "see where any of the city ordinances have been violated, or why the incident should be taken up with the city."[5] The Good Neighbor Commission simply had no power to affect the climate of hate in Texas. Its own bias plus the determination of state officials to maintain power over Mexican Americans created an "opportunity" for the G.I. Forum. They would have welcomed help but Governor Shivers' "war on discrimination" was a bloodless affair, and Forumeers understood the nature of their "public servants."

Law and Order

General measures demanded by Forum activists included a Texas law (with sanctions) prohibiting discrimination against Latin Americans in public places. Such a bill had been passed by the Senate in 1944 but not by the House of Representatives; the same fate occurred for the bill introduced in 1951.[6] The Forum campaigned against the use of property as a qualification for voting in certain elections, neighborhood clauses in real estate contracts, and even restrictions on owning property.[7] Segregation in hospitals continued to receive special attention; the Forum called for appointments of Mexican Americans by the governor to the State Board of Health, the Board of Hospitals and Special Schools, and the Hospital Council Advisory Board. State administrators claimed that non-discrimination existed as official policy at all levels but the facts proved otherwise.[8] Other requests included a Fair Employment Practices Commission and investigation of civil rights violations by the Department of Justice.[9] The attack on the traditional Texas bastions of bigotry and prejudice did not produce immediate results, but the difference between this post-war group and earlier organizations lay in its day-to-day endurance. Demands did not cease; valuable experience from these struggles would not be forgotten and the lessons learned in these early years would be put to use in the 1960's.

However, the efforts of the Texas Forum were not confined to more general actions or programs. Combatting individual discrimination produced important results. Many of these incidents involved police brutality in which Anglo police and/or sheriffs took it upon themselves to intimidate and harass Mexican Americans. Time and time again Forum members were subject to savage attack by law officials who felt their traditional powers of control were being challenged.[10]

Clearly, *Mexicano* veterans did not go through a war only to be threatened by people empowered to protect them. Forum attorneys carried many suits against such peace officers to civil and criminal courts; charges usually included "excessive force" and "abusive language." In two particularly notable cases, the Knaggs incident of 1952 and the Vega killings of 1953, the Forum, although ultimately losing in court, succeeded in eventually removing some of the officers involved (Knaggs, because of the negative publicity sustained by Forum actions, was defeated in the next local election).[11] Suspensions and indictments against policemen became less of a rare event in Texas because of Forumeers who actually risked their lives to fight against such treatment.[12] In lesser cases of prejudicial treatment, Forumeers would advise the abused individual of his rights and procedures to follow for redress.[13] This type of help may seem of a minor nature, but it was extremely vital for people who were often responding for the first time to such conditions. The availability of a Hector Garcia, Ed Idar, Chris Alderete, and others constituted support that buttressed individuals who had no such leadership in their own localities.

The incidents did not cease (nor did intimidation), but neither did they go on relatively unnoticed as before. In fact, many Anglo officials in small towns increased their attempts to stop the G.I. Forum. Death threats became a common event for leaders of the Texas Forum; Dr. Garcia missed a possible assassination attempt in Mathis, Texas,when he appeared late for an Auxiliary affair after local Anglo citizens had interrupted the meeting demanding the whereabouts of the doctor. When they discovered his absence, they threatened the women and left.[14] One effort to discredit Garcia by state officials appeared in the form of a publication , El Congreso , which supposedly was financed by a Mexican government official; the magazine praised the governor of Texas and his administration, labeled the doctor a radical and troublemaker, and claimed that Mexican Americans lived in a happy environment undisturbed until prodded by such scurrilous individuals as Hector Garcia. Although it was never conclusively proved that certain officials and farm growers were responsible for the attack, the Forum did establish the fraudulence of the "Mexican" official, and El Congreso suffered an unlamented demise.[15]

New Mexico Delivers

In New Mexico, G.I. Forums acheived some noteworthy results in *la lucha contra discriminacion*, in no small part due to the leadership of Vicente Ximenes. Mexican Americans of that state historically had more political power and strength than in Texas, but it should not be inferred that *Mexicanos* of the state encountered less prejudice; in fact, the degree of such attitudes varied little, but the absence of border conditions of

Texas and the different history of the state (no Alamos in New Mexico), did offer different circumstances. In 1953, the New Mexico G.I. Forum began a campaign to enact an anti-discrimination law in public places, a law with monetary fines, prison terms (30—90 days), and a revocation of license of any public place in violation of this law. The New Mexico House killed the bill with a tie vote,[16] but the Forum did not desist in its efforts to secure such legislation. Working in 1954 to draw up another legislative program, the New Mexico organization geared up for an intense campaign to push the program through the 1955 regular session. Gaining support from the Catholic hierarchy, LULAC, the American Federation of Labor, and the NAACP, a legislative program was presented including (1) civil rights with penalties against discrimination in public places, (2) appropriations for the New Mexico FEPC, (3) prohibitions against insurance sales by small loan companies, and (4) enabling legislation to permit cities to undertake slum clearance under federal statutes.[17] In March 1955, the New Mexico Senate followed the House by passing the anti-discrimination bill, deleting the penalty clause but subjecting any alleged violation to court action and contempt action if individuals convicted of an act of discrimination refused to cease and desist. One of the groups opposed to the new bill was the Motor Hotel Association of New Mexico. It appears that this group did not want Mexican Americans in their bedrooms, but thanks to men and women of the Forum employing coordinated and continuing pressure, plus the aid of other organizations, that desire no longer operated within the law.[18]

A Merit System

Also in New Mexico, the Albuquerque G.I. Forum managed to make inroads in labor rights. In the fall of 1953, the garbage workers of that city, 99 percent of whom were of Mexican descent, were the only city employees not under a merit system. The local Forum appeared before the city commission. Demands included the removal of political pressure from hiring procedures, no dismissal of laborers without just cause, grievance procedures, stabilization of the work force, and the acquisition of seniority. In addition to the absence of these conditions, garbage workers had no sick leave, no paid holidays and vacations, or other benefits that the merit system could provide. The Forum had already dealt with the garbage superintendent when he fired two *Mexicano* workers without cause. The response of the superintendent, besides failing to show justification for the dismissal, was to place the Forum member, who led the appeal and worked in the garbage department, on night duty in order to prevent his full participation in Forum activities. Unintimidated, the Forum gathered signatures on petitions for a merit system. In November 1953, faced with a group prepared to sustain that advocacy, Albuquerque officials granted the request of the Forumeers to incorporate the garbage workers into the city merit system with all benefits.[19]

In following up this accomplishment, the Forum prevented repercussions from city officials. When the garbage superintendent attempted to demote one of the leaders of the campaign, the Forum protested and forced decision of the order. Even more critical for the long-range goal of fair employment practices, the G.I. Forum stopped the dismissal of a *Mexicano* truck driver by the superintendent. Vicente Ximenes represented the worker, proved the justifications presented by the superintendent as fraudulent, and won reinstatement for the worker.[20] Ximenes continued this type of watchful waiting through the winter of 1953-1954 and the city departments finally ceased their harassment of Forum members and workers. This affair prefaced the establishment of union organization for Mexican Americans in Albuquerque and provided valuable lessons for the G.I. Forum. As one of the Albuquerque members put it, "we showed that *la raza se junta y se puede organizar.*"[21]

The New Mexico Forums, much like their Texas counterparts, also protested against individual instances of police harassment and excessive force. Publicizing police brutality and methods such as mass arrests of Mexican American youths ostensibly for "routine investigation of alleged incidents", Forum chapters often provided the only representation for these children or other "suspected criminals." By forcefully articulating the differences between the attitude of law officials toward Anglos and *Mexicanos*, Forum lawyers and activists began eroding the old traditions of Anglo police intimidation. No one should infer from this statement that immediate or complete eradication of such attitudes came about because of these activities, but compared to pre—G.I. Forum days, a significant "dawning of awareness" of "radical Latins" on the part of Anglo officials did occur.[22]

In Colorado, the situation regarding such incidents and attitudes was much the same as in New Mexico and Texas, although to a lesser degree. Forumeers encountered basically the identical treatment from Anglo society and institutions and fought it with the same methods. The state did pass an Anti-Discrimination Act in 1951 and extended the scope of that law in 1955 in contrast to the refusal of the Texas Legislature to enact such laws. However, the attitudes of those people covered by the law did not change, and the Colorado G.I. Forum had to struggle for the same civil rights of Mexican Americans as its brother Forums.[23]

The Poll Tax

A most important civil right lacking for most Mexican Americans in Texas concerned voting. The fundamental or at least ideal basis of the American system is the process by which citizens choose their government officials and representatives. The act of voting symbolized the concept that the powers of leadership are vested in the people, not in those who temporarily hold the particular office. But, as in many other areas, this particular privilege did not extend to all people. Mexican Americans in Texas did not possess the same voting rights as their Anglo neighbors, but in this instance, a number of factors accounted for the discrepancy; a subtle and concomitantly more complex obstacle prevented a full participation by *Mexicanos* in the political process—the poll tax.

After World War II, Texas was one of the few states to retain the poll tax as a prerequisite for voting. The tax, a "minimal" fee in the 1950s of $1.75 per year, theoretically represented the vested interest that all "good citizens" must have in their various institutions; however, most states outside the South had voided this fee as a voting qualification. Southern states had used the poll tax for years as a means of disenfranchising certain citizens, therefore little demand appeared for repeal of the tax except from blacks, Mexican Americans, and some Anglos who felt the payment was unfair and had lost its original meaning.[24] The poll tax was a discriminatory requirement affecting those at the lower end of the economic scales, again mostly blacks and Mexican Americans. In 1948 the median yearly income of *Mexicanos* was $980 or approximately $19 per week; obviously, from this perspective, $1.75 becomes an important sum.[25] Coupled with the lack of faith of most *Mexicanos* in the democratic system and a reluctance to participate without more benefits and hope, the poll tax was a formidable obstacle. Nonetheless, from its inception, the G.I. Forum began a serious campaign to rid the state of this tax while conducting poll tax drives to enable Mexican Americans to become qualified voters and express and secure their own needs by developing political strength.

The Forum and other organizations made minimum progress regarding the elimination of the poll tax. Some Texas legislators introduced various resolutions and bills calling for its repeal, but no real impetus developed from the dominant Anglo political sector. The "devotion" of Anglo liberals to the deprived and underprivileged of America was still in the future, and those who most desired the abolition of the poll tax were those who lacked the political strength to effect that goal. Consequently, the Forum could do little more than keep the issue alive by constantly proposing repeal and supporting those individual legislators who also advocated elimination. Continual resolutions for repeal at the state conventions maintained the movement toward eradication.[26] The G.I. Forum, LULAC, and the NAACP did provide ammunition in the post-JFK years when federal administrators were willing to lend their support. Indeed, political activities by G.I. Forum leaders in the Kennedy and Johnson presidential campaigns contributed information to Robert Kennedy and others who sincerely did not understand the problem. But that was in the future—in the formative years of the G.I. Forum, repeal remained an unreachable goal.

The main effort of the American G.I. Forum in Texas on voting was directed at campaigns to get Mexican Americans to pay their poll taxes and become registered voters. Such drives were conducted at various times during each year and provided information on the procedures necessary to purchase the "permit". Dances, barbeques, radio programs, rallies, and other tactics (such as the simple service of providing transportation to pay that tax) contributed to the poll tax activities.[27] These efforts brought a substantial increase in the numbers of Mexican American voters, and this increase did not always receive the praise of Anglo politicians who otherwise favored the right of every citizen to exercise his or her franchise.[28] The best example of this conflict, as well as the real potential of the political strength of *la gente*, occurred in the 1955 to 56 poll tax drives in the Rio Grande Valley, an area where "Latin Americans" made up 40 to 80 percent of the various counties.

"Un-American"

The G.I. Forum sponsored a poll tax drive from November 1, 1955, through January 1956, supported by the American Federation of Labor, the Congress of Industrial Organizations, and the Railroad Brotherhoods. A temporary organization was established, the Rio Grande Democratic Club, in order to simplify and coordinate the various activities of the groups working for voter registration. Robert P. Sanchez of McAllen, Texas, an attorney and Forumeer, headed the Valley-wide drive in the counties of Hidalgo, Cameron, and Willacy; many other people labored in the campaign as volunteer workers and poll tax deputies. Employing the techniques of previous drives, the effort produced a significant change in the voting balance of the Valley. At the beginning of the drive the Mexican Americans of these counties, 75 percent of the population, held only 43 percent of the poll taxes, but at the end of the Forum campaign, they had 53 percent of the total. For the first time in history those voters of Mexican descent possessed a majority of the poll taxes and for the first time the poll tax lists more nearly reflected the population make-up. The immediate result saw Mexican Americans elected to local offices never previously held and the election of candidates sympathetic to the needs of those of Mexican descent. This was a major success but only part of the story. This effort by the American G.I. Forum to incorporate American citizens into the basics of the democratic system engendered an enormous and (even in Texas) incredible opposition from Anglo elements of the Valley communities.[29]

The most vocal outrage came from the so-called "freedom newspapers" of the Valley area, the *Valley Morning Star* of Harlingen, the *Valley Evening Monitor* of McAllen, and the *Brownsville Herald*. The crux of the three-month journalistic onslaught concerned the participation of the AFL-CIO and railroad unions, which these newspapers described as evidence of a union conspiracy to take over the Valley. Labeling U.S. Senator Dennis Chavez of New Mexico, a guest speaker of the Forum at the poll tax rallies, as a traitor to the American farmer, editorials also accused the G.I. Forum of promoting class and racial warfare.[30]

Further opposition came from state senator Rogers Kelley, who represented a constituency of 75 percent Mexican Americans and whose actions were more conspicuous than those of other opponents because of his long-standing support of previous Forum activities. However, this time the senator assailed the "misguided or selfish forces which seek to divide us, to play up racial, religious differences in order to stir up strife and trouble."[31] Kelley made these remarks at a suddenly revived LULAC council in Harlingen, but this obvious attempt to divide Mexican Americans failed when LULAC national president Oscar Laurel of Laredo pointed out in a letter to Ed Idar that LULAC had conducted many poll tax drives in the past and was not opposed to such efforts (although Laurel did not condemn Kelley's attack).[32] The Texas legislator had no rebuttal to LULAC nor to the Forum criticism that he was one of many Valley politicians who maintained power by employing the ancient divide-and-conquer strategy among Mexican Americans.[33]

Probably the most petty act by the Forum's opposition was the refusal of the American Legion, the Veterans of Foreign Wars, and a national guard unit to march with the American G.I. Forum on Veterans Day; they claimed the Forum was a political faction and not a veterans organization. Ed Idar replied to that rationalization:

> We have come to a sad day in Texas democracy when an organization of veterans cannot join in efforts to promote—of all things—the sale of poll taxes to citizens in an area where the record shows that the majority of the citizens never have qualified themselves to vote.
>
> Apparently, Lt. Werner (the National Guard commander) ignores the fact that members of the G.I. Forum paid for the right to participate in poll tax drives with the blood, the guts and the lives of many of their comrades left overseas . . . and only a warped and twisted logic can come out with the principle that National Guardsmen who are subject to pay the same price in the future must not march shoulder to shoulder with men who already have done so in a day set aside to commemorate the sacrifices that American's fighting men of all backgrounds made to make such commemoration possible.[34]

The outrage of Kelley and the Valley newspapers reflected the fear that the traditional feudal agricultural empire of the Rio Grande was being threatened. Voter strength translated into political power could affect the grower-dominated, twenty-five-cent-per-hour labor system which depended on *mojados* (illegal workers) and *braceros* (contract workers) from Mexico. The very idea that 5 percent of the population, which had historically controlled the remaining 95 percent Mexicanos, might actually have to share political power was intolerable. As the *Texas Observer* said in a Veterans Day editorial:

> What the upshot is we are not sure, but we hope they sell a lot of poll taxes. Maybe then Latins in the Valley will get to go to school more than the three and a half years they now average. Maybe then they will get paid more than 30¢ an hour for which they now must cower. One never knows of course, but it is conceivable that democracy in the Valley may, at some future date, include the Latin Americans.[35]

Lest it be assumed that Anglo society accepted the success of the drive with grace, many local McAllen merchants who had contributed generously to the previous year's G.I. Forum Christmas party for under-privileged children refused to do so in 1955. The McAllen Forum had participated in the poll tax drive.[36]

One parting shot came from those who simply would not countenance a new spokesman for the usually voiceless Mexican Americans. Governor Allan Shivers accused the American G.I. Forum and the AFL of "urging people to pay the poll tax necessary for voting."[37] The governor demanded an investigation of the Rio Grande Democratic Club, including its role in the "controversial" poll tax drive by the G.I. Forum, controversial because it had actually influenced previously unqualified Mexican Americans to vote. (The governor knew that in Texas that vote would be against the traditional power blocs.) Bank deposit slips were stolen from G.I. Forum files in an effort to discredit the organization by proving the misuse of union and possibly federal funds.[38] No evidence as to the identity of the thief was gathered, but Shivers somehow acquired information regarding the financial operations of the Forum. This act highlighted the real fear of some Anglo leaders that they would be accountable to their Spanish-speaking citizens; Dr. Hector Garcia also demanded the investigation, and the attorney general's office completely cleared the G.I. Forum of any illegalities.[39] The only misuse of leadership in this affair was on the part of Valley newspaper editors, growers, and others who would not tolerate any challenge to their political and economic policies.

"A Class Apart"

In the legal arena, the outstanding contribution to the full enactment of civil rights for Americans of Mexican origin took place in 1954 (twelve days before another historic decision, *Brown* vs. *Board of Education* in Topeka, Kansas). The United States Supreme Court declared that Mexican Americans were entitled to a jury of their peers and their exclusion from any juries was unconstitutional and illegal. That decision came after a three-year struggle by American G.I. Forum attorneys to finally obtain the recognition of the right of Mexican Americans to enjoy the fundamental and constitutionally described jury system.

In September 1951, Pete Hernandez allegedly killed Joe Espinosa in Edna, Texas. He was arrested, detained by police, and charged by Jackson County attorneys of murder with malice. Hernandez labored as a cotton picker in an area not well known for an enlightened view toward Mexican Americans (in the adjoining county, Congressional Medal of Honor winner Marcario Garcia was refused service in a restaurant and beaten by Anglos for his protest and resistance to such treatment). The Hernandez family, part of the migrant labor force, did not initially have the money nor could they raise a sufficient amount to hire an attorney for the defense of Pete.[40] Fortunately for these people and indeed for all Mexican Americans, Gustavo C. Garcia learned of the Hernandez situation and agreed to represent the accused without fee in order to test in court the systematic exclusion of persons of Mexican origins from all types of jury duty in at least 70 counties in Texas.[41]

Gus Garcia had considerable experience by 1954 in the fight for Mexican Americans in Texas. Born in Laredo in 1916, Garcia lived most of his childhood in San Antonio, where he attended Jefferson High School, acquired championship skills as a debater, and graduated as valedictorian. Attending the University of Texas on a scholarship, he won further honors (his debate partner was John Connally) and reputation for his abilities. In 1938 Garcia passed the bar exams and began his career as a lawyer in San Antonio as assistant district attorney for Bexar County, handling criminal cases. During World War II, he served as a first lieutenant in the U.S. Infantry and later in the judicial branch; afterwards he returned to San Antonio and joined LULAC, where he became very active with the problems of education for Spanish-speaking children, fully aware of the vast gulf between Anglo and *Mexicano* schooling.[42] In 1948 this young attorney represented a group of Mexican American parents in Bastrop County, protesting the arbitrary segregation of their children by Bastrop County officials. During the many meetings and fund-raising efforts by LULAC and the G.I. Forum for the court costs, Gus met Dr. Hector Garcia and joined the Texas G.I. Forum.[43] The victory in the court case established a new chapter in the conflict between Anglo school policies and *Mexicano* demands for equal education; it also highlighted a new figure in the ranks of Mexican American advocates for justice in

American society. Working with the American G.I. Forum and LULAC, Gus Garcia continued to be active in school segregation and other problem areas for the Mexican American. The Hernandez case of 1951 -1954 offered ample opportunity for such a cause.

Prior to the trial of Pete Hernandez, Garcia filed a motion against the indictment of the migrant on the basis of the exclusion principle of the Fourteenth Amendment. Garcia maintained that the constitution prohibited the denial of equal protection of the laws on the basis of race, color, or *class*. Contending that the jury selection of Jackson County violated this principle because it excluded Mexican Americans from jury service, Garcia requested the presiding judge to quash the charges against Hernandez. In presenting the supportive evidence for his pretrial motion, the San Antonio lawyer enlisted the aid of John Herrera, a lawyer and first national vice-president of LULAC, and James De Anda, a lawyer and member of the G.I. Forum. They investigated Jackson County school census rolls, court documents, business reports, and other official reports to convince the court that an attitude and environment of hostility existed for Mexican Americans in that area of Texas. By accident Herrera discovered signs on the court restrooms reading, "Men, Colored Men, and *Hombres aqui*." (It should be noted that the lawyers for Hernandez were not excluded from this hostility; Garcia and his colleagues considered it safer to commute 200 miles *each day* to and from Houston rather than stay in Edna.) The summation of Garcia's final argument included three critical points: (1) no persons of Mexican or of other Latin American descent had served as jurors, jury commissions or had even been called for jury service in Jackson County for the preceding twenty-five years, (2) those Spanish-named individuals denied this opportunity were qualified for the activity, and (3) discrimination and segregation were common practices in Jackson County where Mexican Americans were treated as a "race, class, or a group apart from all other persons." The court rejected these contentions, denied the motion and proceeded with the trial, during which further evidence was presented and the motion once more denied; Pete Hernandez was found guilty and sentenced to life imprisonment.[44] But Gus Garcia intended to make this case a test on the discrimination practices of Anglo law officials, and test cases do not end in district courts.

With the appeal of the verdict to the Texas Court of Criminal Appeals, a fourth lawyer joined with Garcia, Herrera, and De Anda. Carlos Cadena of San Antonio shared a major portion of the appeal efforts including the briefs and oral arguments.[45] The appeals court upheld the lower court decision on the grounds that the Fourteenth Amendment included within its contemplation only two classes—white and Negro; Mexican Americans were legally considered as "white" and did not receive treatment as a class apart from "whites"; therefore, the Texas statutes regarding jury activities made no discrimination toward Latin citizens of Texas.[46] The only option open to those determined to pursue the issue now lay in an appeal to the United States Supreme Court. Gus Garcia filed an application for a *writ of certiorari* on January 19, 1953; the Supreme Court accepted the case later that year and requested an immediate $900 for costs; at this point the LULAC council provided the money from its scholarship fund, a vital service at a critical time. After the initial $900, the Texas G.I. Forum provided additional funds for court costs and traveling expenses to Washington, D.C. In addition, the Texas state chairman of the G.I. Forum Chris Alderete, joined the team of attorneys who presented their arguments before the Supreme Court on January 11, 1954.[47]

Carlos Cadena presented the opening argument for *Pete Hernandez, Petitioner* vs. *The State of Texas*; Gus Garcia delivered the primary contentions of the petitioner, that the Fourteenth Amendment was not directed solely against discrimination within a "two-class" theory, "white" and Negro. Garcia acknowledged that the Texas system of selecting grand and petit jurors by the use of jury commissioners was fair on its surface and capable of use without discrimination.[48] But those who administered the law did not introduce discrimination because of the exclusion of otherwise eligible individuals solely due to their national origin. Such exclusion was unconstitutional because it violated the principle of no group or class discrimination. Garcia introduced evidence supporting this charge, much of which had been originally presented at the 1951 Edna trial; in addition, it was established that 14 percent of the population of Jackson County were persons with Mexican or Latin American surnames, with 11 percent representing Spanish-surnamed males over 21.[49] Even the State of Texas admitted that "for the last twenty-five years there (was) no record of any person with a Mexican or Latin American name having served on a jury commission, grand jury or petit jury in Jackson County." The parties also agreed that qualified males of Mexican or Latin American descent did live in Jackson County, and by virture of being citizens, freeholders, and other legal prerequisites were elibigle for participation in the jury system.[50]

However, according to the State of Texas, the Fourteenth Amendment covered only white and Negro, and Mexican Americans were white; the State of Texas further contended that Mexican Americans were ·not designated consciously or otherwise as a separate class, nor did any actions by Anglo society so delegate them to that status. Claiming that the absence of certain ethnic surnames did not in itself prove discrimination, the State claimed that the lack of these names from the Jackson County jury rolls was coincidence; the acceptance by the State of the presence of qualified Mexican or Latin Americans in the county showed the good faith of the officials of Texas and Jackson County. Therefore, jury discrimination against Mexican Americans did not exist in Jackson County in any facet and Pete Hernandez was given a jury of his "peers".[51]

During the questioning period following the oral arguments between the bench and attorney Garcia, Justice Potter Steward asked whether Latin Americans were newcomers to Jackson County and could speak adequate English. Garcia vigorously answered with a tone of irritation and pride.

> Your honor, my people were in Texas 100 years before Sam Houston arrived . . . Sam Houston was just a wetback from Tennessee to the real citizens of Texas but (today) Latin Americans are denied the right to jury service.[52]

On May 3, 1954, Chief Justice Earl Warren delivered the unanimous opinion of the Supreme Court. Briefly reviewing the appellate history of the petitioner, Warren pointed out that the Supreme Court had rarely dealt with the direct question of class exclusion depriving citizens of equal protection of law; even the Texas courts had assumed this broader view of the equal protection clause, excepting the exclusion of persons of Mexican descent. Warren stated that "when the existence of a distinct class is demonstrated, and when it is demonstrated that laws, written or applied, create unreasonable and different treatment for that class not based on a just classification, then the guarantees of the Constitution were violated"—so much for the "white and Negro" argument. The Chief Justice's opinion accepted Garcia's substantiation of the charge of group discrimination. The attitude of the community as described by "responsible officials and citizens" contained the admission that citizens of Texas and Jackson County did distinguish between "white" and "Mexican". The lack of participation of Mexican Americans in business, the fact of school segregation and the presence of public discrimination constituted ample proof of this attitude, one that the State of Texas did not convincingly rebut.[53]

Chief Justice Warren then addressed his opinion to the State's contention of "chance" as a viable factor explaining the lack of Mexican Americans on juries:

> Circumstances or chance may well indicate that no persons in a certain class will serve on a particular jury or during some particular period. But it taxes our credulity to say that mere chance resulted in there being no members of this class among the over six-thousand jurors called in the past 25 years. The results bespeaks discrimination, whether or not it was a conscious decision on the part of any individual commissioner. The judgement of conviction must be reversed.[54]

Finally, Warren dealt with the essence of the jury system and the rights of every citizen to participate in and receive the benefits of this aspect of the law:

> To say that this decision revives the rejected contention that the Fourteenth Amendment requires proportional representation of all the competent ethnic groups of the community on every jury ignores the facts. The petitioner did not seek proportional representation, nor did he claim a right to have persons of Mexican descent sit on the particular juries, which he faced. His only claim is the right to be indicted and tried by juries from which all members of his class are not systematically excluded — juries selected from among all qualified persons regardless of national origin or descent. To this much he is entitled by the Constitution.[55]

The immediate effect of this decision was a new trial for Pete Hernandez. The verdict remained the same but the sentence was lessened to twenty years with opportunity for parole. The lasting influence must be considered incalculable.[56] At last the Supreme Court, the highest arbiter of the laws of the United States, had recognized that Mexican Americans did not receive equal treatment under law entitled to all American citizens. Those Anglo institutions that would retreat into the "white equals Mexican—therefore no discrimination" syndrome were put on guard. The heavens did not fall nor did the earth shake, but the Supreme Court had established an extremely valuable legal precedent. Gus Garcia, the *Mexicano abogado* (lawyer) who received plaudits from his colleagues for the articulate and brilliant presentation of the Hernandez Case, did not live to see the full implications of his victory; he died a disillusioned man in 1964 on a San Antonio park bench, essentially alone in bitterness and cynicism produced by the frustratingly slow progress his people were making.[57] But the memorial to his work has become more and more vital in the struggle to reach equality for the Mexican American people. In 1954 that battle had really just begun, but Gus Garcia and the American G.I. Forum had provided a contribution that could not be deluded.

The organizational abilities of the G.I. Forum were aptly demonstrated by the most successful work dealing with the many problems facing Mexican Americans. The failure of other groups to make more substantial inroads in these areas reflected their inability to effectively motivate and sustain the grass roots segment of the Mexican American people. The leadership of the G.I. Forum depended on the support of the poor and "second class" Mexican American. Without them, the effort in confronting police brutality could never have passed the point of simple protest. Without the tangible backing of the *pobre Mexicano*, the Hernandez Case would never have reached the Supreme

Court. The American G.I. Forum did not attempt to "appeal to the better element" of Americans of Mexican origin. But it did strive to lift the Mexican American people in these early years out of conditions formulated by a society that cared little for its "other" elements. The Forum could not change the attitudes of Anglos and *Mexicanos* overnight, nor did economic and social conditions miraculously improve, but events were acquiring a momentum that would substantially affect *la vida de la gente* in the next ten years with the G.I. Forum remaining in the forefront. A part of that momentum involved the fight for equal education.

CHAPTER VII

Education is Our Freedom

Part 1 - Back to School

Improvement of the status of Mexican Americans involved better education. Attendance in the schools was an obvious necessity. Dropout rates were appalling. Skills necessary to cope with an often hostile Anglo society could not be learned. If for no other reason than the facile nature of the activity, back-to-school drives were the first major education program of the Forum chapters. Used to emphasize and sometimes convince Mexican American parents of the value of registering and keeping their children in school, they became an important event for local chapters in all Forum states. Forumeers often encountered stubborn resistance from a family to the removal of a child from labor in order to attend school because that child could contribute to income. But if *Mexicanos* were ever going to exhibit any efficient opposition against dominant Anglo instutitions, education was absolutely necessary. The effort needed to obtain the required results called for "repetition, constant campaigning and follow through."[1]

The first step in the campaign involved the establishment of a full-time education, back-to-school committee in the local Forum which could contact community organizations such as LULAC, The Knights of Columbus, church organizations, and possibly other veteran groups. In August, just prior to the opening of school, the Forum coordinated its campaign with these groups in sponsorship of dances, tamale sales, solicitation drives among local business and other fund raisers to provide the necessary monies for media advertising.[2]

The publicity for the back-to-school drives made use of various types of media. Forum members printed stickers and signs and distributed them in key neighborhoods, usually those with low attendance records (knowledge easily obtained from local school officials whose state appropriations teacher's salaries, and other funds depended on the average daily attendance during the school year). School administrators did not care much about the attendance after registration due to the easily circumvented "daily attendance" figures, but initial registration *in the district* was important to them; therefore, local school administrators often cooperated with the Forum. Radio stations became a vital part of the campaign, particularly after the Federal Communications Commission required every local station to dedicate a percentage of its air time to public service announcements at no cost for certain civic projects. Twenty-or thirty-second spot announcements usually began a week before the opening of the schools, sometimes followed by five or ten minute talks by local personalities. Especially vital to this part of the media projects were the Spanish-speaking stations so prevalent in South Texas and other states where local Mexican American communities were large enough to "merit" such programs.[3]

The climax of the campaign or drive involved a major community rally in which newspaper and radio advertisements publicized the gathering. School authorities were requested to aid in distributing information pertinent to registration and attendance. Police authorities were requested and sometimes attended the meeting to explain the state compulsory attendance law, but this help depended on the city's or town's administrative attitude. In many states, particularly Texas, enforcement of such laws was non-existent. Main speakers for these rallies included the more well-known personalities of the G.I. Forums: Dr. Hector Garcia, Gus Garcia, Vicente Ximenes, Dr. George I. Sanchez, Alonso Perales and many other Mexican Americans devoted their time, effort, and finances to the back-to-school drives.[4]

The activities did not end with rallies. House-to-house canvassing and small neighborhood gatherings occurred immediately before and after the beginning of classes to attempt to follow through any initial success in registering *niños y niñas* (boys and girls). Welfare agencies and personal Forum collections were used for supplying destitute families with shoes and clothing for their children in order that they could attend school without the loss of dignity deprivation might cause. To provide some incentive and aid for higher education, scholarship funds became a corollary to the back-to-school program. Individual G.I. Forum chapters in all Forum states raised money for hundreds of scholarships during the first ten years of the organization. Dances, barbeques, dinners, king and queen contests, and other activities produced thousands of dollars for young Mexican Americans.[5] Most of those people could not have attended college and universities without the Forum support.

Other problems concerning education for Americans of Mexican descent compelled attention. As mentioned, truancy by *Mexicano* children did not bother Anglo officials; indeed, it was often used to the benefit of the Anglo schools, but compulsory attendance was the law. The G.I. Forum in Texas demanded compliance. Aside from the first priority of keeping kids in school, it wanted equal distribution of funds, and a "supportive" program for Mexican American parents who might not know the law (or if they did, would not comply without legal sanction). In 1953, the Texas Education Agency sponsored a stronger law developed by Forum leaders, an acknowledgement of both the correctness of the group's position and a recognition of an assertive representative of *Mexicano*. Attempts to increase the availability of pre-school training in the form of kindergartens had limited success, but this and the other efforts by the G.I. Forum were important precisely because they were done.[6]

Much more can be said about these programs than the fact that they were done. Attendance did increase in most of the regions and states where back-to-school drives were enacted. Year after year these activities occurred and year after year a few more children went to school. For a people whose education attainment was so dismal, this fact was critical to any long-range betterment of their lives. The improvement is obvious in the statistics presented by various studies such as the census data gathered by the federal government and other demographic information researched by various bodies. The levels still remained low, but the idea was implanted that conditions could change and Mexican Americans were not restricted to 3.5 years of school and $980 per year income.[7]

Part 2 - Delgado to Sandia

While back-to-school drives were important, their success did not disturb the traditional place of Mexican children in the Texas educational system. Social prejudice by Texas-Anglo society, reflected by politicians and administrators, resulted in a segregated school system. A viable solution for eradication of this segregation seemed to lie in the legal arena where prejudice and bigotry could more easily be overturned by facts. The American G.I. Forum focused its program to achieve equal education for Mexican Americans on the school system of Texas which deprived children of Mexican descent from the facilities and opportunities readily available to Anglo Americans in the state.

The Treaty of Guadalupe Hidalgo expressly granted all rights guaranteed by the Constitution of the United States to any Mexican citizen who remained in the new territory acquired by the United States after the Mexican War. Implicit in that agreement was the notion of full participation in the various institutional systems of this country, including the public school facilities.[8] The Texas Constitution of 1809, written under the guidelines of Reconstruction officials, distributed educational financing equally among all school districts, without any racial or ethnic qualification and did not mention or provide for separate schools. However, the Texas Constitution of 1876, designed to restore racial restrictions, did stipulate that "separate schools shall be provided for the white and colored children and impartial provision shall be made for both."[9]

These legal guidelines contained the connotations and the elements of what would become a "separate but equal" doctrine. But the qualifying phrase, "white and colored," proved to be a mode of challenging the segregation of *Mexicano* children precisely because of the racial distinctions. Mexicans and Americans of Mexican origin were "scientifically" considered Caucasian stock; in 1930 Mexican American attorneys representing parents in the Del Rio school system argued that school officials were arbitrarily and illegally depriving Mexican American students of facilities used by *other white races* in the same school.[10] Contending that the plaintiffs were segregated solely because of their Mexican origin, attorneys in *Independent School District* vs. *Salvatierra* demanded the end of this unauthorized activity by the Del Rio officials. The trial court agreed with Salvatierra's lawyers and granted an injunction against the separation of *Mexicano* and Anglo children within the school system. Curiously, the Texas Court of Civil Appeals upheld the concept that this segregation of Mexican children was unlawful but reversed the trial judge and voided the injunction. In its ruling, the appellate court stated that without *proof of intent to discriminate* (emphasis mine), segregation of the first three grades in separate campuses due to pedagogical judgement was not an unreasonable or unwarranted exercise of the school board's authority. In this case, correction of language deficiency *as determined by the educational experience of the Del Rio administrators* (emphasis mine) was deemed adequate justification for separation.[11]

The court did rule that such testing had to be administered to all students on an equal basis, but local school authonomy received a boost from this decision as well as an apparent court acceptance of the "other white" theory.

Few legal or other activities were pursued following this decision. Any opportunity to further challenge the system became impossible when the Great Depression eroded any leverage that Mexican Americans might have won. Alien deportation programs by federal and state agencies ostensibly to improve the employment opportunities of American citizens intimidated *Mexicano* society. As the general repatriation campaign dispatched Mexicans and Mexican Americans, the social and political climate became nonconducive to integration programs on the part of "suspect" minorities.[12] Nonetheless, one low-key protest did come in 1940 from LULAC when the Ozona School Board was accused of practicing arbitrary segregation. LULAC attorneys carried their case to the Texas state superintendent of the public schools who in turn ruled that " . . . under the laws of this state (Texas) children of Latin-American extraction were classified as white and therefore have a right to attend the Anglo-American schools in the community in which they live."[13] The importance of this ruling would not be felt until after World War II when the practices of the Anglo school systems in Texas came under intense attack.*

In October 1947, three University of Texas student groups, the Laredo Club, the Alba Club, and the American Veterans Committee issued a press release on five school districts. Their report charged that the school administrators in Beeville, Sinton, Elgin, Bastrop, and Cotulla were segregating children of Mexican descent in grades one through eight. The superintendents of the Beeville and Sinton schools defended the practice and insisted that the "educational opportunities offered Latin Americans (were) equal to those offered Anglo Americans." As soon as language handicaps were overcome, "it is the desire and policy of both schools, to move them into classrooms with the Anglo Americans."[14] The Texas State Department of Education concurred in its own investigation, stating that "provisions for the Latin American school-building equipment measure up favorably with the best the supervisor has found in 54 counties."[15]

This all-too-usual attitude might have continued except for two other segregation-related decisions in 1947. In California, the Ninth Circuit Court ruled in *Westminister School District* vs. *Mendez* that certain California school districts were improperly separating Mexican American and Anglo children. Segregation was permissable, but only between the races, and because *Mexicanos* were part of the white race the practice was unconstitutional.[16] In Texas, Gus Garcia questioned Attorney General, Price Daniel, whether segregation was permissible unless the separation due to language deficiencies was based on "scientific tests" and applied to all students regardless of racial ancestry. Daniel fell right in, answering, "I am certainly pleased to know that your interpretation of this opinion agrees with ours. We meant that the law prohibits discrimination against or segregation of Latin Americans on account of race or descent, and the law permits no subterfuge to accomplish such discrimination."[17]

The impetus from these two events made a school suit against Mexican American segregation more propitious than at any other time in Texas since 1930. With the aid of LULAC and the support of the Alba Club at the University of Texas, Garcia became the attorney for Minerva Delgado and twenty other Mexican American parents who did not appreciate the second-class nature of their children's education. These people brought suit against the Bastrop Independent School District, the Elgin ISD, the Travis County Schools, and L.A. Woods, state

---

*Some curriculum changes emphasizing Latin American history, were instituted in Texas during the war. Workshops for teachers also attempted to improve the educational climate for Mexican Americans, but "reform" did not take place.

superintendent of public instruction. Garcia employed the "other white", "absence of law" concepts and lack of equally applied tests as proof of the charge that the Bastrop ISD was arbitrarily and illegally depriving *Mexicanos* of equal facilities, services and education instruction.[18]

Dr. Hector Garcia immediately became involved in the Delgado case. As a result of the Beeville-Sinton exposé, he had already involved himself with the educational difficulties encountered by most Mexican Americans. As an active member of LULAC, he assumed the responsibility of raising funds in the Corpus Christi area for legal expenses. (With an initial goal of $2,500, the doctor's committee acquired $1,689 within three months and $2,000 by March of 1948.[19]) During that time Hector Garcia met Dr. George I. Sanchez, a noted historian at the University of Texas, a lifelong advocate for *la gente*, and the Texas chairman of the fund committee for the *Minerva Delgado et al* vs. *Bastrop ISD et al* segregation case. Naturally, the doctor also became good friends with Gus Garcia, and these three men would remain intimate colleagues until Gus Garcia's death in 1964 and Dr. Sanchez's demise in 1971.

After its formation in March 1948, the American G.I. Forum joined with LULAC in the activities so necessary for the pursuit of the Delgado court procedures. Gus Garcia repeatedly emphasized the necessity of maintaining unequivocal support of the twenty-one parents, who, until this point in their lives, had accepted the restrictions of a small-town, Anglo-controlled environment. The parents were performing a very courageous act in opposing the Anglo concept of equal education, and the task of LULAC and the G.I. Forum was to demonstrate that they were not alone (as well as to provide financial needs). Dr. Garcia and the G.I. Forum were instrumental in doing just that by eliciting support and aid from the numerous communities in South and South Central Texas.[20] When Minerva Delgado and her compatriots presented their case in the United States District Court in Austin, Texas, they were representing the hopes (and fears) of many more Mexican Americans than just those in Bastrop, Texas.

Judge Ben H. Rice rendered his final judgment on June 15, 1948 and found that the defendants were in violation of the constitutional rights guaranteed to every citizen by the Fourteenth Amendment of the Constitution of the United States. The final judgment issued an injunction that

> . . . permanently restrained and enjoined from segregation pupils of Mexican or other Latin American descent in separate schools or classes within the respective school districts of said defendants and each of them, and from denying said pupils use of the same facilities and services enjoyed by other children of the same ages or grades.[21]

Judge Rice also prohibited the state superintendent from "in any matter, directly or indirectly participating in the custom, usage, or practice of segregating pupils of Mexican or other Latin American descent in separate schools or classes." Any school district not in compliance with the above judgment had until September of 1949 to correct discrepancies.[22]

Even though this decision undermined the rigid segregation of the pre-1948 Texas school system, a loophole did appear in the final court order that gave school districts opportunities to circumvent the intent of the *Delgado* decision. Judge Rice allowed the defendant school districts, and by inference, all school districts, to maintain separate classes *on the same campus and in the first grade* (emphasis mine) "solely for instructional purposes" as determined by "scientific and standardized" tests, equally given and applied to all pupils to determine their understanding and competency in the English language.[23] This provision, and a pro-segregation attitude of state authorities enabled local school boards to procrastinate on desegregation and provided innumerable problems for G.I. Forum integration struggles.[24]

Nonetheless, to his credit, State Superintendent Woods issued very explicit instructions to all public school officers and school districts. He pointed out that segregation of children of Latin American origin for reasons of race or descent was considered unconstitutional by the state and federal court. Three strongly worded instructions were authorized and so directed:

> Segregation of Mexican or Latin American descended children in separate classes or schools was forbidden.
>
> Separate classes on the same campus for instructional purposes for any students with language difficulties was permissible but only as determined by equally applied language tests; all pupils were entitled to the use of the same facilities, i.e., cafeterias, playgrounds, and participation in the same functions such as school contests, bands, etc.[25]
>
> 'You will take all necessary steps to eliminate any and all segregation that may exist in your school or district contrary to instruction and regulations.'[26]

Many school districts paid little or no attention to these instructions because of professed ignorance of the law and an unwillingness to correct years of "practice, custom and usage."[27] One of the more stubborn was Del Rio, a town in West Texas across the border from Ciudad Acuña. On January 7, 1949, Christobal Aldrete, an attorney and citizen of Del Rio (and a member of the Forum) protested segregation of *Mexicanitos* in the elementary grades of the Del Rio ISD. L.A. Woods sent an assistant state superintendent to investigate and report his findings. He made a telling statement. Two school campuses were separated by railroad tracks. The north elementary school campus was reserved strictly for Anglo children, although zoned for all students in an area where many Mexican American children lived. The south campus had four buildings, two of which had *Mexicano* students only. Latin American teachers taught only in these schools, being unwelcome and unacceptable in Anglo schools by the Del Rio board, even though many were deemed "good teachers" by board members. The assistant state superintendent recommended a removal of accreditation from the district until correction was made in the school organization. Woods withheld punitive action, at the request of the Del Rio Board of Trustees, until Judge Rice could review the case. But after notice from the judge that the Delgado case would not be reopened every time the state superintendent delivered an administrative interpretation, Del Rio was removed from the accredited list of Texas schools. Appeal was denied, in part because of testimony by Dr. Hector Garcia and attorney Gus Garcia.[28]

Del Rio was not the sole school district in violation of state law after the *Delgado* decree and the Woods instructions. G.I. Forums made numerous inspections of various communities where members of the Forum or citizens of the locale complained of continual school segregation. One such trip in February 1949 in Live Oak County (the constituency of J. F. Gray of Longoria "fame") produced the rather remarkable statement from the principal of a segregated Mexican school that he knew of and admitted the separation of Latin children up through the sixth grade despite the instructions by L.A. Woods. It was wrong, but what could a person do? The school board authorities wanted integration but had no plans or program. American G.I. Forum representatives made the suggestion that integration could be achieved by mixing the children on the same campus. They even offered to pay for necessary expenses, but that was a radical step for the concerned and "hopeful" officials.[29]

A more extensive inspection tour by Dr. Garcia and various individuals provided evidence of ruses, actions, and schemes which circumvented the Rice decree and the Woods instructions, actions consciously done "to deprive the Latin American children of their God given right of the advantages to which they are entitled under our . . . Constitution." Robstown, George West, Mathis, Orange Grove, Bishop, Driscoll, Sinton, Faft, Three Rivers, Edcovah, Encinal, Beeville, Rio Hondo and Del Rio were actively practicing segregation of children of Mexican descent despite promises to change their systems.[30]

The result of these confrontations was a heightened and, for many people, a developed sense of outrage against the treatment of Mexican Americans. The American G.I. Forum (and LULAC) were not going to accept the pre-war world of second-class conditions. But neither were the political powers going to permit a "bunch of Latinos" to tell them how to conduct "their business". In June of 1949, the Texas Legislature used the newly created office of Commissioner of education to subsume the functions of the state superintendent of public instruction. L. A. Woods, a man who had demonstrated his intentions of complying with the spirit and letter of the Delgado decree, was demoted to the position of temporary advisor to the new commissioner. J.W. Edgar, with the overwhelming support of the legislature, received the appointment, a fact that did not argue for the future of Mexicano education. The new commissioner immediately assumed office (the Legislature deemed the act an emergency measure). The Del Rio ISD reappealed its discreditation to the State Board of Education and won.[31] More opposition by the Texas school system came in a reply to Dr. Garcia regarding his complaint to the Good Neighbor Commission about segregation in the Santa Cruz Independent School District. The GNC acknowledged that it appreciated the information , promised an attempt to resolve the issue, but hoped that the courts would only be the last resort.[32]

The G.I. Forum continued its efforts to publicize the educational condition in the state. The 1949 American G.I. Forum convention adopted resolutions that called for suspension of all federal funds to schools that practiced segregation, and demanded investigation of a number of school districts. The Forum went on record as opposing the concept of "free choice" which enabled Anglos to keep their children out of "Mexican schools". Finally, the state unit issued a report detailing segregation in Lubbock, San Angelo, Samora, Ozona, Sanderson, Alpine, Pecos, George West, Morathon, Rock Springs, Santa Cruz, Kyle, Beeville, Taft, Sinton, Robstown, San Marcos, Bishop, Odem, Edcouch, Del Rio, Harlingen, Lockhart, Cotulla, and Cuero — a notable "honor roll".[33]

Perhaps the highlight of this year (1949), and certainly an action worthy of its author, was a proposal by Congressman J.F. Gray to give county boards of education, school boards and ISDs the power to locate schools and place pupils wherever the authorities wanted. No appeal would be possible except by re-election or defeat of the local officials.[34] The act did not pass, and the transparency of the scheme was both ludicrous and sad. But J. F. Gray did not give a damn—and the G.I. Forum did—that was the difference in Gray's view of racial harmony and also the fear of this Texas legislator.

In 1950, J.W. Edgar carried out the role assigned to him by the Texas Legislature. Obviously the local authorities would continue their intransigence as long as tacit approval flowed from the highest state officials. Acts such as denying the use of school buildings to local Forums were frustrating as well as expected, but a citizen does have the right to depend on public officials to administer the law of the land.[35] A directive by the Texas State Board of Education and a follow-up letter by Commissioner Edgar in June to all legal school authorities indicated that the intent of the law and the qualities of justice extracted from the same law might be separate.

The policy statement recognized the responsibility of the State Board to administer the public program of Texas in accordance with constitutional and statutory authority and that "any form of segregation not authorized by the Constitution and laws should be eliminated."[36] The statement directed the local administrators and boards of trustees as the primary source of initiative and change, but the subsequent letter provides a more enlightening glimpse of what the Texas Board had in mind:

> We believe that it is highly desirable for local boards of trustees to be given every opportunity to administer the local school program in accordance with provisions of the statutes. *Consistent with this desire to promote strong local administration of the school program* (emphasis mine), and in order that local authorities may discharge their legal responsibility, the following procedure has been adopted to handle cases where it is alleged there exists the practice of segregating Latin American children from Anglo American children in the school program.
>
> 1) When complaints alleging segregation of Latin American children contrary to the provisions of the statutes are made to the Commissioner of Education without evidence of previous action of the local board of trustees these complaints will be referred to the local school authorities of the school district involved in order that appropriate action may be taken.
>
> 2) The local board of trustees receiving such referral has a legal responsibility for determining whether or not Latin American children are being segregated from Anglo American children in the school program of the district. If the local board finds that such segregation is being practiced, it is their duty to make the necessary adjustment in their administrative policy to eliminate this practice. . .
>
> 3) . . . Upon receipt of an appeal from the action of the local board of trustees the Commissioner of Education will give full consideration to the facts in order to determine whether or not *in his judgement* (emphasis mine) there has been violation of the statutes or of constitutional rights. . .[37]

The implicit motive of these statements, especially when considered in the light of the Del Rio reversal, was to impede the attempts of the G.I. Forum and other organizations to eliminate segregation of Mexican American children. If Commissioner Edgar had the power or prerogative to determine what "previous action" existed that might contribute to "violation of statutes", then civil rights advocates had a formidable opponent. Indeed, the concept of "previous action" as a determinant in any segregation case does not make sense. Whether unequal education by practices such as segregation was intended or unintended, what did it matter? The goal by the G.I. Forum was to eradicate those customs, not to demand apologies or waste time assessing blame.

Perhaps Mr. Edgar and other persons did not understand the Forum's motives, but it is apparent that the May and June directives were a direct reaction to efforts by Dr. Garcia and his organization. A letter and report by the doctor on April 13, 1950, to the State Board and the Commissioner in which various localities are accused of segregation is forthright:

> . . . In general, it can be stated that in the majority of places where we have people interested in stopping segregation, it has been stopped usually by continuous pressure methods against the school officials. We are indeed ashamed to state that the majority of the school boards still believe that segregation is American and *unless they know there is a higher authority than their own local school boards* (emphasis mine), they have no intention of stopping this cruel segregation as has been ordered since last year. . . . In spite of the *Delgado* decision, an instruction sent out by the former superintendent of Education, the local school boards still believe that they are justified in continuing segregation because they have done it legally in the past.

The report listed twenty-two cities and towns in violation of the *Delgado* decree (many of them making repeat appearances from other such reports), and concluded with a "request" to the commissioner that he do something. Edgar's answer was the policy statements that strengthened the position of the local boards.

Forumeers continued to file complaints but without meaningful response from those who were able to effect any change. This lack of attention did not deter the Forum's general practice of putting pressure on local school administrators and state officers, but it did not help the morale of those Mexican Americans who were receiving the brunt of the struggle. Such tactics as gerrymandering and "free choice" plus outright opposition appeared to be succeeding. For instance, a school board would zone a school by requiring all children living "south of a particular street" to attend a designated school. Perhaps such wording did not explicitly segregate *Mexicanos,* but the obvious fact that all of the children living south of that street were Mexican American and were already attending the designated school does not seem a matter of coincidence.[39] Nor does a superintendent who claims "such letters and demands are not in keeping with the true objectives of the PTA organization" (in response to a request by a PTA to cease use of a wooden-frame building that was extremely dangerous and inadequate — and used mostly by children) appear reasonable.[40] Nonetheless, the battle went on.

The emphasis of the Forum strategy at this juncture was to expose the glaring inequities between the "Mexican school" and the "Anglo school". While establishing the legal proof of segregation was difficult as long as Edgar and people of his sentiments ruled the education system, verification of maltreatment or at least the indifference of Anglo officials toward *Mexicanos* was a different matter. A good example of this tactic was a report by the Corpus Christi G.I. Forum on the Sandia school system of Sandia, Texas. A Mexican American committee from Sandia asked the Forum to investigate the school situation because of its belief that discrimination was the predominant policy of the Anglo trustees. Dr. Garcia personally led the Forum committee and issued a public report.[41]

The Sandia school system consisted of a Mexican ward school and the Anglo school. While the main Anglo school building was a two-story brick building with good a playground, the Mexican classes were held in a frame building that by 1952 was no more than a shack with poor ventilation and improper heat; the playground was a field with several craters. *Mexicano* elementary classes through the third grade had twenty-five students and one teacher, whereas the corresponding ratio for the Anglo school was ten to one. Dr. Garcia recommended the "Mexican" building be demolished, the students incorporated into the Anglo school, and ". . . all the white children can be together and have the same facilities and advantages as given them under the Court of Texas and the Fourteenth Amendment to the Constitution of the United States."[42]

A trend was created from these events that make the out-of-hand dismissal of Forum complaints more and more difficult. Beginning in late 1952 and ending in 1957, a series of desegregation cases finally removed the psuedo-legal rationales of Texas educators for the maintenance of separation of children of Mexican descent from the facilities and instruction available to Anglo Americans. While not solving the problem of equal education, they would force a shift in Anglo obstruction that would have seemed impossible only a few years before.

Part 3 - Pecos to Driscoll

The Pecos Independent School District of Pecos, Texas, proposed in 1952 to zone the Mexican neighborhoods in an area which would require the children to register at the East Pecos Junior High and allow all other students to attend Pecos Junior High. This plan produced *de jure* segregation based on a *de facto* housing pattern. The G.I. Forum and LULAC proposed a new zoning plan or relocation of the new junior high that would reflect the *Delgado* decision. In addition, the Forumeers demanded the elimination of the segregation in the elementary school system. This separation forced Mexican American children into Earl Bell and West Pecos Elementary, which deprived them of other facilities. Finally, the organizations called for an end to the "free choice" plan which perpetuated this segregation.[43] Commissioner Edgar did not accept the arguments or demands as valid and approved the Pecos plan, which instituted the zoning change and maintained the traditional elementary school divisions. Despite appeals by G.I. Forum and LULAC attorneys, the State Board of Education sustained the ruling in April 1954. In a parting shot, the attorney representing the Pecos ISD said, "I don't think the Pecos Board of Trustees is going to abdicate its authority to the American G.I. Forum or LULAC."[44] However, the Forum pursued other assaults on the staunchly dedicated officials of the Texas school systems. Chris Aldrete filed a perfected petition against the Sanderson, Texas, system in August 1952, alleging that first graders were illegally segregated and that grades two through six were segregated by achievement grouping. Edgar did sustain these charges after lengthy deliberation and ordered an end to such practices.[45]

More significant was the decision by Commissioner Edgar in the *Orta* vs. *Hondo Independent School District* of September 1953. He upheld the contentions by Forum attorneys that the Hondo ISD had illegally separated children of Mexican descent on a campus known as the West Ward. In the hearing before the commissioner, the Hondo superintendent testified that children at the West Ward school were there by choice or were placed there because of their language deficiency as determined by oral tests. Forum counsel pointed out the absence of scientific testing and the existence of a separate campus, both in violation with the *Delgado* decision.[46] Besides ordering full compliance with the *Delgado* decree, Edgar ordered the cessation of the two-year first grade concept and the implementation of equally applied language tests.[47]

A momentum of events, influenced by the continous pressure applied by the American G.I. Forum, was taking effect. Forum attorneys filed suits against the Carrizo Springs ISD, the Kingsville ISD, and the Mathis ISD which increased the tempo of the organization's anti-segregation program. A major effect of these cases was to modify the time-consuming procedures required by Commissioner Edgar in challenging a local school board.[48] The delay tactics of local negotiations produced a new Forum strategy which allowed only a minimal time for resolving local intransigence before proceeding to the federal courts. The results were amazing.

Cortez vs. *the Carrizo Springs Independent School District* began in April 1955. The plaintiffs charged that the Carrizo Springs Board of Trustees and Superintendent had adopted a plan by which Mexican American children were prevented, solely because of their ethnic origins, from attending certain schools and using certain facilities which were maintained exclusively for Anglo American students. Due to "absence of law", the lack of due process and equal protection of laws, these persons were deprived of their rights as citizens of the United States. Commissioner Edgar, with full knowledge of this condition, condoned illegal acts by his refusal to carry out the decrees of *Delgado* and the guarantees of the Fourteenth Amendment. Because all parties intended to continue these practices, the Carrizo Springs plaintiffs asked for a permanent injunction to end the deplorable harm done to children of Mexican descent. On June 13, 1955, the federal action was dismissed when the Carrizo Board agreed to end the segregation of Mexican American pupils.[49]

A similar case developed in the Kingsville ISD when the school board adopted a zoning plan in 1954 in which (1) one of the junior high schools would have all Spanish-named students, and (2) the Anglo children would have "freedom of choice" in order to escape the prospect of attending the Mexican school. G.I. Forum attorneys Gus Garcia and Carlos Cadena "took 'em to court",[50] and established in the Commissioner's hearing that segregation had existed in Kingsville since 1914. Garcia also contended that the post-*Delgado* actions of the Kingsville officials were designed to perpetuate that tradition. Mostly by cross-examination, Garcia showed that discriminatory practices and bigoted attitudes permeated the Kingsville board. In one exchange, a board member remarked that no controversy would exist "had the people not been stirred up by outside influences"; the board member added that he was referring to Dr. Hector Garcia and the G.I. Forum.[51]

The commissioner would not be rushed into any hasty conclusions, and, furthermore, the stenographer who recorded the hearings did not transcribe the testimony. Therefore, the commissioner explained that he could not deliver a ruling until proper transcriptions arrived; but four months later he had taken no action.[52] That nonsense did not work — the G.I. Forum filed a suit in federal court on April 23, 1955.[53] Commissioner Edgar may not have been disturbed, but the Kingsville School Board was shaken by the fact of federal court proceedings. It modified its zoning plan to integrate *Mexicanos* in the new school, and, after observation, the plaintiff's attorneys expressed satisfaction. Meanwhile, federal judge James V. Allred ordered Commissioner Edgar to get his job done.[54]

If an award could be given for recalcitrance, the Mathis Independent School District of 1954—1956 would win. Dr. Garcia had investigated the schools in Mathis as early as 1948. His detailed report proved conclusively that the segregated "Mexican" school existed, that the buildings were extremely dilapidated and that health facilities were very inadequate. He concluded that the educational progress of *Mexicano* children was considerably harmed. The reaction of school officials can be summarized as, "So?"[55]

In 1954, with considerably more experience, the Forum once again moved against Mathis officials. At stake was not the existence of segregation but the matter of when it would end. The school superintendent claimed the old West Ward campus (a target of Dr. Garcia's 1948 report) had to be open until the new building was complete. But Forum attorneys insisted on a hearing with Edgar to expedite the removal of the Mexican school, an act opposed by the Anglo board.[56] Edgar did urge the superintendent to end the segregation by eliminating the separate campus and to comply with court rulings on language tests, but the school district did not take him seriously.[57] The commissioner ruled in May 1955 that it was not necessary to study the record; he was aware of the facts and did not need the stenographic transcript. With this noted departure from previous precedures, Edgar ordered the end of the Mathis West Ward segregation by September 1955.[58] But the Mathis officials paid little attention to the directive, and the American G.I. Forum did not waste its time waiting for any positive response from Edgar. Trinidad Villarreal and others filed against the Mathis ISD of San Patricio County.[59]

Pre-trial memoranda, grievance lists, motions to dismiss, and defendant replies made up a ponderous list of Anglo obstinancy and *Mexicano* determination. Testimony by the Mathis superintendent illustrated a logic that justified second-grade placement in segregated classes solely because of first-grade status. He also felt the old elementary building had its redeeming feature—age or "the test of time." Separation did not really exist because the buildings were only 150 feet apart and no fences stood between them.[60] Commissioner Edgar, a co-defendant entered a motion to dismiss because, among other reasons: (1) the attempt to involve the federal courts was "frivolous in concept, nebulous in form, lacking in substance, (and) unreal", (2) the defendant was described as a resident of Travis County, therefore, not in the jurisdiction of the federal court of the Southern District of Texas, (3) "no statement is made showing how this defendant ever acted or failed to legally act in any manner to damage any of the plaintiffs, (therefore) no showing is made of this defendant ever depriving any plaintiff herein of a civil right."[61] Forum attorneys had their answer:

> It is one thing to segregate specific pupils as a result of individual testing at a time when they are being taught the language (just as in some schools slow readers are in one group and fast readers in another during the time of reading lesson). It is quite another to completely separate them for *all purposes*, and thus to deprive not only the Mexican children but also the other children, of the benefits of the commingling process, held by the United States Supreme Court in *Sweatt vs. Painter*, to stand at the very heart of the right to be free from discrimination because of ancestry. This is so because otherwise the segregated student is kept 'in isolation,' and deprived of the benefits of contact with those with whom, as a citizen of a community, he is expected to live.[62]

The Mathis Superintendent and Commissioner Edgar were surely "inspired" by this action because the Mexican school was closed and the district ordered to comply with *Delgado*, even though the suit was dismissed due to the reluctance of an expert witness to testify. The reasons for the orders are vague, and the results still saw a considerable number of Mexican American students segregated, but the triumph was nonetheless real and significant.[63]

The culminating event of these ten years of persistent, sometimes frustrating, but always important confrontations occurred· with the Driscoll decision of 1957. The case represented the final attempt of the Texas school system to cling to its "language" rationale in order to maintain legal segregation of Mexican Americans.

In September 1955, Dr. Garcia of Corpus Christi communicated a formal complaint to Commissioner Edgar about the practices of the Driscoll Consolidated ISD. The founder of the G.I. Forum charged that *Mexicano* children were placed in a segregated system. They were classified in a "beginners' class" for their first scholastic year, passed to "low first" in their second year, moved to "high first" in the third year, and finally graduated to a segregated second grade class in the fourth year of their elementary scholastic schedule. Apart from the *prima facie* absurdity of this situation, the doctor also alleged that the students did not receive proper testing as required by the *Delgado* decision. Mexican American children who could speak excellent English were subjected to four years of supposed training in their language.[64]

Even Commissioner Edgar recognized the strength of the Forum's position and urged the Driscoll officials to comply with the *Delgado* decision. The district superintendent gave the standard reply that the board of trustees would do so but needed time to construct new buildings (even though they were able to reduce "training" to three years).[65] That game had been played too often; Herminia Hernandez and others, represented by Forum attorneys James De Anda and Gus Garcia, filed suit in January 1957.[66]

Testimony by the Driscoll superintendent demonstrated the all too usual complacency and ignorance of Anglo educators:

> It's been our (Driscoll) experience that it took a majority of the students longer to do what an English-speaking child would accomplish in one year.
>
> Question (De Anda): Any special tests for English?
>
> Answer (Supt.): No, but they will be used. (It had been 9 years *Delgado*).
>
> Question: Aren't Latins offered pre-primer ahead of Anglos just starting?
>
> Answer: Yes, in some respects.[67]

The defendants' counsel employed his own unique logic in answering the suggestion by Judge Allred that a Latin child in an Anglo class might be an incentive or merit-inducing device. The counsel replied:

94

> If the court will give that thought further consideration, we believe it will be seen that such a method would call for a recognition of a difference in descent, and would imply that those who are not of Latin descent are superior to those of Latin descent and their company should be preferred. When we are seeking to do away with distinctions or differences resulting from racial or ethnic differences, we would be defeating our purpose if we follow a plan which caused small children to think that it is a desirable reward to be taken out of a group which happens to be of Latin descent and placed with a group which happens to be of Anglo descent.[68]

If a stenograper had not been present to transcribe this idiocy, it would be difficult to believe; Allred indicated as much.

While the defense itself might have been De Anda's best weapon, the presence of Linda Perez was incontrovertible proof of the Driscoll system's inadequaces. This young Mexican American student spoke nothing but English, yet was automatically placed in the "Mexican" first grade to learn that language.[69]

Judge Allred found for the plaintiff. His memorandum reached the center of the issue at hand. After a brief outline of the history of the case, Allred emphasized a number of points:

> The foregoing is a generally correct statement of the issue but it overlooks the fact that the Driscoll school authorities have drawn the line, not only for beginners, but through the first and second grades, not on a basis of individual aptitudes or attainments, but against all children of Latin American extraction *as a class*. This is a modified continuation of the old policies under which all such children once were segregated in separate campuses through the first six grades. That the line is drawn on a racial rather than a merit basis is evidenced by the overall facts and the refusal in September 1955, to place a beginning Latin child, Linda Perez, who could speak no Spanish, in the Anglo section until after a lawyer's services had been secured. In the twelve years that the present superintendent has been at Driscoll, this is the only Mexican child that has been placed in the Anglo section and then only after the parents' intervention.[70]

The conclusion of Judge Allred's findings found the Driscoll grouping *of separate classes* arbitrary and unreasonable:

> . . . They are hereby enjoined and restrained and permanently enjoined and restrained from grouping in separate classrooms plaintiffs and other students of the class of person they represent upon any basis other than as herein above set forth.[71]

The ultimate significance of this statement lay in the removal of the legal entanglements first confronted by Gus Garcia in 1948.

A major and positive shift in Mexican American education in Texas (and the Southwest) occurred because of the efforts and programs of the American G.I. Forum from 1948 to 1957. By introducing the federal court strategy also used by the black civil rights movement, the G.I.

Forum established *la causa* on another front. The 1954 Supreme Court decision which ruled legal segregation of black students unconstitutional did not apply to Mexican Americans. In Texas, President Eisenhower implicitly supported the anti-integration actions of Governor Allan Shivers (Texas Rangers appeared at Texarkana Junior College and Mansfield High School to "assure" segregation). In a tour of the South, the president expressed his belief that racial reform should occur at the local level and by state initiative.[72] The federal troops at Little Rock, Arkansas, would not have been there if the governor of Arkansas had not blatantly defied the Supreme Court dictate. If Mexican Americans wanted to eliminate desegregation, they would have to do it themselves and they did. Unfortunately, the "other white" and absence of law strategy limited the extension from desegregation to integration. When *de facto* segregation became the main target of civil rights activists, the "other white" concept allowed the grouping of Black and Mexican American children to circumvent the spirit of integration laws. However, the G.I. Forum's achievements from 1948 to 1957 are not diminished by that fact. With the Hernandez decision in 1954 and the school cases, *de jure* segregation by language separation suffered a lethal blow.

Other effects became noticeable in the latter part of the 1960s when young Chicanos "suddenly" began voicing their opposition to a system that had basically ignored their needs. While many *Mexicanos* still lacked a high school degree, a significant number did achieve educational goals undreamed of in 1945.[73] Youth movements in Southwest universities began articulating a virulent anger toward institutions engrained with a tradition of neglect and ignorance of the needs and aspirations of the Mexican American. There can be little doubt that many of these students received better education as a direct result of the desegregation struggle.

But what about the more ephemeral effect? An activist of today might criticize these accomplishments of the 1950s as less than complete and cite statistics showing the same gap between Anglo and Mexican American scholastic attainment in 1960 as 1950; or argue that Anglo administrators still maintained segregation in many systems and were unresponsive to Forum pressure.

The answer to such criticism must be based on the context of the period in which these events took place and the historical process of integration. Surely an individual with six or eight years education was better equipped socially than a person with 3.5 years. For example, the ability to add, subtract, or read a contract is critical if one is to pevent hostile or indifferent parties from taking advantage of a situation, such as cheating on a paycheck. The so-called "gap" might remain the same, but the impact of those additional years were vital to many people. Certainly, many, if not most, Anglo administrators remained unresponsive but compared to what? The educational rights of Mexican Americans in 1957 were much different than in 1948. That difference reflected the determination and ability of Mexican Americans and their organization. The issue was identified and the campaign long and demanding. The results speak for themselves.

CHAPTER VIII

Muchos Mojados y Otras Cosas

By 1953, American G.I. Forums were firmly established in Texas, New Mexico, and Colorado. Texas had established its predominance, but New Mexico and Colorado held their first state conventions in 1953 and had added to Forum experience with their own. The triumphs of these units and the zeal of the first organizers were manifested in the addition of three new states in 1954: Ohio, Utah, and Kansas. Texas leaders played a major role in establishing this expansion, but the initiative lay largely with the native inhabitants, a fact that pointed out the general need and basic similarity of the issues concerning Americans of Mexican descent. The proven ability of the G.I. Forum in producing incipient solutions and the desire of Dr. Garcia, Vicente Ximenes, and other leaders to engage in expansion contributed to the growth. With the expressed willingness of other *Mexicanos* to participate in *la lucha*, the results were most encouraging. In 1955 and 1956, Nebraska and California saw the development of American G.I. Forum state constitutions and charters. By December of 1957, with the addition of Arizona, Missouri, Michigan, Illinois, and Wyoming, the National American G.I. Forum represented thirteen states with approximately 20,000 members.[1]

The first national convention elected Hector P. Garcia of Corpus Christi as national chairman, an honor and deserved recognition for the founder. The national constitution retained the fundamental tenets of the original 1949 Texas document with some modifications to incorporate broader membership. The national office was fixed as the clearing house of basic guidelines, but the local units lost none of their autonomy or independence. Vicente Ximenes was chosen national chairman at the 1957 convention and Dr. Garcia re-elected in 1958, a reflection of the still-growing Forum and the reluctance of the membership to trust the top positions to new people. Expansion continued at an accelerated pace as new elements swelled the ranks. The tenth anniversary in 1958 produced a national convention in Corpus Christi (a celebration of the birth in 1948), attended by 2,000 delegates who represented eighteen states (seventeen official charters) and 25,000 members.[2] Three accomplishments in these years demonstrated the maturity, cohesiveness, and regional distinction of the G.I. Forum.

Part 1 - Daughters of the American Revolution

The Colorado Industrial School for Boys scheduled a Lincoln Day celebration for February 12, 1957, sponsored by the Daughters of the American Revolution with the usual flags, speeches, and general American hoopla. A "disconcerting" aspect of the celebration compel led the local DAR chairman to speak out. The school was a state correctional institute for young boys assigned by juvenile and county courts and, according to the local chairman, "at least half are Mexicans." She presumed that most of the "Mexicans" were born in the United States but of parents "who came here from Mexico — they were Mexican boys, not American boys" and she would not permit a Mexican to carry the American flag.[3] Reporters verifying this statement were answered with a question, "I wouldn't want a Mexican to carry Old Glory, would you?"[4] Art Tafoya, Colorado state chairman of the American G.I. Forum, had an answer. Tafoya and Frank Duran issued a statement of outrage to the Denver newspapers. They notified national chairman Vicente Ximenes, who then wired Board chairman Dr. Hector Garcia. Telegrams immediately went out to all state organizations with information of the incident and with requests to send protests to all congressmen. Thousands of messages alerted these representatives to the presence of a prejudiced attitude in the DAR. (The DAR had once prohibited Marian Anderson, a world-famous American gospel singer, from giving a concert at Constitution Hall in Washington, D.C., simply because she was black.) Senator Dennis Chavez of New Mexico responded with the thought that 576 "Mexicans" were among those at Bataan in World War II and asked the local Colorado DAR, "What makes you think they can't carry it (the flag) just as proudly in Colorado?" Dr. Garcia sent a special telegram to President Eisenhower stating, "We carry our flag with the same dignity, honor, and love that we used when we draped the caskets of thousands of our own soldiers, the Americans of Mexican origin, when we brought them back to bury them in the land that we love so much". The governor of Colorado ordered cessation of DAR activities pending scrutiny of their attitudes and feelings.[5]

The Daughters of the American Revolution was acutely embarrassed The national office of the Forum provided an escape clause by expressing a belief in the general patriotism of the organization, and Mrs. Frederic Graves, national DAR president, jumped at it. Enunciating profound gratitude for this "expression of confidence", a questionable interpretation at best, she disowned the local Colorado leader, offered a goodwill gesture involving an exchange of large American flags, and praised American soldiers of Mexican origin. Ximenes accepted the gesture. Governor McNichols rescinded the ban on DAR work, and the organization was thoroughly vindicated, according to DAR officials. As a Lubbock, Texas, member put it, in reference to their work with "Latin Americans", (we) thoroughly enjoyed drinking coffee, eating tacos, and meeting friends at your last fiesta. We are really interested in your citizenship endeavors. After all, Jesus Christ probably had darker skin than the average Anglo."[6]

This type of incidents did serve a purpose. If some Mexican Americans became satisfied with initial progress, a local DAR individual's insensitivity could dispel any notion of success in eliminating discrimination. The immediate challenge of the G.I. Forum to this type of attitude, and the organizational abilities displayed, particularly in Colorado, indicated something new in the Southwest. Traditional practices toward Mexican Americans such as the DAR insult would not remain unanswered; passivity among this minority was a thing of the past if, indeed, it had ever existed.

Fair Employment

The second episode concerned the concerted campaign of the New Mexico G.I. Forum to secure labor rights for Mexican Americans. Having won many labor disputes, in addition to playing a major role in the passage of an anti-discrimination law in the state legislature, this Forum kept a surveillance on possible discriminatory practices. One such infraction, discovered in August of 1956, concerned a passage in the constitution of the Brotherhood of Locomotive Firemen and Enginemen. The passage defined membership:

> He shall be white, born of good moral character, sober and industrious, no less than 16 years of age, and be able to read and write the English language and understand our constitution. Mexicans or those of Spanish extraction are not eligible. [7]

Vicente Ximenes filed an immediate complaint with the New Mexico Fair Employment Practices Commission with a demand for investigation. In reply to FEPC questions, the union denied the existence of the clause and refused to supply a copy of the constitution, but did so when threatened by a subpoena. The national office also requested the President's Committee on Government Contracts to pursue an investigation and received a favorable response. All state Forums were instructed to follow the progress of the affair and lend support.[8]

In November, Senator Dennis Chavez and Senator Ralph Yarborough offered to lend their offices in support of the President's Committee. The New Mexico FEPC found the union in non-compliance with state law but encountered an obstinate "Brotherhood". At this point, the

Forumeers began the standard practice of letter writing to congressmen. As usual, the defendants managed to stall the proceedings, in this case by reference to a federal court case in Ohio covering the same issue. The New Mexico union requested a delay until that case was decided.[9]

Meanwhile, not to be outdone by the railroad union, the manager of the Belen, New Mexico, depot had a sign posted prohibiting the use of Spanish in the station and on adjacent property. Ximenes and state chairman Louis P. Tellez vigorously protested and alerted the newspapers, which gave the story good distribution. The sign was removed, but the Forum had exhausted its patience with railroad people. In January 1958, an official complaint to the New Mexico FEPC demanded removal of the offending and illegal clause. Apparently, the union recognized a lost cause and finally agreed to delete the statements forbidding Mexican American membership.[10]

A postscript to this incident demonstrated the collective opposition toward the idea of equal rights. A Forumeer in Saginaw, Michigan, supplied the local newspaper with information of the successful New Mexico developments and asked that it be published. An individual in charge of publication refused, saying that the news was too old, was not local, and probably not true.[11]

Giant

In 1957, the Texas Legislature made its stand against the 1954 Supreme Court ruling in *Brown vs. Board of Education of Topeka, Kansas* (separate is not equal and unconstitutional). Displaying a less than fervent desire to follow the law, a bill was proposed in the Texas Legislature that would prevent integration by supplying the local boards with the right to assign students to schools of the trustees' choosing. On the surface, this act seemed democratic, but it was the old "freedom of choice" method faced by the G.I. Forum in its own struggle against segregation. Although this bill was directed toward black children, the Texas G.I. Forum fought the proposed legislation as an effort to prevent any type of segregation, regardless of race.

The numerous activities of this state unit in the previous ten years had paid off in developing contact with state representatives. A strategy of procrastination was conceived by these legislators as the most likely method of blocking the proposed bill. A Forumeer from San Antonio, Henry Gonzalez, had been elected to the Texas Senate and, with Abraham Kazen, took charge of the opposition team. Another contribution involved testimony by Forum members who pointed out the past history of "freedom of choice." They also demonstrated the fallacious logic of a bill that, in effect, delegated to the administrators in the school systems their own power of appeal because of a grievance procedure which prevented parents from going beyond the local school boards for redress. The majority of the legislators were not interested in logic, but experience had taught these *Mexicanos* to touch all bases. The final gamble proved to be the most desperate of measures, Senate filibuster. In a very dramatic incident, and in many ways a turning point for Texas society, senators Gonzalez and Kazen were able to severely weaken the strength of these segregation bills and undermine the Southern concept of law and order. Some flexibility as to freedom of choice was permitted as a compromise but nothing to the extent of the original proposals. (A typical reaction came from a *Houston Post* letter column directing Gonzalez and Kazen to join the NAACP.)[12]

Other Forum states were engaged in many programs, each confronting their particular problems and pursuing their own solutions. Californians geared up for state elections and questioned some companies about hiring practices. Ohio and Kansas Forums investigated possibilities of increased political representation for Mexican Americans; Colorado members pressed for compliance of the anti-segregation stance of public school officials; Utah fought for continual organization and expansion of the G.I. Forum.[13] But the most difficult struggle for the second decade of the national organization would be the attempt to control the open border and protect the domestic farm worker of the United States from exploitation, a campaign actually born with the first Texas G.I. Forum, but in the end, a national matter.

Part 2 - "Grapes of Wrath"

After substantial expansion from the original Texas experience, the leaders in the various states felt that the strength and size of these groups required and indeed compelled a more ambitious program developed not only on a regional but on a national level as well. The local and state units still maintained their own regional identity and characteristics, but with the creation of a broader program, the Forum was able to work in a potentially more productive area — congressional legislation. While many problems and issues required and received attention, the most immediate focus of the national organization became the critical needs of the domestic farm workers, most of whom were Mexican American, and the attendant issues of the *bracero* or Mexican contract worker and his brother, the *mojado* or illegal alien. The inherent and traditional Southwest relationship of cheap labor and large-scale agriculture had a detrimental effect, especially on the Mexican American farm laborer. The presence of the *mojado* and *bracero* maintained and exacerbated this condition. Because the agri-business sector engendered strong support from many government officials, the possibility of improving life standards of the migrant workers was not promising. In addition, the complexities of the economic and international facets of the farm labor issue made it a difficult matter to resolve.

The first efforts of the American G.I. Forum in confronting this problem came from Texas. However, the other border states (Arizona, New Mexico, and California) rapidly involved themselves as the Forum expanded and acquired more cohesiveness. The nature of the migrant work (travel to other states following certain seasonal crop harvesting) made the issue a national as well as regional concern. The G.I. Forum pursued various goals and programs, including repatriation of illegal aliens, increased border surveillance, strict enforcement of *bracero* contract restrictions, improvement in migrant benefits and working conditions, and a long and often frustrating campaign to eliminate the *bracero* agreement, Public Law 78. A final victory would come with that elimination in 1964. However, an important story emerges from the struggle, not just the outcome; the foremost and immediate problem was the *mojado*.

Workers Aplenty

Mojados were not a new phenomenon in Texas. Throughout the border area their presence was acknowledged, but during World War II, the Mexican government contracted with the United States for workers to replace agricultural laborers who had gone into the armed services. Texas did not receive any of these *braceros* because of discrimination practices against Mexican nationals and Mexican Americans; Texas was blacklisted in June of 1943. Despite this well-known situation, thousands of Mexican citizens did cross the border illegally, mostly due to the increase in the cost of living in Mexico, the scarcity of work in Mexico, and the availability of jobs from American growers and farm managers. The Mexican government did little to stop this immigration, and in many instances Mexican border officials literally rode herd on groups of *mojados* to assist Texas farmers in delegation of labor. They did so for two reasons: money was paid to these people and a tacit understanding existed in Mexico that this flow of workers relieved some political pressure on the Mexican government.[14]

The responsibility for preventing this migration fell to the United States Border Patrol under the jurisdiction of the U.S. Immigration and Naturalization Service. The Service accepted the dubious claims of the growers that labor shortages and the related threat to the harvest overrode the blacklist. The presence of *mojados* went "unnoticed" unless they were conspiciously in a town or city. In order to avoid accusations of non-enforcement of border regulations, the patrol would then conduct a roundup and release on the Mexican side; often the *mojado* would be back across the river before the immigration officer arrived back at his checkpoint.[15]

Texas government authorities blatantly ignored the ban on illegal alien recruitment and in some cases worked with the agricultural "executives" in supplying this labor. In April of 1947, this hypocrisy became law when employers were allowed to take their workers to designated ports of entry (Reynosa, Mexicalli, Ciudad Juarez) for legalization; at that point, these entrepreneurs certified the prevailing wage rate in the Lower Rio Grande Valley (the predominant location for *mojado* work) at twenty-five cents per hour. (In California the wage scale went as high as sixty-five cents per hour). In September of 1947 the Mexican government ended the legalization process, but the trend had been well established and the absurdities were just beginning.[16]

In October 1948, West Texas cotton growers claimed a need for Mexican contract labor at a wage scale much lower than that in other states. When refused, these citizens convinced the El Paso Immigration Service and the Director of the U.S. Employment Service that the cotton was "awasting" in the fields. Determined to prevent this national catastrophe, they stared adversity in the face and did not blink. The El Paso border sprang open like a dam and 7,000 Mexicans poured across, where they were "arrested", loaded into trucks, and delivered to West Texas farmers. The governor of Texas and the Good Neighbor Commission remained silent despite scores of protests from the American G.I. Forum, LULAC, the AFL, and the Mexican Consular Service.[17]

Many critics of *mojado* employment claimed their presence inhibited union organization. In November of 1948, illegal aliens were used to disrupt a National Labor Relations Board-supervised election at the Rio Grande Valley Gas Company in Harlingen, Texas, where most of the employees were Mexican Americans or Mexican nationals. Just before the election began, border patrolmen entered the plant and arrested ten of the workers. The intimidation produced a company victory for union relations. (The men were back the next day.) Mexican nationals were imported into Nuevo Laredo to break a strike of employees of several export-import firms and also to break a strike by the Amalgamated Clothing Workers in El Paso.[18]

The end result of these incidents was a policy of intimidation and repression. Americans of Mexican origin who at one time made up most of the agricultural forces simply had no rights in the view of the growers. The need for labor did not exist after World War II when hundreds of thousands of men came home, but in 1949, 400,000 *mojados* crossed the border. If the native worker protested, he could lose his job. The wage scale remained outrageously low (fifteen to twenty-five cents per hour) because the *mojado* would do the work. If an agricultural worker wanted employment, he was often forced to join the migrant trail and pick cotton in Texas, Arkansas, or New Mexico; or harvest and pack citrus fruits in California; or gather the sugar beets in the North. Health care or employment benefits such as social security were non-existent; education remained a fantasy; public discrimination was the rule. The ludicrous irony of this existence was the fact that the *mojado* suffered the same conditions. But the pillars of agrarianism were always maintaining that these workers were better off than in Mexico, and, by no coincidence, Valley farms had a 30 percent higher income than the rest of Texas agriculture.

Forumeers and Growers

Leaders of the Corpus Christi Forum were intensely aware of the Valley situation. Dr. Garcia had witnessed the migrant trail as a child and had noticed the abysmal life standards of the people. As a young doctor in post-war Corpus Christi, he often treated families of domestic workers and *mojados* and was appalled at their living conditions. As founder of the G.I. Forum, the doctor had more reason to become involved in this desperate issue. His group discovered that the "wetback (*mojado*) problem which tends to lower the standards of living of American citizens in the Valley appears to be the biggest incentive for organizing" in the Rio Grande Valley. The incidents involving strikes and illegal state cooperation in furnishing "wetback" labor reinforced his view that the presence of the *mojado* had serious implications for the ability of the Mexican American to improve his own environment and standard of living. Consequently, the Forums in Texas began actively opposing the open border and the attempts of Valley agri-officials to perpetuate their lucrative practices.[20]

One of the first significant opportunities to challenge these traditions came in the investigations of the hearings of the President's Commission on Migratory Labor. The commission wanted to determine the effect of Mexican contract labor in the United States as a factor in the decision to extend Public Law 78, the basis for *bracero* agreements. The impact of the *mojado* acquired importance in these deliberations. Numbers were increasing so rapidly that even the lukewarm efforts of the Border Patrol would result in 280,000 apprehensions in 1948—1949.[21] Many reports were circulated (which the growers immediately labeled as leftist propaganda) testifying to the exploitation of Mexican labor. But Dr. Garcia presented a more eloquent statement to the President's Commission as a representative of the G.I. Forum.

Dr. Garcia characterized the exploitation of the *mojado* as the fundamental cause of the low standard of living for the domestic Mexican

American farm worker, including the attendant problems of high infant mortality and high tuberculosis rates. The doctor felt that low wages, high unemployment, and minimal educational attainment were in part a result of the presence of the illegal aliens. As the doctor asked, "Would 30,000 Americans migrate out of this area if they did not have to? Would they expose their children to sickness and death if they did not have to? Would they leave their homes and schools to migrate to uncertainty if they could make a living at home?"[22]

After additional testimony and deliberation, the commission issued its report in April 1951; it recommended extension of contract agreements but severely criticized the exploitative practices of growers. The claims of agrarian supporters on the need for massive numbers of Mexican workers were severely questioned.[24] The American G.I. Forum had made its point but did not overcome the basic strength of the agricultural lobby. It was clear, however, that the impetus for open borders and administrative negligence was weakening. Unfortunately, the Korean War created new rationales for *bracero* and/or *mojado* demands, as new labor "shortages" developed. Suddenly, picking the crops was "critical to national interest" and Mexican labor was the only available option in the view of the grower. The Forum and other organizations maintained surveillance, but were unable to affect much change due to the exigencies of the Korean War and the preoccupation of the Truman administration with internal politics such as the upcoming presidential campaign. Agricultural lobbyists "permitted" passage of a law making importation or harboring of illegal aliens a felony but prevented the passage of sanctions against hiring of illegal aliens. The growers generally blunted efforts by the G.I. Forum and other groups to lessen the illegal immigration.[25]

The election of Dwight David Eisenhower as president of the United States seemed to indicate a change in national policy. Eisenhower was on record as highly critical of "wetback" exploitation (although Vice-President Nixon was very favorable to growers), and his newspaper statements indicated sympathy for those opposed to the existing situation. Legislation against the smuggling of *mojados* was passed in Congress to strengthen the administrative and enforcement powers of the border patrol. Strenuous criticisms of congressional backing for agribusiness interests became more prevalent.[26] *Business Week* carried an article describing the illegal alien presence as the most important problem facing the nation. Attorney General Herbert Brownell, after a tour of the Southwest border areas, said that laborer smuggling "has mushroomed into a grave social problem involving murder, prostitution, robbery, and a gigantic narcotic infiltration. . . a malignant threat to the growth of our society."[27] While this characterization is extreme and missed the point of the real impact of the *mojado* it at least signified an official condemnation of the immigration; one million *mojados* were apprehended in 1953, although approximately two million were undetected. Labor Department officials felt that as many as five million illegal residents could be in the United States. The economic advantages for the farmers were enormous in that they were saving substantial labor costs (as much as $1,000 on fifty bales of cotton) by using the low wage scales; some refused to pay their workers and instead turned them over to federal officials after the harvest. Counter arguments pointed to the annual thirty-million- dollar remittance to Mexico by these people as a drain on the American economy (and the third largest source of income for Mexico). But despite his earlier statements against the employment of illegal aliens, Eisenhower angered the Forum and other anti-*mojado* groups when he reduced the size of the Border Patrol.[28] The surveillance and enforcement of immigration laws lessened, and the struggle against the open border intensified.

A good example of the chaotic nature of this struggle was the attempted appointment of James Griffin to the post of agricultural advisor to the Secretary of Labor or assistant immigration commissioner. Griffin, a farmer, former border patrolman, and past president of the American Agricultural Council, had publicly campaigned for a cessation of immigration regulations and had allegedly obstructed enforcement of immigration laws. Yet this individual could be in the position of being responsible for that enforcement. Ed Idar, president of the Texas Forum, successfully appealed to Senator Lyndon Johnson and other Texas representatives to block the appointment. At the same time, the Forum intensified its campaign to enlist the aid of national legislators against the continued influx of the illegal Mexican worker.[29]

"What Price Wetbacks?"

An important part of the campaign came in October 1953. Ed Idar and A.C. McLellen conducted a two-month survey of several Forums in Texas from El Paso to Brownsville. They interviewed many *mojados* on their wage rates, living conditions, and means of transportation to various border localities for work distribution. The two men also took several hundred photographs as evidence to document their written conclusions. The publication *What Price Wetbacks?* outlined problems of law enforcement, inadequacies in existing border statutes, and the economic influences on American wage earners and business of the border area. This project was conducted at no small risk to Idar and McLennen; discovery by ranch and farm managers might have placed their lives in danger.[30]

A controversial factor in the production of *What Price Wetbacks?*, concerned the involvement of the American Federation of Labor. Union organizations often elicited savage response from the conservative Texas establishment, a condition that the G.I. Forum could ill afford. But the State Federation of Labor of the AFL had expressed opposition to the presence of the *mojado* as a threat to American workers, a belief that Idar, Dr. Garcia, and other Forum leaders concurred with easily. The state union was also willing to support the Forum with money for publishing costs, a sum that would have been difficult to raise from Forum members (approximately $8,000). Therefore, the Forum leadership decided to accept the AFL offer and, *What Price Wetbacks?* became a co-publication.[31]

Major conclusions of this work were: (1) wetback wages ranged between 25 and 30 cents per hour; (2) the presence of the wetback lowered health standards for American citizens in the border areas. Idar and McLennen found that illegal border crossings were minimal until 1941, when wartime agreements and better economic conditions produced a sharp increase; in 1953, one million illegal aliens were arrested. The report also concluded that retail business suffered in the areas of wetback employment, a fact highlighted by the sharp decline in retail sales in McAllen, Texas, during the peak cotton harvest months. In an attempt to engender the broadest possible support, the survey also suggested that the open border posed a threat to the internal security of the United States due to the possibility of communist infiltration, a weak contention at best, but all-too-usual in the era of the Joseph McCarthy spy-hunt. Finally, the report criticized the lack of enforcement of immigration laws by state and federal agencies and called for severe surveillance by such officials. Every congressman and many administration officials received a copy. It was well reviewed by scholastic and judicial parties interested in the labor situation of the United States. (For instance, the *Stanford Law Review* used *What Price Wetbacks?* as a major source in its own legal interpretation of the options for stopping illegal entry.)[32]

Congress finally held hearings on the issue of the illegal alien in 1954. Assistant Secretary of Labor Rocco Sicilliano described the disadvantage of the farmer who did not hire illegal aliens. He also emphasized the absence of any real justification by employers to hire illegal entrants; in 1953, 200,000 *braceros* had worked in the United States; any farmer could take advantage of the program. A much better witness, Ernesto Galarza, discussed the culpability of employers who hired the *mojado* and dismissed the familiar farmer excuses as pretext and hypocrisy; citizens deserved the protection of their government and the right to compete fairly on the job market. A representative of the Texas Sheep and Goat Raisers' Association bemoaned the loss of "the principal source of labor'' (Mexican Americans) for the ranches and farms of the Southwest to the industrial sector. The Mexican national was the only worker available but the contract labor agreements were much too complicated.[33]

"Operation Wetback"

Congress produced no legislative solution, but even those normally indifferent to the presence of the *mojado* felt the "invasion" had become intolerable.[34] In July 1954, Major General Joseph M. Swing, head of the U.S. Immigration and Naturalization Service, personally warned American farmers in the Southwest that an intensive drive would be undertaken to evict the thousands of illegal aliens in the country. Ample precedents existed for such a campaign. On July 17, 1954, "Operation Wetback" commenced; the Border Patrol, assisted by county, state and federal authorities, began apprehending and deporting illegal aliens. Hundreds of thousands of individuals were arrested or intimidated and sent back to Mexico; this period also saw an increase in the numbers of voluntary departures. Opposition to this "maximum effort" came from many civil liberties groups who felt that the lack of due process for extradition undermined constitutional guarantees to American citizens. Some Mexican Americans rightly complained that immigration officials did not discriminate in arrests and deportations. As in the 1930s, many American citizens of Mexican origin were caught up in the border sweep. The American G.I. Forum expressed approval of the project but also worked with immigration agencies to assure compliance with due process and constitutional rights. But it is clear that the Forum had little sympathy for those who were concerned with civil liberties but ignored the domestic effects that the exploitation of Mexican labor had produced.[35]

The response by the Anglo citizens of the Rio Grande Valley was blatantly anti-federal. Newspaper headlines "screamed" of an "occupation army". Allegations of a communist conspiracy and "declaration of war" between state rights and federal intervention appeared in editorials throughout the Valley. Rumors of atrocities by Border Patrol officials were given strong emphasis, and sympathy for the "poor Mexican" suddenly materialized. This campaign lasted well into 1955. "The wetback was an innocent and poor individual who came from poverty and knew no other life. His work is tied up in his sarape; his pleasure is today, his problems are *mañana*." He was not competing for domestic agricultural labor because native American workers did not do "stoop labor" (the notorious short hoe became a symbol for the plight of the migrant). The dastardly Border Patrol was an agent of the unions who were intent on closing the border to un-organized labor.[36] This typical rhetoric had little effect on those Mexican Americans who had experienced the results of *"los trabajadores de espalda mojada"* and the border *was* closed.[37]

After Operation Wetback, the apprehension of illegal aliens substantially lessened because illegal crossings decreased. While the motivations for this action are controversial, there is no question that it succeeded. There is also no doubt that a division was created among Mexican Americans. The position of the exploited *mojado* created a confrontation of Mexican against Mexican American. Because of the geographic proximity of Mexico and the United States, many Mexican Americans saw close relatives deported as illegal residents; this, in turn, produced a certain ambivalence toward the anti-*mojado* groups. Hypocrisy existed among a majority of state and government officials who tolerated the employment of these people as long as the economy permitted, and only became alarmed by the political repercussions of recession and unemployment (as took place in 1953 and 1954). The prevalent official policies also reflected satisfaction that illegal immigration usually meant only temporary labor employment and not permanent settlement with the attendant ethnic and racial connotations. As long as the flow of illegal migration from Mexico could be controlled, the open border policy demonstrated a "profitable means of acquiring needed labor without incurring the price that characterized the immigration, utilization, and the eventual settlement of European and Oriental immigrants."[38]

An important qualification to this conclusion involves the real damage that the use of the *mojado* produced. *What Price Wetbacks?* is clearly an unfair and racist diatribe against the *mojado*. It does not present a balanced account of illegal immigration, and that is precisely why it is important. It is not a rationale by nativists, anti-immigrationists, or political flunkies seeking simplistic answers. Rather, the views expressed represent a fact that has not been adequately addressed by immigration studies. Recent accounts ridicule the claims that undocumented workers or illegal aliens undermine American workers. Overwhelming evidence concludes just the opposite. But that analysis, as accurate as it may be, does not answer the realities of the Southwest in the 1950s. Whatever the attitudes of Congress, executive administrations or other influential institutions, people like the members of the American G.I. Forum witnessed first-hand the repressive political and economic effects of the total Anglo exploitation of cheap labor. Mexican Americans bore the effect of illegal labor; Mexican Americans lost jobs or were forced to work for depressed wages. Many had to leave their homes and subject their families to the cruelties of the migrant trail.

Operation Wetback was a throwback; the precedent of repatriation is all too clear. It is all quite evident that the *mojado* was a scapegoat sacrificed to Anglo authorities who acted for their own self-interest. In this case, the threat of more deportation might produce Mexican American support of a better *bracero* agreement with Mexico. But to denounce Operation Wetback as a misguided and coopted act misses the point. The American G.I. Forum understood the motives of its Anglo "allies"; it did not enjoy the spectre of repatriation. The difficult decision to cooperate in the roundup is still controversial and not easily defended. But to concentrate on the exploitation of the *mojado* during this period without also examining the effect on Mexican American labor is too easy and simplistic. The event was not a noble moment for any of the participants. Twenty years later such a "solution" would not receive support from any Mexican American organization, only severe opposition. But today is not yesterday, and the two-edged sword is easier to grab. A less controversial approach and, in essence, a "better way" was the elimination of the *bracero* agreement.

CHAPTER IX

Public Law 78

World War II and the labor shortages created by recruitment and conscription brought demands from American agricultural and nonagricultural segments for individuals to replace those laborers lost to the war effort. Because Mexico had traditionally supplied cheap labor for the large agricultural enterprises, and because the American government had usually supported this tradition (such as the exemption from head tax provisions and alien literacy tests), a restoration of this relationship seemed natural. The new attitudes of conciliation and reciprocation between the two governments, were exemplified by the economic agreements of 1941 and 1942.* Mexico's full fledged participation in the Allied policies against the Axis powers buttressed the idea of mutual cooperation.

However, President Manuel Avila Camacho did not adopt the sanguine view of those American businesses who desired this labor supply. As stated in Chapter I, the United States had repatriated hundreds of thousands of Mexican citizens residing in the U.S. during the Great Depression without regard to legalities. During the same period, constant protest by Mexican consuls against the treatment of Mexicans and Mexican Americans reinforced the concern Avila Camacho felt for Mexicans in the United States. The president of Mexico insisted on contract labor arrangements which included protection from Anglo discrimination.

The agreement of 1943 between the U.S. and Mexico guaranteed transportation and living expenses to and from the workers' place of employment. They could not be used in the military nor could they displace domestic workers (who were mostly Mexican American). Discrimination was forbidden on penalty of forfeiture of contract. The Farm Security Administration, a New Deal creation with a liberal reputation, was given responsibility for overseeing the *bracero* agreement. It required all employers to sign individual contracts with their employees

---

*The economic agreements concerned oil payments for the 1938 expropriation, agrarian issues and claims of American citizens, export-import loans, and credit establishment.

and guarantee fulfillment. A prevailing wage of thirty cents per hour was established as the pay scale in agricultural work. (Texas did not receive any *braceros* but increased its exploitation of the *mojado.*[1])

This agreement operated fairly well during the war years, but in 1946, the U.S. State Department notified all concerned parties that termination was -imminent. Agricultural interests vigorously opposed the cessation and instead demanded an extension of the original international policy. Congressional and private-sector pressure produced a new agreement through 1949. In 1947, the legalization of *mojados* reduced the "need" for *braceros*, but in 1948, a new Mexico—United States *bracero* policy did not cover the illegal alien and Mexico abrogated the relationship. However, a revision of the "wetback" policy occurred in 1949 and all such persons (87,000) were legalized and contracted through 1950. A review by the President's Commission on Migratory Labor produced a substantial change in the 1951 *Bracero* Contract Agreement. Public Law 78 stipulated:

> No workers shall be for employment in any area unless the Secretary of Labor for such area has determined and certified that 1) sufficient domestic workers who are able, willing, and qualified are not available at the time and place need-ed to perform the work for which such workers are to be employed and 2) the employment of such workers will not adversely affect the wages and working conditions of domestic agricultural workers similarly employed and, 3) reasonable efforts have been made to attract domestic workers for such employment of wages and standard hours of work comparable to those offered to foreign workers.[2]

Other stipulations of this law provided emergency medical care, decent reception centers, transportation reimbursement by the employers, the right to choose the type of work and employer, healthy living quarters, injury compensation and exemptions from federal or state taxes. The new agreement also permitted the use of *mojados* who had been in the United States since 1946.[3]

Using the basic law, 4,336,785 *braceros* were hired from 1951 through 1964 compared to 430,000 from 1942 through 1950, with four of those years under wartime conditions. This fact by itself questions the justifications for the *bracero* importation, as well as *los mojados*. The complications of their effect on domestic farm workers, such as displace-ment of workers, caused hardship. Low wages and forced migrant employment exacerbated the detrimental aspects of the policy.[4] Many in-dividuals and organizations engaged in a long struggle to correct and resolve the situation. The American G.I. Forum was one of the first and most enduring.

The fundamental objection of the G.I. Forum to the *bracero* program was its effect on the domestic farm worker. In the schemes of the employers, the *bracero* assured not only a low prevailing wage, but often a non-existent prevailing wage rate. The official scale of thirty cents per hour was essentially a public relations facade; actual rates were much lower. Complaints to raise the standard brought cries of outrage and protest from growers and ranchers. Their standard arguments centered around the rationale that the agricultural industry was a seasonal enterprise subject to the vagaries of climate and weather, therefore the risk of investment was abnormally great. One of the means of saving money was low labor costs and any increase in wages would offset that advantage. In 1959, this reasoning meant that forty cents per hour (the official minimum wage) was already too high for the return of profit (a blatant misrepresentation), and a proposed seventy-five cents per hour minimum wage law would bankrupt the growers in the Southwest. In addition, the growers would lose a 28-week exemption from the wage-hour law, an obvious loophole for maintaining low wages. Spokesmen for the growers association claimed that the existing wage (as if they actually paid it) was sufficient because Latin Americans took home fruits and vegetables for consumption; they did not require more money. These men also opposed the idea of a guaranteed amount of work because of the seasonal aspects of their industry.[5]

The G.I. Forum countered these claims with facts demonstrating two realities: (1) enough workers lived in the agriculture area to prevent any importation of contract labor and (2) the work conditions for these people included the real wage of twenty-five cents per hour and indecent, unhealthy work quarters. The Forum demanded a humane rate of seventy-five cents and elimination of the conditions that forced 300,000 Mexican Americans to leave the state for the migrant trail. Forum representatives also accused the Texas Employment Commission of serving the Rio Grande Valley farmers and shippers by establishing a prevailing wage of less than twenty-five cents per hour.[6] Unfortunately, the Mexican American worker did not "merit" the protection of the Congress, and the farm worker received scant attention while the *bracero* became the concern of both countries.

Regardless of this defeat, the G.I. Forum continued to press for other rights of *Mexicano* farm workers, including education. Approximately 100,000 Mexican Americans did not attend school in 1949, most of them children of migrant workers or state agricultural workers. The Forum fought for a state law compelling a minimum amount of education, but little happened until the federal government passed the Fair Labor Standards Act in 1949. Effective in 1950, the new law made agricultural employment of children under sixteen illegal during school hours. Although it did not apply to a farmer's own children, most *Mexicanos* did not own land and their children were covered by the new law. With this weapon the various Forum units worked for compliance by political persuasion and education. The agri-business powers objected to the law because it deprived them of their labor, due in part to the refusal of labor leaders to transport families with children under sixteen.

Besides attacking this law, the Texas Farm Bureau, in their convention of 1952, went further in criticizing the *Bracero* Agreement of 1951, which, among other things, established a prevailing wage of thirty cents per hour. Demanding a "white card" plan by which Mexican citizens could work in labor-short areas without contracts, representatives of the Bureau expressed the belief that "Mexicans, Latin Americans, or whatever you call them, they all talk alike, act alike, think alike, and almost look alike when they're traveling over the country picking cotton" and "a Mexican with a contract is like a woman with a marriage license, she changes after she gets it."[7] This time, Congress did not agree with such arguments and retained the child labor laws and the thirty cents per hour wage rate; but farmers learned that *braceros* could be manipulated as easily as illegal aliens.

If any meaningful gains or even attempts to improve the migrant situation were to occur, organization was required to oppose P.L. 78 and advocate for the domestic farm worker. In March 1953, the first Southwest Regional Conference on Migrant Labor was held in Albuquerque, New Mexico. Attending were representatives from Arizona, California, Colorado, Nevada, New Mexico, Oklahoma, Texas, Utah, and Wyoming. Also present were the executive director of the Bishop's Committee for the Spanish-Speaking and his assistant, Reverend Erwin Juraschek (the eventual National G.I. Forum chaplain), reflecting a somewhat tardy interest by the Catholic church for the plight of the migrant. Heading the American G.I. Forum delegation was Vicente Ximenes, then New Mexico State chairman. The only significant accomplishment of the meeting was that it was held.[8] It was the beginning, in a sense, of a general liberal movement that would culminate in the late 1960s and 1970s with legislation for the betterment of conditions for migrant workers. But it was also an incipient attempt to educate the American people to the paradox of the migrant existence in the wealthiest nation on earth.

An incident in 1955 in Denver, Colorado, demonstrated the need of this knowledge. Fifty-four men, women and children in a cattle truck with a forty-six-steer capacity overturned twice — an eleven-month old baby (Daniel Lucio) died and sixteen others were injured. These migrants had come from Texas to work in the sugar beet fields. The employment service said the truck should have held twenty-five adults and ten children. Colorado governor Edwin Johnson ordered the State Patrol and the Colorado Employment Service to enforce provisions (or just good sense) on overloading trucks carrying migrant workers. Texas governor Allan Shivers professed unawareness of the condition of migrants once they left South Texas, and the Texas commissioner of agriculture wanted to know how he could attract the Mexican American vote in the upcoming gubernatorial election. The Colorado Senate defeated a House resolution (inspired by the Lucio incident) to study migrant camps because migrants would be out of their element living under modern conditions.[9] One suspects that farmer-grower pressure was active.

Despite this attitude, the G.I. Forum did not lessen its efforts to enlighten people about the migrant existence and the effects of the *bracero* agreement. Vicente Ximenes conducted a study as an associate of the Bureau of Business Research at the University of New Mexico, demonstrating the lack of participation by *Mexicano* farm workers in the normal institutional processes of government benefits. Migrants rarely served on juries or voted; they (and all Mexican Americans) lacked the political clout to strengthen or enforce Fair Employment Practice acts or anti-discrimination laws. Because of low wages and long periods of unemployment, the farm workers were eligible for welfare, but due to their own ignorance and the indifference of public administrators, very few benefited from this tax-supported device. Social security and compulsory education meant nothing to the domestic agricultural laborer. The result became starvation wages, little medical attention, minimal (if any) education, and sub-standard housing. But Anglo politicians could express pride for those areas with a low rate of welfare recipients. The availability of *braceros* increased the overall problems for these Mexican Americans.[10]

In 1957, the state of Texas created its own Council on Migrant Labor, partly from the pressure of the Forum and other supporters, and perhaps in an attempt to better the state's relationship with Mexico. An old friend of the organization, Senator Abraham Kazen, proposed a council to promote the formulation of rules to improve migrant travel and living conditions, analyze federal and state laws, hold public hearings, and advise and consult with state agencies. The bill received only tentative support from the G.I. Forum because of a fear that a new "Good Neighbor Commission" was being set up. Endorsement was based on assurance by Kazen of eventual Mexican American representation on the council and a commitment for a "beginning of the improvement of migrant workers and families."[11] However, this act was not viewed as a solution to the migrant problem. Forum leaders were now convinced that national

116

legislation was the only means of achieving meaningful reform. As the *bracero* became more and more identified as a cause of the migrant problem, that legislation was envisioned as termination of the *bracero* agreement. To engage in that struggle would produce a collective effort by a minority of concerned people against a smaller but disproportionately powerful group who did not discriminate — people who would exploit a *bracero* or a migrant without prejudice.

"Availability Certified"

Southwest G.I. Forums had clearly outlined their opposition to the importation of *braceros*. As the Eisenhower administration began, this resistance became formidable; more Forums produced more voices and consequently more attention. Operation Wetback was to an extent a result of that pressure as well as the economic slump. Quixotically, during the debate for renewal of P.L. 78, the Texas, New Mexico, and Colorado units found themselves supporting the *bracero* agreement because of a proposed congressional bill to recruit agricultural workers in the absence of an agreement with Mexico. Forum experts felt that passage would once again establish the open border of the 1940s and early 1950s. Because the budget of the Immigration Service was being reduced by Eisenhower in an effort to economize, even more trouble could result. The bill did not pass; Forum research (*What Price Wetbacks?*) and Forum support was of no little consequence.[12]

When it soon became evident that the reduction of *mojados* meant more *braceros*, G.I. Forums had to concentrate on undermining the rationales for their presence. One of the steady "complaints" by the farmers was the refusal of domestic laborers to work for the prevailing wage. Pronouncing these individuals as lazy, obstinate, or absent, the growers would request and obtain *braceros*. Forum units began conducting surveys pertaining to the exact number of domestic workers in a given area and the wage needed by the workers. This data was available from the state employment commissions but based on information that was contradictory to actual conditions. Forum chapters also signed up domestic laborers willing to work for the specified minimum rates stated in the *bracero* work contracts, figures that growers claimed were unacceptable to Mexican Americans. Some of the surveys also indicated the loss of business revenue in areas where *braceros* came in and native workers were unemployed, but the important contribution lay in the proof of the availability of the local resident laborer.[13]

A few officials in charge of the *bracero* program paid attention to these efforts. Often they expressed dismay at the mistrust that many farm workers felt toward the employment commission, a complaint that brought patient but obviously exasperated explanation from Forum leaders who diplomatically placed the blame for the suspicion on state and federal administrations. At other times, however, these officials sought G.I. Forum help in getting information to the worker concerning his rights and options. On many occasions Forum chapters actively recruited workers for the available jobs and always kept people informed of the state or public job opportunities. Along with this positive aid, the G.I. Forum managed at times to block the request for alien labor by the agrarian operators. One of those rare but significant events took place in July 1956, when a committee headed by national chairman Vicente Ximenes turned back a demand by New Mexico farmers with a petition signed by a substantial number of American-citizen farm workers indicating that outside labor was not needed.[14]

Another incident that illustrated a typical Forum effort in these years occurred in Mathis, Texas, an area that had failed in its attempts to segregate *Mexicano* school children because of G.I. Forum intervention. In 1957, the F.H. Vahlsing Incorporated Company brought in a number of *braceros* to ostensibly fill a shortage created by the lack of domestic labor. A group of Mexican Americans, organized into the Farm Truckers and Farm Workers Association of Mathis, requested Dr. Garcia to lead their opposition in what they perceived as an injustice. These men claimed that the Vahlsing manager did not properly advertise the available jobs as required by the 1956 *Bracero* Agreement. Claiming a lack of domestic laborers, the manager hired *braceros* and gave the more difficult work to Mathis residents. These Mexican Americans received lower pay than the minimum wage guarantee without the unemployment compensation and free medical care available to the *bracero*. The Mathis group also complained of the inexpensive injury and life insurance available to the alien worker that was not allowed to the American laborer.[15] At the same time of this protest, the doctor was representing Vahlsing *braceros* who accused the company of continued abuse and exploitation involving wages and incorrect weight scales.[16]

After a period of three months, the Forum demand for investigation finally produced dividends. Two members of the regional office staff of the Department of Labor personally met with Dr. Garcia after a discussion with the Mexican consul of Corpus Christi. The investigators did uncover a faulty procedure by which Vahlsing weighed the harvested crops in order to determine the proper amount of money earned. It was "discovered" that the control weights were "light". The company was forced to dismiss the official in charge of the Mexican nationals and ordered to reimburse the *bracero* workers for the sum of $3,509.27. This was the second such incident involving the Vahlsing Company, but it would not be the last.[17]

118

The matter of false certification of *bracero* need did not fare so well, but the success in protecting the *bracero* highlights a much misunderstood fact. The American G.I. Forum was not interested in depriving the Mexican citizen of an economic opportunity. To the contrary, the organization did its best to protect the alien worker in a foreign country, knowing full well the exploitative practices of the contractors. Yet the Forum sincerely believed that the native Mexican American came first and priority lay with his welfare. If the *bracero* (or *mojado*) had to suffer because of this belief, that was unfortunate; but so was the *Mexicano* who could not feed his family because of their presence.

During the Vahlsing incident, a rather interesting case developed from the same conditions that predicated the Mathis affair yet involved the use of Japanese. Approximately 1,000 Japanese citizens had been imported to the United States for various type of work that supposedly could not be supplied by American labor. When the G.I. Forum complained of this situation, the reply from the state officials in charge was unusual, to say the least.

> Dear Dr. Garcia:
>
> I was pleased to receive your letter of June 25 and I have noticed your request concerning the importation of Japanese workers. It just happens that today we have received an order for 6 chicken sexers for work in Dallas or Chicago. The rate of pay is 3/4 cents to one cent per chicken. A competent chicken sexer should average about $500.00 per month.
>
> A chicken sexer determines the sex of day-old chickens by visual examination of genital organs, skin structures, and certain bodily features. His or her determinations must be 98% accurate. He will be expected to travel to chicken hatcheries in the middle U.S.A. as arranged by the employer.
>
> We have been unsuccessful in locating qualified workers to date. The employer is desirous of importing 6 Japanese chicken sexers if we are unable to find experienced workers. The minimum experience required is one year in a chick-sexing school and three years as an apprentice.
>
> We have already canvassed our Agricultural Colleges and are informed that all qualified chicken sexers are employed.
>
> If you know of any qualified chicken sexers or are able to find any, please ask them to contact the nearest office of the Texas Employment Commission and ask that their application be submitted to me in Austin.
>
> Very Truly Yours,
> Henry LeBlanc, Chief
> Form Placement Dept. [18]

Mr. LeBlanc was not a devious man and had proved his willingness and determination to carry out the law as it was actually written. But the doctor and his organization were not concerned with chicken-sexers. They wanted to know why four thousand *braceros* were needed in 1957 and why government officials were so indifferent to human suffering. They were determined to prevent 1,000 Japanese (or 1,000 Martians) from being used when American citizens could not find employment. These *Mexicano* activists were also becoming increasingly weary with tiresome rationales by government bureaucrats.

One such justification from federal officials for *bracero* importation bears examining. Government bureaucrats pointed out that as wages for the harvesting of certain crops in the North increased during World War II, Texas workers left their homes to make more money. This produced the flood of illegal aliens into South Texas, which prevented the returning servicemen from finding a job. When the *mojado* was finally "eliminated", the growers were *forced* to sign contracts. After violations of the *bracero* agreement were discovered and rectified, the problems of the agricultural employment situation were eliminated. There was still a need to find work for the number of seasonal workers not employed in the off-season, but the government was attempting to meet its obligation with information exchange among all state employment services.[19] What about low wages? What about false certification of labor need? What about low schooling? What about the social and psychological effects? If all of this resolve was true, why did the American G.I. Forum fight so hard for reform?

A different and more sinister objection to the activities of those who opposed the *Bracero* Agreement has never been better articulated than in an editorial in the *Dallas Morning News*.

> Immigrant labor is a Texas asset. Few controversial subjects resolve themselves comfortably into clear blacks and whites, but sloganeers habitually try to fit their aims into what seems in mere words, a praiseworthy objective. Applied to facts, the outcome is somewhat different. Sunday, the American G.I. Forum in Dallas phrased one resolution that can be endorsed on its face. Underneath the surface it is not so readily acceptable. It should not be worked into fact without safeguards and provisions. This is the demand: that alien labor wherever employed never be permitted to lower the working standards of the natives of this country. That reads well. You react to it favorably. What makes America is its standard of living. We are all against starvation wages and peonage. But a free economy has to keep a weather eye on inordinate demands that may seek to create a higher standard (of) living in terms of bigger wages that can be borne safely by the economy. That is where you need ifs, ands, and provisos against the G.I. Forum's standards for alien labor. Still more needful of security is the Forum blanket rejection of immigrant Mexican labor and demand that it be excluded. Oddly, the Forum itself seems to be Latin American composed. Hence, the beneficiary in one way or another of immigration privileges. To insist arbitrarily that the flow cease, is to bar new arrival without exception. Why?[20]

Not all responses, as indicated, were so transparent. In September of 1956, Congress passed Public Law 939, permitting the Intestate Commerce Commission to regulate the interstate and foreign transportation of migratory agricultural labor, a proposal long advocated by the Forum in the hopes of supplying protection and aid that was not forthcoming from state government. The national office also stepped up its campaign against the international labor arrangements between the United States and Mexico. In September of 1957, Texas state legal advisor Frank Piñeda conducted a series of interviews with congressional legislators in Washington, D.C. The results were statements of interest and commitments to the Forum program by a number of senators and representatives. Piñeda also discerned a real lack of knowledge on the part of these national legislators and suggested the need for the G.I. Forum to become a conduit for that information. While expressing a concern about the possibility of any immediate change or action from Congress, Piñeda felt that maybe there was some hope.[21] Other groups were beginning to express the same frustrations and outrage that the G.I. Forum had articulated for ten years. Mexican bishops and some labor unions did not appreciate the exploitation and the displacement of workers caused by the *bracero* program. Different organizations offered their own aid or accepted Forum coalitions. Migrant labor protection and *bracero* repeal became popular issues in 1957 and the "bandwagon" became crowded.[22] The American G.I. Forum welcomed the company.

Federal Support?

G.I. Forum leaders knew James Mitchell quite well. Constant communication with the Secretary of Labor since 1956 regarding *bracero* certification or migrant labor problems had established a formal connection. For instance, in May 1957, the Corpus Christi Forum requested a branch office of the Department of Labor to provide wage and hour supervision for *braceros* and domestic workers and enforcement of child labor laws. Secretary Mitchell believed in the existing field organization which decided not to provide a Corpus Christi office.[23] But the Secretary took the time to explain the decision, and the Forum accepted the sincerity of Mitchell and his program. This confidence was buttressed by an attempt to remove the Wage and Hour Division from that area. John Stanfield, the local supervisor, had performed admirably in preventing violations by growers in the Arkansas Valley but received criticism. The Colorado unit notified Dr. Garcia and other leaders who immediately questioned their representatives and sympathetic legislators, including Mitchell. The response from the Department of Labor emphatically supported Forum requests for maintaining the office.[24] That act boded well for upcoming events.

Opposition to the *bracero* program and demand for migrant labor protection increased in 1957—1958. California authorities imported 12,000

121

Japanese laborers with plans for many more; Texas brought in 21,000 Mexican *braceros*. Meanwhile, many American citizens had lost jobs in a serious recession; 500,000 *braceros* and 5,000,000 unemployed seemed inappropriate. Farmers and citrus growers had millions of dollars to "impress" influential legislators with their "needs", while groups such as the G.I. Forum had only their own human resources. They emphasized the absence of any protection for migrants who were not covered even by the federal minimum wage law, while underlining the increase in at least theoretical benefits for *braceros*. These organizations called for workmen's compensation, better child labor protection, improved housing, education programs, and extension of the minimum wage. A report requested by Eisenhower on domestic migratory farm labor recommended these reforms and a review of *bracero* effect on American labor conditions. In addition, twenty-one state migrant committees developed out of the early efforts of the first advocates (the Texas Council on Migrant Labor had at last issued its conclusions and solutions, the same basic proposals that the Texas G.I. Forum had made ten years earlier). In January of 1959 the National Advisory Committee on Farm Labor solicited the help of the Forum in researching various aspects of the migrant scene. The number of resident workers, migrant workers and imported aliens, wages and wage trends, the abuse of contractors, and the impact of these conditions on the human beings living with them would be strong evidence for congressional committees.[25]

The same National Advisory Committee held a conference in February of 1959. The chief speaker, Secretary of Labor James Mitchell, presented a startling speech. His opening remark gained the immediate attention of the audience.

> Twenty and more years of rhetoric have not made much improvement in the plight of the migrant farm worker. I have no desire to add more rhetoric this evening.

Alluding to improved conditions for imported alien workers, the Secretary delivered a shocker:

> It is my conclusion that the migrant farm worker will never take his place as a fully useful citizen, and never be able to successfully resist exploitation, until, first, federal legislation guarantees him a decent minimum wage upon which he can build a decent and independent life; second, unless he has fairly continuous employment; third, until he receives the equal protection of all Federal and State laws, such as enforced housing codes, enforced safety codes, accessible health services, and protection for his person in the form of compensation for injury and unemployment.[26]

Additional remarks elaborated on the above but the bombshell had been delivered.

American G.I. Forum response was immediate and unmistakable. Letters of support came in from all parts of the United States. Forum leaders were taken by surprise with this unqualified statement from a high ranking cabinet official, but they were naturally gratified and increased their own efforts on behalf of the migrant worker.[27] Dr. Garcia, speaking as the founder of the Forum, appeared in many areas and delivered a very moving description of migrant life:

> The children of migrant parents are born into a world completely of their own. An anemic mother, and possibly a tubercular father — a life that will take him into this world, where he may possibly die within one year, either from diarrhea, tuberculosis, or malnutrition. His infancy would be a very close association with his brothers and sisters. Their home would be a one or two room shack with no inside running water and no flush toilets.
>
> If he lives to be of school age, he could possibly go to many schools on different occasions at different places, but will never average more than three years of schooling in his lifetime. His future life will be one of wondering, poverty and more sickness.
>
> I am still haunted by that remembrance of a day ten years ago when a little boy came to my office to ask me to go and see his mother who was sick. I went to his home — a one room shack. I found a dead mother with six children lying in the same bed, all covered with blood from the hemorrhage of a dying tubercular mother.[28]

While these particular hearings were being conducted, G.I. Forums continued their other projects for migrant workers. Some state legislators, reflecting Forum goals, tried to incorporate domestic farm laborers into minimum wage protection. Most importantly, Secretary Mitchell named a "distinguished committee" to investigate the *bracero* program; a member of that group was the chairman of the Texas Council on Migrant Labor.[29]

The chief executive apparently decided that it was time for him to exert his "moral leadership". Eisenhower sent a message to the Senate subcommittee headed by Senator Harrison A. Williams (D-NJ) to end the "poverty and degradation." This committee had already begun to investigate several proposed bills to increase pay and better working conditions. A presidential spokesman even urged the Congress to enact an administration bill to impose federal regulation on the conduct of labor contractors and crew leaders who recruited and transported American farm laborers. In addition, a Labor Department directive issued standards, albeit weak and minimal, for farmers to meet in order to use the Farm Placement Bureau for recruitment.[30]

G.I. Forum strategists were a definite part of these activities. The federal government requested a Forum representative to testify before the Williams subcommittee; Attorney Robert Sanchez, a long-time expert on this matter drew the assignment. His own statement was an endorsement of Secretary Mitchell's regulations but went much farther. Sanchez asked that migratory workers be given (1) a minimum number of weeks employment in any given area, (2) a definitive minimum wage schedule, (3) the same housing guarantees as foreign workers, (4) transportation reimbursement by the grower, (5) protection for "outspoken workers", and (6) a general preference over foreign farm workers. Senator Williams contacted Sanchez after his testimony and discussed his own new special labor subcommittee on migratory problems. The members included Barry Goldwater and Everett Dirksen, not the most sympathetic legislators. Nonetheless, Sanchez felt encouraged by Williams's concern and receptiveness to Forum ideas. Secretary Mitchell reiterated his own belief that reform was absolutely necessary and also praised the G.I. Forum for being one of the first to focus attention on the plight of the migrant and for Forum efforts to improve that condition.[31]

The climax of these efforts came in the debate over a series of bills to extend P.L. 78, in particular the one offered by a committee on migratory labor and developed by Congressman B. C. Gathings of the House Agriculture Committee. (The Forum wanted Department of Labor supervision of these matters but the Harrison subcommittee did not play a role in the Gathings affair.) This legislation was designed to accomplish the major objectives of the American Farm Bureau Federation, an organization of growers and agri-business interests. It removed the power of the Secretary of Labor to regulate employment of domestic farm workers, substituted Agriculture Department rather than Labor Department statistics as criteria for wage adjustments, delegated *bracero* certification to the Secretary of Agriculture, and extended the *bracero* program for two years. The American G.I. Forum directed its entire organization to oppose this transparent farm interest act. Forumeers supported a substitute bill by Senator George McGovern that followed the Mitchell-G.I. Forum policy and provided for elimination of P.L. 78 within five years.[32] This Congressional battle produced some bitter disputes among certain individuals who had professed support in the past for better enforcement of P.L. 78 restrictions. Perhaps the actual prospect of the defeat of the commercial power structure and agriculture's own increased pressure against the McGovern bill frightened these men. Their reluctance to push for the anti-grower legislation did not engender "friendly" response from G.I. Forum members.[33]

The new allies stood firm against the orchestrated attempts of the agricultural bosses to destroy the McGovern legislation. The box score showed a reaffirmation of the Labor Department's power to supervise interstate recruitment of domestic farm workers. Perhaps the most

124

significant decision was the six-month extension of the *bracero* agreement. This replaced the customary two-year extension, which had passed so easily in 1954, 1956, and 1958. Among those who helped defeat the two-year extension were Senators George McGovern, Eugene McCarthy, Hubert Humphrey, Harrison Williams, and Jacob Javits. (Every congressman received two typed letters from the national Forum while those in the twenty-four G.I. Forum states got five letters and two telegrams; every senator was sent three letters with Forum senators getting five letters and three telegrams.) The next major struggle would come in January of 1961 with new hearings over the *bracero* concept.[34]

Kennedy and Repeal

A new president assumed office in January. John F. Kennedy won one of the most closely contested presidential elections in American history, due in large measure to the support of the Spanish-speaking people of the United States. G.I. Forum strategists expected administrative backing in the attempt to eliminate the *bracero* law. Despite extensive evidence demonstrating the adverse effect of these agreements on American laborers (including personal G.I. Forum testimony), the Kennedy people did not fulfill the total expectations of the migrant worker advocates. Amendments added to the bill extending P.L. 78 installed minimum wage provisions and other fringe benefits for domestic farm workers, but they were removed in House-Senate conference. The only apparent "reform" was a restriction of operation of power-driven machinery by *braceros*. The international treaty was extended for two additional years.[35]

In fact, the new bill represented a turning point for those who had worked so long to overturn the *bracero* laws and improve the lot of the migrant laborer. President Kennedy signed H.R. 2010 with the public statement that his administration was committed to protection of domestic agricultural workers. His spokesman, Assistant Secretary of Labor Jerry Holleman, a new appointee and longtime ally of the G.I. Forum, made it clear that wages would increase, conditions improve, and the struggle would continue. He declared that groups seeking the reform of P.L. 78

> ... while not winning some important improvements, nevertheless, accomplished a great deal, much more than is apparent on the surface. It is important that all organizations participating know this because it was their power that made it possible. They should be made to recognize how much power for good is within them. It is to their efforts that we must look for the muscle that will complete this legislative task.[36]

With Kennedy's approval, the Williams subcommittee on migratory labor finally produced its recommendations for eliminating or at least lessening the difficulties encountered by the migrant farm workers and their families. The senators suggested five separate bills to (1) extend child labor laws, (2) establish health programs, (3) regulate labor contractors, (4) provide federal aid for education for migrant children, and (5) create an advisory council on migrant labor. These recommendations were enacted over the next few years. It does not belabor the fact to once again point out that the G.I. Forum had fought for these measures for fourteen years. Ed Idar and Chris Aldrete presented testimony before new Department of Labor hearings in December of 1961. Criticizing the Texas Employment Commission for collusion with the agricultural employers, the two Forum leaders demanded full enforcement of *bracero* restrictions. In Utah, Frank Jamie, president of the Utah Forum, spoke for *braceros* on miserable living conditions; an Ohio unit provided funerals for *braceros* killed in an automobile accident; Oklahoma Forumeers continually requested investigation of contractors and growers in their exploitation of all Mexicans and Mexican Americans; New Mexico and Texas chapters pressed for decent lives for Mexican farm workers.[37]

In Laredo, Texas (a large Southwest border city designated as the poorest city in the nation), Forum units began a new campaign against the commuter system that permitted Mexican citizens to cross the border for employment as long as they returned before night. A lawsuit in a federal district sought interpretation of immigration laws to resolve the situation, but Kennedy officials, fearing economic retaliation from Mexico, intervened and blocked any action. The work-visa program and the return of the *mojado* replaced the *bracero* as a major threat to any potential economic gains for the Mexican American farmworkers.[38]

"Replace" is the key word. In October of 1963, Public Law 78 was not extended, and it expired on December 31, 1964. The leaders of agri-industry did not succeed in renewing the program despite a last -minute scramble to produce national security threats and economic rationales.[39] The American G.I. Forum had no illusions. George Murphy, an ex-tap dancer, won a California senatorial contest in November 1964. He favored renewal of the *bracero* treaty for "easily understood" reasons:

> You have to remember that Americans can't do that kind of work. It's too hard. Mexicans are really good at that. They are built low to the ground, you see, so it is easier for them to stoop.[40]

Conclusion

The repeal of Public Law 78 removed another obstacle supported by

126

American industry that repressed the economic opportunity of the domestic farm worker. The continuous pressure by these corporate powers was matched by the determination of the many individuals and groups who believed in equal opportunity for all American citizens.The American G.I. Forum remained in the forefront of those who would not be discouraged by the power of agri-business. Finally, these Mexican Americans were joined by people who believed in the goals and programs established by *Mexicano* activists in the 1940s. The experience of the migrant worker developed by their collision with the *bracero* system is now contributing to farm worker organizations; the American G.I. Forum gave much to those policies.

CHAPTER X

The New Frontier, the Great Society

In the development of the American G.I. Forum as a viable, activist, Mexican American organization, a key ingredient was the political perception that grew out of the experiences of confronting Anglo-oriented power structures. If any self-interest group was to achieve any success in American society, creative participation in the political processes of that society was absolutely essential. That participation could simply center around traditional political methods involving influence and exertion of power. A minority body had the additional burden of overcoming the inherent prejudice in the established Anglo institutions. The political apathy in the oppressed group, in this case, Americans of Mexican descent, presented more problems. Any success would also encounter more opposition from a forewarned "opponent"; success could also increase the expectations and ambitions of the activists without any real prospect of meeting those hopes immediately. The ultimate synthesis produced by this deliberate psychological situation became a combination of endurance, determination and practicality.

A restriction of the first state constitution, adopted by all other state units, and accepted by the 1956 national convention of the G.I. Forum, prevented any local, state, or national Forum member or chapter from endorsing a political candidate or organization. Many present day critics of the Forum accuse it of being apolitical and point to this prohibition as proof. In 1948 this rule was considered critical in eliminating potential divisions of the state chapters and in protecting the novice minority organization (with all the connotations of such an endeavor) from the automatic hostility of Anglo political powers. That it worked is proven by the continuing presence of the G.I. Forum in 1982; but to maintain that the people in the Forum were apolitical is a position that can only be termed historically improper.

G.I. Forum activists in the field of anti-discrimination legislation, veteran benefits, immigration, and civil rights displayed a full cognizance of political requirements. Poll-tax drives, often very dangerous because of the real threat they posed to traditional institutions, took place precisely because of the understood need for political power. The best and most descriptive label that can be applied to the results is political consciousness. While learning from experience and persistence despite amazingly stubborn opposition, many Mexican Americans of the G.I. Forum, acting as individuals, participated in political acts. With expansion and growth, political relationships developed in local, state, and national settings. Beginning with the 1960 presidential campaign and culminating with the LBJ years, the American G.I. Forum achieved gains quite unforeseeable in 1948. Proceeding from a somewhat low-key attitude in the sense of being unwilling to risk open or prolonged political combat, G.I. Forum *Mexicanos* eventually expressed a public independence and willingness to openly resist what they considered a malicious indifference on the part of national "leaders".

Part 1 - Political Education

The initial efforts of the Texas G.I. Forum brought political contact. Veteran Administration officials were more subject to political pressure than the simple pleadings of a small pressure group; the subsequent events such as the Felix Longoria affair, the hospital closings and general civil rights activities increased and capitalized on those first relationships. Most of the reaction to the Forum demands were negative, especially from the higher state offices. An attempt to pacify these new "upstarts" took place in 1950 when Governor Allan Shivers created a Council for the Study of Human Relations to improve relationships between English-speaking and Spanish-speaking peoples of Texas. When certain members did not follow the Shivers line, they were not reappointed. Afterward, the state's administrative attitude toward the G.I. Forum was openly hostile, although some legislators did display a supportive view.[1]

Forum leaders believed that positive political influence was necessary to improve the status of Mexican Americans. An incipient national recognition did come in the 1952 presidential campaign when Forum members, acting independently of their organization, supported Democratic nominee Adlai Stevenson. Hector Garcia, Gus Garcia, Dr. George I. Sanchez, Richard Casillas, Albert Peña and Chris Aldrete enabled the party to retain the Spanish-speaking vote, promoting the standard idea that the Democratic Party represented the common man vis-a-vis Republican interest with big business.[2] It might be surmised that Dr. Garcia and others did not envision any sudden reciprocation in the form of social programs, but they did consider the 1952 campaign as a particularly apt period to demonstrate the potential of the Mexican vote.

Such publicity and the continued expansion of G.I. Forums with concomitant success in different areas did gain the "attention" of various political figures. Local and state officials started attending Forum functions to solicit Mexican American support. Not coincidentally, individual members of the Forum, reflecting the experience acquired in their own chapter programs, had some success in "making their vote count" for those for and against the interests of their people. The state and national conventions became especially convenient "Forums" for candidates and incumbents to sell themselves. This situation did not violate the constitutional law against political endorsement because no Forum chapter gave official approval to any person. At the same time the willingness and, in some cases, eagerness of politicos to appear before these audiences illustrates an increase in the value of the vote.[3]

A by-product of these events was the decision of many Forumeers to seek political office. Although not receiving any chapter endorsement, these people did count on the support of their colleagues, which they received. Victories did not come immediately, nor did so-called "liberal" elements rush to the aid of Mexican Americans. It did not secure the help of the many sincere people who became a part of the black civil rights movement of the early 1960s. Mexican Americans won or lost by their own resources; political concerns did continue. In 1956 appointments to the State Democratic Advisory Council and the National Advisory Council of the Democratic National Committee recognized forum efforts. The experience and expertise developed from their work in the Forum; an obvious product of their activities was this heightened political consciousness.[4]

The campaign for the domestic farm worker gained more national attention for the American G.I. Forum. Senators, congressmen and executive officials learned about this minority group and its ability to produce. Many liberal and some conservative legislators established at least pro forma communication with the various men and women who lobbied for the elimination of P.L. 78 and better conditions for the migrant labor population. These contacts benefited the National Democratic Party in 1960 when John F. Kennedy ran against Richard M. Nixon for president of the United States. The American G.I. Forum played a significant and major role in one of the most exciting political contests of American history.

Part 2 - Kennedy's Decision

Theodore White spends a fair amount of space in *The Making of the President, 1960* discussing John Kennedy's appeal to black people and their response to his candidacy; White rightly believes that their overwhelming vote for JFK was vital to his victory. Unfortunately, but not surprisingly, he did not seem aware of the Latino (Mexican American and Puerto Rican) participation in that campaign. Most so-called Anglo liberals did not learn about the Latino until late in the decade. But John Kennedy considered the Spanish-speaking population a critical source for Democratic votes. Because Mexican Americans traditionally supported Democratic candidates and did not oppose Catholic office-seekers, they played an important role in the presidential campaign. Even John Kennedy could not have known how much they would contribute.

Viva Kennedy

Kennedy knew of the American G.I. Forum as a result of his senatorial service during the *bracero* debates, the Stevenson campaign when Dr. Garcia and other Forum leaders did not betray the party, and certainly in 1959 when the "Irish mafia" geared up for the presidential primaries. In August of that year, Senator Kennedy sent a particularly warm message of congratulations and admiration to the National G.I. Forum convention in Los Angeles, California. His personal representative was Carlos McCormick, a charter member of the Washington, D.C. American G.I. Forum.[5] In June 1960, the senator became a full-fledged member of the Forum, a "splendid veterans organization of Spanish-speaking ex-servicemen."[6]

Senator Kennedy continued his pursuit of the Spanish-speaking vote in the hearings of the Democratic National Committee and the subsequent platform presented at the convention.[7] Dr. Garcia delivered a rather strong statement to the committee, chastising the party for its failure to answer or even attempt to meet the needs of American minorities. Calling for more Latin American representatives at different party levels, the founder also requested a strong civil rights plank, a minimum wage for all Americans, and protection for migrant workers. The Democratic convention of 1960 responded to the issue of civil rights and promised that the new administration of 1961 would pursue the policy of school desegregation established by the Supreme Court. Equal employment opportunity, fair housing, and voting rights were also designated as areas of concern for the federal government. In addition, the party included in its platform a pledge to develop comprehensive legislation for migrant farm workers. (This was the first official platform attention for farm workers in American history.) Immediately after the convention, Robert Kennedy, JFK's campaign manager, asserted to a Spanish Harlem audience in New York City that his brother was determined to appoint Americans of Mexican extraction as ambassadors to Latin American countries.[8] The Kennedys were touching all the bases in their efforts to get those votes.

Along with these overtures, a more precise instrument was devised to obtain as many Latino votes as possible. Carlos McCormick organized the first Viva Kennedy Club in Tuscon, Arizona. Because McCormick had worked very hard as Chairman of the Forum Legislative Committee, he had good connections with Forum leaders. He enjoyed a more than formal relation with the Kennedy organization as a member of the senatorial staff. The Viva Kennedy concept, born before the convention, became a logical and ideal means for Forumeers to endorse and, more importantly, work for Kennedy's election without compromising their non-partisan charter restrictions. By the end of the election campaign, organizers estimated that thousands of clubs had been formed throughout the nation.[9]

The chief goal of the Viva Kennedy Club drive was the registration of Spanish-speaking voters. Senators Dennis Chavez and Joseph Montoya served as honorary chairmen and traveled extensively for Kennedy. A great deal of the work was done by political activists who happened to be officers and members of the American G.I. Forum. McCormick acted as national coordinator; among the national co-chairmen were Forumeers Henry Lopez and Edward Roybal of California, Jose Alvarado of Illinois, John Mendoza of Nevada, Filo Sedilo of New Mexico, Stanley Valdez of Pennsylvania, and the Texas representatives, state senator Henry Gonzalez, Albert Peña, and Dr. Hector Garcia. Leadership at the state level read like an honor roll of G.I. Forum members. All of these men, especially Dr. Garcia, spoke in many parts of the country for the Democratic nominee.[10] Amazing increases in the numbers of Spanish-speaking voters were registered during a relatively brief period after the convention until the election. In California, 135,000 new citizens appeared on the registration rolls; in Southern California, Nixon had to actually campaign in his own territory because of this new threat.[11]

The effects of these activities were little short of phenomenal. Large numbers of Latinos, especially Mexican Americans, actively participated in a national campaign with a real hope of electing a president who would be sympathetic to their needs. When John Kennedy won the incredibly close contest, these people felt they had been responsible; the victories in Texas and New Mexico were, in large part, attributable to the Viva Kennedy Clubs. Nationwide, 85 percent of the Mexican American voters went for Kennedy. In Texas, 91 percent voted for Kennedy with a 200,000 plurality; he won the state by 50,000 votes. In New Mexico, the respective figures were 70 percent 20,000, and 2,000. John Kennedy's total plurality was 119,000 out of 68,000,000 votes. Robert Kennedy publicly stated it had been the votes of Mexican Americans and other Latin Americans in the United States that elected his brother; John Kennedy expressed his gratitude.[12]

Mexicano political activists sincerely believed they had earned a place in government affairs. Some theorists feel that all segments of a given population should enjoy actual representation; some require deeds as a criterion; Mexican Americans had fulfilled both qualifications. Kennedy offered ambassadorial posts to Hector Garcia and Henry Gonzalez, both of whom had other commitments. Dr. Garcia did accept a temporary assignment as envoy in a special delegation which negotiated a mutual defense and aid treaty with the Federation of West Indies Islands. However, there were many other capable Americans of Mexican origin who could carry out more substantive assignments. Very early in 1961, Senator Dennis Chavez accused President Kennedy of holding back on his campaign pledge.[13]

A very bitter experience further convinced many Mexican Americans that their president was somewhat less committed than they originally believed. When federal judge James V. Allred (of the *Driscoll* decision) died in September of 1959, many people felt that a Mexican American should be appointed for the vacated judgeship. A very concerted effort was made by Dr. Garcia and other Forumeers, acting independently from the G.I. Forum, to have Judge E. D. Salinas of Laredo, Texas receive that position. High officials in the Eisenhower administration, including Secretary of the Treasury Robert Anderson and members of the State Democratic Committee, also highly recommended Judge Salinas. As the issue carried profound importance to *Mexicanos,* it was also a case where a highly qualified individual merited and received the support of many individuals. Eisenhower left the matter to his successor, who was well aware of the situation.[14]

After the successful 1960 campaign, those who were pressing the appointment felt some confidence that Kennedy would make Salinas the first American of Mexican descent to hold a federal judgeship. Senator Ralph Yarborough of Texas, the legislator responsible for the state where Salinas would serve, ostensibly supported Salinas, a vital requirement in such a case. Therefore, all concerned were taken aback when Kennedy nominated a Republican Mexican American for the position. Dr. Garcia professed pleasure that a man of Mexican origin had received the post, but clearly, many people were outraged and rightly so. Kennedy had ignored the advice and consultation of individuals who labored very hard for his election and who also possessed a thorough knowledge of the political needs of their people.[15] Kennedy did recognize the ethnic importance of a patronage position but from the Anglo stereotype that "all Mexicans are alike." Therefore, a Republican was as good as a Democrat. Kennedy dismissed the needs of people who had been very important in giving him the opportunity to appoint federal judges. Mexican American Democrats were left twisting in the wind.

These feelings were expressed at a conference of Viva Kennedy Club leaders in March 1961. Called as a means of maintaining the organization created during the campaign experiences, the conference became the precipitating event for the creation of an independent, Spanish-speaking, political organization. The most obvious complaints of the people at the meeting centered on the perceived callousness of the new administration. Many Forumeers attended and presented their own feelings of betrayal and outrage. The consensus rapidly developed that *Mexicanos* must attempt to divest themselves of national party independence. Dr. Hector Garcia was nominated and elected by acclamation as the national president of the new Political Association of Spanish-Speaking Organizations; other officers were Ed Roybal and Henry Lopez of California and Carlos McCormick, all of whom were members of the American G.I. Forum.[16]

California and Texas PASSO groups had tremendous initial success; in California, Ed Roybal became the first Mexican American congressman of that state; Henry Gonzalez also had the same experience in Texas. John Tower won a special Texas senatorial election for Vice-President Johnson's vacated seat, becoming the first national Republican office holder from that state, largely because of the withdrawal of Mexican American support as a demonstration of their political power.[17] Many Anglo liberals also deserted the Democratic Party by believing that Tower would only be a one-term senator. But Texas liberals were constantly outsmarting themselves. Mexican Americans were attempting to make a point with a not-so-usual tactic. The Texas PASSO had other triumphs, particularly in the Crystal City elections of 1963. Unfortunately, the conservative, Anglo-controlled Democratic Party simply had too much power. Despite the Crystal City experience, the election of John Connally as governor in 1962 signalled at least a temporary setback to the type of independence that the men who originally created the organization envisioned. Internal disputes added to the complexities of attempting to develop strength and unity from a less than powerful base.[18]

And yet there is another vexing factor in the analysis of JFK. He was far more accessible to Mexican Americans than any previous president. He did provide some reforms, albeit timid, for migrant workers, and the *bracero* program ended under his administration. His personality did contain elements of "con" or deceit. But the tantalizing feeling did exist that if John Kennedy could obtain more than a paper majority in Congress, he would create more progressive and far-reaching legislation. The 1964 Civil Rights Act was largely his own proposal, and evidence that his promises were more than political enticement. The men and women of the American G.I. Forum were not novices or naive social dreamers. They had learned very bitter lessons over a long period of time. They criticized the Kennedy failures but did not denounce the Kennedy intent. On a practical level, such a statement might have been political suicide, but from a more intangible perspective Mexican Americans had the legitimate belief and hope that federal direction would come. Hector Garcia and his organization felt a certain trust in John Fitzgerald Kennedy. It probably was misplaced. On November 22, 1963, the presidency passed to Lyndon Baines Johnson. His administration produced benefits and controversy of equal dimensions.

Part 3 · LBJ

Lyndon Baines Johnson had a very distinct and long-running "affair" with Mexican Americans and the American G.I. Forum. In 1939 Congressman Johnson spoke for minimum wage that would eliminate the seven-cents-per-hour horrors of the San Antonio pecan industry. His contribution on the Felix Longoria case earned the friendship of many Forumeers; his help during the South Texas hospital crisis was most welcome; in 1953 he presented the chief speech at the Texas G.I. Forum convention. The relation was not always conciliatory, as in 1954 when the Texas Forum criticized his somewhat tentative efforts in support of better border control and his persistent attempt to blame the agricultural problems on the Eisenhower administration without including Democratic congressmen in his indictment. But generally Senator Johnson was responsible in serving his Mexican constituency on many individual cases such as veterans benefits or other issues.[25]

Johnson did not conduct a very shrewd campaign in his attempt to win the 1960 Democratic nomination as president. However, his presence on the ticket was a definite plus for the Viva Kennedy Clubs. The senator from Texas had displayed a more than casual understanding of the issues most important to Mexican Americans and rendered good service to Kennedy as an attractive factor in the close election. As vice-president, LBJ continued to correspond and meet with G.I. Forum leaders on matters such as equal employment opportunity or Mexican American representation in federal government. When Johnson became president, he received the support from Forumeers across the country.[26]

In early 1964 the National American G.I. Forum opened a Washington, D.C., office to lobby for the interests of Mexican Americans.[27] Other special events of that year included the appointment of Dr. Garcia as special ambassador to the inauguration of the new Venezuelan president, and the passage of the most comprehensive civil rights act since Reconstruction. The two were related in the sense that President Johnson recognized the obligation of the Democratic Party and the federal government to acknowledge the contribution of Mexican Americans. He clearly included Mexican Americans in his definition of the economically and socially oppressed people in the United States. The 1964 Civil Rights Act embodies that opinion.[28] Part of the legislation included the Economic Opportunity Act, which created the Office of Equal Opportunity, VISTA, the Community Relations Service and other far-reaching social programs. The president named, among others, Dr. Hector Garcia, Louis Telez, Larry Ramirez, and Rodolph "Corky" Gonzalez (all Forumeers) to a national committee to augment the work of the Community Relations Service. He appointed Edward Terrones, national vice-chairman of the American G.I. Forum, to a high federal position on the staff of the assistant postmaster general. [29]Vicente Ximenes and Rudy L. Ramos, director of the D.C. office, acted as national and deputy national coordinator of the Viva Johnson Clubs for the 1964 Presidential campaign.[30] Johnson's extraordinary victory promised good things for Mexican Americans — or did it?

War on Poverty

The creation of a federal OEO seemed to indicate tremendous changes for minorities in American society. By inserting itself into the private-sector practices, the federal government lent great weight for more egalitarian employment practices. Sadly, the operation encountered difficulties from its inception because of the reluctance to allow minority groups a strong voice in administering the program.

G.I. Forum activists were not comfortable with the trend in the initial stages of the anti-poverty structure. Spanish-speaking groups did not receive the opportunity to draw guidelines for a realistic application of OEO to problems "in the field". The Washington, D.C., office of the National Forum quickly protested this direction of the equal opportunity programs. Forum members were invited to a White House meeting to review the various "Great Society" programs and to lend their own expertise to the many avenues of approach to the problems of poverty. However, the question remained as to how much advice the federal administrators were willing to consider.[31]

A major concern of the 1966 National G.I. Forum convention was the failure of the local War on Poverty officials to delegate policy-making positions to the Spanish-speaking. At a White House conference on equal employment opportunity, Dr. Garcia presented a statement signed by most of the major Mexican American leaders in the nation calling for a Mexican American appointee as presidential assistant for the

136

purpose of establishing a more fruitful communication between the Mexican American community and the federal government. While this request was being considered, a few Mexican Americans, including Corky Gonzalez, received more responsible positions in OEO programs. (Gonzalez became head of the Denver War on Poverty after the internal ouster of the previous director.) The national director also pledged a more responsible director for the program, but these "statements" did not produce much confidence from those most involved.[32]

A more specific protest occurred in Santa Clara County, California when two G.I. Forum chapters aligned themselves with eight other Mexican American organizations and picketed an Equal Employment Opportunity Commission (EEOC) meeting while other supporters made their voices heard in the meeting place. The Anglo director had denied the need for a Spanish-speaking deputy director and generally undermined the grievances of these people, who felt they were not being served by the local office. Forumeers had rarely engaged in demonstrations; the EEOC directors drew up a new commission with better representation and a deputy director.[33].

This type of situation indicated to Forumeers and other Mexican Americans a degree of indifference on the part of the federal government. The Washington, D.C., office of the G.I. Forum delivered well-qualified applicants for Great Society programs time and time again without subsequent or adequate reply. Many were convinced that federal authorities were as discriminating as Anglo society. The proverbial lid almost blew in 1966. Johnson announced in February the formation of a council to the White House Conference, "To Fulfill These Rights." A cross-section of representatives from the nation's leading industrial, labor, and civil rights groups was named to a body "to help the American Negro fulfill the rights which after the long time of injustice, he is finally about to secure."[34] Mexican Americans were outraged at this "insult by omission," and hinted at massive demonstrations.

A most important event took place after Johnson's statement. The next month, several groups attending a Southwest regional EEOC meeting (including the American G.I. Forum, LULAC, and PASSO) abruptly walked out, charging discrimination in the highest circle of EEOC. Albert Peña presented data indicating 800 southwestern companies with 600,000 employees and no Mexican Americans· on the payrolls. Yet the Johnson administration could not see fit to appoint a single Mexican American EEOC commissioner. A Mexican American Ad Hoc National Joint Committee was formed, with National G.I. Forum president Augustine Flores as chairman, to seek solutions. The Washington, D.C., Forum office threatened to file an injunction against the use of public funds by the EEOC unless an appropriate response (a

White House conference on Mexican American needs) was forthcoming from the federal government.[35]

President Johnson replied in a press conference that he had done all he could to promote better understanding between the Spanish-speaking and his administration. However, if a conference was needed, then a conference would be held. A temporary but disquieting truce developed. Eight thousand people marched on Sacramento, California on behalf of the National Farm Workers Association (the G.I. Forum state chairman and other members marched with Chavez). Corky Gonzalez was fired as director of the Denver Neighborhood Youth Corp. Many Forumeers were disenchanted with the Texas White House.[36]

Meanwhile, the relationship between John Kennedy and his Viva Kennedy supporters acquired an ambivalent tone. It was obvious that substantive recognition of Mexican Americans as first-class citizens was not going to happen in that administration. The Justice Department under Attorney General Robert Kennedy did not pursue investigations of violations of *Mexicano* civil rights; the Labor Department remained somewhat vague on the *bracero* issue despite ringing declarations of the intent to protect all citizens. Administration advisors seemed concerned about the potential loss of Latin American voters but did nothing significant about it.[19]

Nonetheless, the American G.I. Forum continually pledged its confidence to Kennedy. It supported him after the Bay of Pigs fiasco. The psuedo-attention to Latin America in the Alliance for Progress did not alienate Forumeers. The somewhat questionable actions of the president in the 1962 Cuban missile crisis received praise and statements of confidence from Forum leaders and chapters. High-ranking Forum officials sometimes accompanied the president on Latin American excursions or on public-relations trips involving Mexican Americans.[20] These matters were largely cosmetic, but the very fact of the adminstration's desire to maintain cordiality implied a recognition by the Kennedy organization of the need to maintain political ties with the Spanish-speaking.

In July of 1963, Attorney General Robert Kennedy delivered the principal address at the national convention of the American G.I. Forum. The event was a momentous occasion for all Forumeers and not unfelt by the attorney general. Pledges of friendship, trust, and hopes for the future were exchanged by the delegates and Mr. Kennedy.[21] The second term of John Kennedy would be a better time for all.

Deceit vs. Hope

John Kennedy has been perceived as a president sympathetic to the grievances of those Americans who did not share in that enigmatic (yet

138

dogmatic) idea known as the American Dream. The symbol of that commitment was his efforts on the issue of civil rights. Theodore Sorensen described Kennedy as the first chief executive to apply the full power of the presidency against discrimination.[22] But did he? What was the nature of his program? Did other options exist for the improvement of minority groups and did he employ them?

Compared to Dwight Eisenhower, John Kennedy accomplished much on civil rights during the "one thousand days". Whereas Eisenhower would not even publicly support the 1954 *Brown* decision, President Kennedy made his approval very clear. His administration produced progress in education, public housing, voting rights, public discrimination, and employment. However, the procedures used involved personal or executive action, not substantive legislative proposals and programs. In a somewhat acerbic analysis called *The Kennedy Promise*, Henry Fairlie indicts the use of personal response as a means of coopting civil rights advocates; by displaying presidential concern, JFK undermined what otherwise would have been a ringing condemnation of the failure of his administration to fulfill its pledges toward minority groups. But William O'Neill, in *Coming Apart*, describes the symbolism of Kennedy's action as important as substantive support. He particularly emphasizes the integration of the University of Mississippi and the University of Alabama as evidence that "public relations bridged the gap between promise and performance."[23] But even those actions were forced by the determination of black Americans to coerce response from Kennedy.

There is no question that the Camelot facade has obscured the realities of John Kennedy's three years as president. The style and rhetoric of that period were much more complicated and flawed than the martyred image would allow the American public to perceive. But the very fact of a president of the United States lending the considerable moral force of his office to the matter of civil rights is important. The lack of successful legislative support to that moral pressure is partially explained by the conservative nature of the Congress during Kennedy's three years. Integration of the University of Mississippi and the University of Alabama were not unimportant, even as symbols.[24] Unfortunately, the failure of Kennedy to acknowledge his debt to Mexican Americans is not so easily understood. Political appointments are the very type of executive or personal forms of leadership that Kennedy did exercise toward black Americans, but not Mexican Americans. Such appointments would have also provided valuable recognition of the abilities and needs of Mexican Americans without pursuing "legislative" answers. John Kennedy failed and in a sense betrayed the *Mexicanos* who gave him their loyalty and their labor.

By September of 1967 the promised conference had not been held, and Mexican American spokesmen were angry at Johnson's callous treatment. Complaints about the failure of the OEO to prevent or even investigate discrimination increased. Yet in that peculiar manner that LBJ often employed, a potentially significant opportunity for the betterment of the Mexican American community did occur. In April, Johnson appointed Vicente Ximenes to the Equal Employment Opportunity Commission and in June 1967, the president named the Forumeer as the head of a top level inter-agency committee on Mexican American affairs. In addition, President Johnson rescued a long-stagnant federal project (suggested by Mexican American organizations) to attack poverty in the southwestern states of Arizona, California, New Mexico, Colorado, and Texas. Project SER (Service, Employment, and Redevelopment) was conceived as a means of training Mexican Americans by other Mexican Americans who understood the community, its culture, and needs. The project was supposed to have started in 1965, but bureaucracy would not cooperate. Finally, on Johnson's direct order, five million dollars was allocated with the American G.I. Forum and LULAC as the principal directors.[37]

These acts by Johnson did not diffuse the criticism directed at his lack of candor on the conference issue, nor did they blunt the more militant advocates of change. Jose Angel Gutierrez of Texas, Reies Tijerina, Corky Gonzalez, and Bert Corona of California were the more well-known spokesmen for more rapid reform by the federal government. A declaration by the National American G.I. Forum rejecting civil disobedience as a means of achieving civil rights goals did not set well with these individuals. Nor did the announcement of the long-awaited conference arouse shouts of praise.[38]

The conference, as presented in October 1967, was not exactly what Mexican American groups envisioned. Four members of the Cabinet and other federal officials attended hearings held simultaneously in five hotels in El Paso, Texas. They were divided into areas of Health, Education and welfare, housing and urban development, agriculture, labor, War on Poverty, and economic and social development. The chairmen of the more well-known Mexican American organizations monitored the individual hearings. Representatives of the "radical" groups (as perceived by the White House) boycotted the session and held their own rump convention. President Johnson "dropped in" on the hearings accompanied by Governor John Connally of Texas, an absurdly insensitive act since Connally had widely denounced striking farm workers in Texas. The reception in El Paso was not polite.[39]

The whole experience acquired a perplexing tone. President Johnson, who could be so eloquent in his perception of the problems of minority

140

citizens, could also contribute to the perpetuation of prejudice by acts such as the Connally fiasco. Still, if he had held the conference when he first promised to do so, such arrogance might have been overlooked. The inter-agency committee, which held the responsibility for the conference, would have received a great boost if the president had more actively participated, but Johnson foolishly undermined his own creation. Finally, and most important, the El Paso conference contributed to a division between the older Mexican American groups and the newer organizations that developed during the decade's social turmoil. Both sides had important ideas, but Bert Corona, among others, charged that the grassroots and militant Mexican American organizations had been bypassed by Washington for the conference.[40] By implication, Corona was criticizing the G.I. Forum for lending its support to the conference, thereby giving credibility to an obviously condescending hand-out. This incident revealed conflict between Mexican American and "Chicano" perceptions. Both sides were right and both were wrong in their condemnation of each other. LBJ's paternalism and insensitivity certainly made the more established groups appear naive and manipulated.

For all intents and purposes, Johnson's "commitment" lessened in 1968. As a personal tribute, the president appointed Dr. Garcia as special delegate to the United Nations and as the first Spanish-surnamed member of the U.S. Commission on Civil Rights.[41] The campaign for the 1968 presidential election marked a distinct change in the federal government's attitude toward Mexican Americans, blacks, and other minority groups in the United States. Richard Milhous Nixon began his imperial presidency.

The LBJ era was a time of rapid change and, in many cases, violent events. Lyndon Johnson was the most qualified man ever to assume the office of president. His grasp of social problems and willingness to use the government as an instrument of social reform could be inversely matched by his pettiness or resentment at some imagined slur.[42] The concept of the "Great Society" was as rich and far-seeing as his inability to understand, until too late, the complications of the VietNam War. And yet the politician could also surrender the power and office that he most cherished when he felt that he could no longer govern effectively (contrasted with Mr. Nixon and his last months in office). No chief executive was as knowledgeable of Mexican American society or more open to its advocates. Contrary to present-day theories which debunk the "Great Society", the programs had a profound effect in raising the status of many Mexican Americans.[43] Sadly, Lyndon Johnson never transcended his own limitations or the restrictions of his political world and, Mexican Americans paid the price.

CHAPTER XI

New Allies, Old Veterans

During the last few years, new trends and new forces developed within the Mexican American civil rights movement. The Chicano movement has provided an urgency to *la causa* that reflected political consciousness. Some of these "radicals" carried their slogans, raised their fists, and learned new handshakes; on the other hand, Cesar Chavez, Jose Angel Gutierrez, Corky Gonzalez, and others produced new options for Mexican Americans. Chavez, particularly, has displayed a dedication and profundity not often found in any movement. The American G.I. Forum remained a constant and dynamic force, in some cases adopting to the new direction, in others refining techniques and strategies long employed by the members. Even as tension developed between the new radicals and the old hands, the Forum and Chicano groups managed to work together on many issues.

All of the various G.I. Forum programs and activities of the preceeding twenty years continued. Forum chapters throughout the nation fought for better education and against *de facto* school segregation. Migrant worker problems, veterans rights and benefits, and public discrimination retained their priority. In addition, the G.I. Forum maintained its efforts to secure more political representation on the local, state, and national scene. Nixon played politics with human rights (as he did with every other social problem), but interesting things did happen.

Part 1 - Radicals?

In March of 1968, Mexican American high school students of seven minority communities in Los Angeles boycotted their classes in protest of low-quality education and the oppressive and discriminatory attitude of school authorities. The exact demands were smaller classes, new buildings to replace condemned ones, larger library facilities, curtailment of the use of sheriffs on the campus, fewer locked classrooms, more counselors, and better qualified teachers. The boycott was a challenge to the traditional and entrenched Anglo school administrators. Police arrested many of the "demonstrators", but after this assertion of authori-

142

ty, officials promised to effect the requests. After the students returned, nothing happened.[1] Nonetheless, this youthful and militant activism marked an important step in the evolution of *la causa*. Young Chicanos indicated their fervent desire to fight for their basic rights as American citizens. The G.I. Forum welcomed these acts; after all, what had they fought for in the United States for the previous twenty years? In fact, as other *Mexicano* students imitated the Los Angeles experience, they often asked Forumeers to speak with them to school authorities.[2]

A few Mexican American leaders denounced these youthful expressions, including the creation of Mexican American youth organizations, which sometimes enunciated violent rhetoric,[3] but the thrust of the young was appreciated by most of the veterans of *la lucha*, as indicated by their participation in such events as the Del Rio protest. In March of 1969, Governor Preston Smith (at the demand of Del Rio city commissioners) expelled VISTA workers from Del Rio, Texas, for "political agitation". Rather than criticize the thirty-two protesters, who were arrested because of a parade against this dismissal, Dr. Garcia, acting as a U.S. civil rights commissioner, intervened at the request of Dr. Fermin Calderon, a member of the Del Rio G.I. Forum. The "criminals" were set free with the city admission that the ordinance they had violated (an anti-parade law) was unconstitutional. While this incident was hardly a victory (the VISTA people were not allowed back in Del Rio), it was a good example of all factions working together.[4]

Another new front in an old war concerned the National Farm Workers Association and Cesar Chavez. This dynamic *Mexicano* had begun the attempt to unionize California's domestic farm workers in 1962 and had confronted all the power that the agribusiness interests could accumulate. His courageous persistence and his technique of boycott and strike produced remarkable gains for the workers, including some agreements certifying the right of collective bargaining and a number of contracts. Although these efforts by no means solved the problems of the laborers, Chavez represented the hope that they could acquire the methods of resolving their own economic needs through unionization rather than rely on federal legislation. The G.I. Forum maintained steady support for Chavez while pushing for legislation to consolidate the achievements of his organization.[5] (One example was the aid of Forumeers at a Holiday Inn incident where the manager "reluctantly" served a UFWOC family. Forum members who patronized the motel set the manager straight.) Commuter programs and "green cards" dramatically increased the number of Mexican citizens crossing the border to work in the United States. Demanding strict enforcement of border regulations, the Forum legislative committees continued their pressure for minimum wage coverage, adequate working conditions, and the same benefits given to industrial labor. In addition, Forum "lobbyists" secured some migrant programs under the OEO guidelines.[6] It is important to remember that migrant workers had begun to receive those rights so long demanded by the G.I. Forum and other pro-worker organizations; nor should it be forgotten that the American G.I. Forum was the first truly activist Mexican American organization, apart from union groups, to fight for those rights.

School integration, a primary goal in the 1950s, remained an important issue, especially in Texas where school authorities never gave up their tradition-based concept of separate school systems. After the *Driscoll* decision, the issue in part became a matter of enforcing court decrees, which invalidated legal or *de jure* segregation.[7] Unfortunately, a new factor of housing patterns as determined by population grouping (*de facto* segregation) severely complicated the problem of eliminating single schools for racial/ethnic groups. The "other white" strategy employed so successfully by Forum attorneys from 1948 through 1957 became, at least temporarily, a weapon of Anglo administrators. Combining Mexican American and black students in one school appeared to fulfill the legal definition of integration while circumventing the true intent of the several federal court decisions requiring desegregation. When Mexican American advocates challenged these tactics, opponents professed an inability to do anything about *de facto* segregation. They questioned the right of federal law to influence the choice of people to live where they chose. (No such question arose when minority children were bused to segregated schools.) Neighborhood schools became a euphemism for the "free choice" tactic used by Anglo school boards in earlier days.[8]

In 1968, Jose Cisneros and twenty-five other Mexican American and black members of the United States Steel Workers Union filed suit against the Corpus Christi Independent School District charging the ISD administrators with operation of a dual school system on a *de facto* basis. (Dr. Garcia had conducted a campaign against the Corpus Christi school system authorities for a number of years.[9]) The attorney for the plaintiffs was James De Anda, a past state chairman of the G.I. Forum, who participated in the 1954 Hernandez case and won the 1957 *Driscoll*decision. The federal court ruled in June 1970 that Mexican American students were separated and segregated to a degree prohibited by the fourteenth Amendment in all three levels of the school system, elementary, junior high, and senior high. Judge Woodrow Seals stated that Mexican Americans had been discriminated against as a class and was convinced that "this history of discrimination as given by Dr. Thomas Carter, Dr. Hector Garcia, and Mr. Paul Montemayor is substantially correct."[10] A federal court had decided that *de facto* segregation was unconstitutional. Perhaps one could be forgiven for

144

assuming that compliance with the court order to devise a plan to correct this situation should have followed, but following is a brief outline of the next *five* years:[11]

July 2, 1971	Judge Seals entered a final judgment and memorandum setting forth a desegregation plan for the 1971—1972 school year.
July 13, 1971	The school district applied to the court for additional time to implement year.
July 16, 1971	A new federal judge, Owen Cox, granted an additional year; the school district appealed the Seals judgment.
July 19, 1971	Cox entered a supplemental order qualifying his previous ruling to eliminate any idea that the schools could do nothing.
July 23, 1971	The plaintiffs appealed the Cox order.
August 5, 1971	The Court of Appeals revoked the Cox order, restoring the original deadline.
August 9, 1971	The school district asked for reconsideration.
August 10, 1971	The Court of Appeals refused.
August 11, 1971	The school district appealed to the Supreme Court.
August 20, 1971	Justice Hugo Black granted a stay until the fifth Circuit Court of Appeals ruled on the merits of the Cox case.
August 23, 1971	Cox issued a new order preventing the reassignment of 1,000 Black students.
February 10, 1972	The fifth Circuit Court announced a delay in its decision until the Supreme Court offered guidance.
April 27, 1972	The fifth Circuit Court enjoined the ISD from constructing or renovating schools until after the appeal decision.
August 3, 1972	The court ruled against the school district, agreeing with the unconstitutional verdict of the Seals decision, and ordered a new desegregation plan.
August 23, 1972	Cox ordered a framework for a plan for the ISD by September 15.
September 15, 1972	The district offered a plan for reassignment of 3,665 students and the closing of one black school, a superficial plan at best.
October 1972	Dr. Garcia and seventeen young Mexican Americans were arrested in a sit-in protesting the refusal of the school board to transfer Chicanos on a majority to minority rule.
May 8, 1973	Cox rejected the plan and ordered a new one by June 11.
June 11, 1973	The ISD entered a new plan of piecemeal boundary change.
June 25, 1973	The U.S. Supreme Court refused to review the case.
December 6, 1973	Cox rejected the ISD attempt to label Mexican Americans as white and transfer them to black schools and ordered a plan of student transfers.

January 1974	The court decided the December plan would not work.
March 1975	
May 19, 1975	Cox ordered a plan to achieve viable integration. The school district replied that residential mix was the only permanent way to achieve realistic integration and forced intermingling was viewed as extremely harmful. However, a new plan was produced.

The effect of these tactics was to delay reasonable progress and better education for thousands of Mexican Americans. Anglo opponents organized the ubiquitous "Concerned Neighbors" efforts to fight federal interference and forced busing. According to their press releases, prejudice or racism had nothing to do with it, only a desire to prevent the decline of their own children's education.[12] The court order remained the same and compliance began, but the power of the federal government hardly manifested itself.

Equal Employment

This same timidity was a characteristic of the Equal Employment Opportunity Commission. G.I. Forum advocates pointed to the reluctance of EEOC boards to prosecute, and to the significant advantage possessed by large companies in money, legal resources, and time. An individual who could not afford the time and expenses required to pursue a decision often dropped the complaint or accepted a less than satisfactory compromise. A more favorable analysis, however, could point out the significant accomplishment of the existence of an EEOC and the essential, although weak, support furnished by federal guidelines.[13]

An illustration of this ambivalence would be the Coors beer boycott, which began in 1968 by the G.I. Forum due to the refusal of the Coors Company to hire Mexican Americans. Efforts by Forumeers to investigate began in 1966, and in August 1970, the Colorado Commission on Civil Rights ruled that the Adolph Coors Company was guilty of racial discrimination in the 1969 dismissal of an employee. The G.I. Forum alleged continued discrimination in Coors hiring practices. The company supplied scab grapes to Colorado in order to break the Chavez (United Farm Workers) boycott against Gallo Enterprises. In 1973, the U.S. Supreme Court overturned a district court order that prohibited review of Coors records by the EEOC (which had no power to conduct its own review). The EEOC promptly began its investigation, and in 1975 compliance seemed to be evolving.[14]

The Office of Equal Opportunity did provide funds for such projects as Model Cities and other programs for community improvement. Although the Nixon administration did its best to dismantle most of the

Great Society programs, pressure from the many groups, including the American G.I. Forum, did salvage and maintain the general focus of those instruments. One of those projects concerned the original rationale for the formation of the G.I. Forum, veterans rights. In January of 1973, a Veterans Outreach Program funded by the United States Department of Labor and sponsored by the American G.I. Forum began an eighteen-city "outreach" counseling and referral service emphasizing the Vietnam ex-servicemen. The specific functions included the identification of returning veterans in need of assistance, mobilization and coordination of available community resources, dissemination of any information pertaining to benefits, intensive counseling, and referral to employment, education, or training programs. After fourteen months, the offices, manned by Forumeers, reached 33,762 veterans, and the Nixon administration eliminated the funding. The Texas G.I. Forum managed to obtain funding from state sources, and the program continued.[15] Along with SER, the Veterans Outreach Program is an excellent example of the ability of the G.I. Forum to "make do" despite the clear lack of help from those federal agencies controlled by the Nixon regime.

Part 2 - Banditos, Beware!

One of the consequences of these years was a determined resolve to defend the cultural pride and dignity of the Mexican American. An obvious target for this determination was that product of a twentieth-century consumer revolution known as advertising. This creative medium displayed an abysmal lack of sensitivity in its brazen portrayal of Mexican American lifestyle to sell a product. The Liggett & Meyers Company presented a Mexican American dressed in sombero, pancho, and bandoliers speaking to his wife with heavy dialect in a dilapidated room. He indicated in an indolent manner that he would fight the revolution *mañana* after he finished his L&M. Another company presented a Mexican character as the ultimate test for its deodorant (Arid). A watch manufacturer in a nationally distributed ad said Zapata 'ould kill for its product. If an ethnic group was truly integrated in a society, these types of descriptions might be viewed as harmless, but if that group was treated as second-class, little humor would be discerned.[16]

In October 1968, Vicente Ximenes wrote to the president of Frito-Lay, Inc., in reference to a character known as the "Frito Bandito", who gained the confidence of an audience and then drew his guns and robbed the viewer of his Fritos; this animated *bandido* wore "Pancho Villa" revolutionary garb and spoke with a noticeable accent. Ximenes informed the Frito king that Mexican Americans did not appreciate this stereotype nor did they enjoy the image of a sneaky, lazy thief. (The

147

original protest had been lodged by a committee called the Involvement of the Mexican American in Gainful Endeavor.) The producer of this valuable product replied that there were no plans to discontinue use of the *bandido* and that the only complaints from the Mexican American market came from organizations like the G.I. Forum.[17]

Other Mexican American groups became involved in the campaign to eliminate the *bandido* and in November 1969, a Los Angeles television station banned the ad; two San Francisco stations soon followed. When two U.S. senators joined the Forum and other concerned Mexican Americans, Frito-Lay, Inc., announced the intention of removing the commercial, or as the spokesman put it, "The Frito Bandito is about to bite the dust." Ten months later the little fellow was still robbing unsuspecting Anglos, and the company claimed in a letter to Dr. Garcia that it could not be expected to abandon an expensive campaign that made money without a suitable advertising replacement. The National Forum office, working with other concerned Mexican Americans who shared the sense of outrage toward this insult, instituted a national boycott of Frito-Lay products. Perhaps even more frustrating was the duplicitous nature of the Frito-Lay communication. Apparently the company grew weary of defending itself, did not appreciate the prospect of losing money, or thought their "Munch for Lunch Bunch" routine was the suitable replacement they so desperately wanted.[18] At any rate, the Frito Bandito died an unlamented death.

A Culture Ignored

This ignorance and apathy toward Mexican Americans did not come only from the commercial class. A more deplorable view, because of its effect on the lives of so many people, was held by the nation's philanthropic foundations that take so much pride in giving help to the country's "underprivileged" or "disadvantaged" people. When Vicente Ximenes, acting as head of the Inter-Agency Committee on Mexican American Affairs, invited fifty of the nation's largest foundations to send representatives to a conference on Mexican American issues, only two accepted. The negative replies were best represented by a letter from the Guggenheim Foundations that noted, "Our program is confined to awarding fellowships through annual competition to advanced workers in science, scholarship, and the arts."[19] Ximenes replied that he assumed that the Guggenheim staff thought American citizens of Mexican descent were stupid, dumb, or maybe foreigners.[20] Maybe the Ford Foundation did not realize that Mexican Americans had any need; out of $5,000,000 in grants announced in 1969, none went to *Mexicanos*, nor did any of the $19,673,963 indicated in a program called "Developing our Wasted

148

Human Resources" go to poor Mexican American people.[21] An appropriate irony of these events occurred when the Ford foundation finally felt compelled to become involved with the Mexican American minority; representatives asked Vicente Ximenes if he knew of any "grassroots" organization that could benefit from the foundation's grant. He did, and it was not the G.I. Forum (which Ford labelled as middle-class) but the Southwest Council of La Raza.[22]

The Master Race

One more example of the largely disinterested attitude of Anglo society toward Mexican Americans will suffice. An incident took place in the Santa Clara Superior Court of California which involved a despicable attitude by a state judge in the incest trial of a young Mexican American boy. Local G.I. Forums immediately organized protests and the affair became a national disgrace for the California judicial system. The following comments of Judge Gerald S. Chargin were the basis of the outrage:

> **The Court:** There is some indication that you (defendant) more or less didn't think that it was against the law or was improper. Haven't you had any moral training? Have you and your family gone to church?
>
> **The Minor:** Yes, sir.
>
> **The Court:** Don't you know that things like this are terribly wrong? This is one of the worst crimes that a person can commit. I just get so disgusted that I just figure what is the use? You are just an animal. Even animals don't do that. You are pretty low.
>
> I don't know why your parents haven't been able to teach you anything or train you. Mexican people, after 13 years of age, it's perfectly all right to go out and act like an animal. It's not even right to do that to a stranger, let alone a member of your own family. I don't have much hope for you. You will probably end up in State's Prison before you are 25, and that's where you belong, anyhow. There is nothing much you can do.
>
> I think you haven't got any moral principles. You won't acquire anything. Your parents won't teach you what is right or wrong and won't watch out.
>
> Apparently your sister is pregnant; is that right?
>
> **The Minor's Father:** Yes.
>
> **The Court:** It's a fine situation. How old is she?
>
> **The Minor's Mother:** Fifteen.
>
> **The Court:** Well, probably she will have a half-a-dozen children and three or four marriages before she is 18. The county will have to take care of you. You are no particular good to anybody. We ought to send you out of the country — send you back to Mexico. You belong in prison for the rest of your life for doing things of this kind. You ought to commit suicide. That's what I think of people of this kind.

149

You are lower than animals and haven't the right to live in organized society — just miserable, lousy, rotten people. There is nothing we can do with you. You expect the county to take care of you. Maybe Hitler was right. The animals in our society probably ought to be destroyed because they have no right to live among human beings. If you refuse to act like a human being, then you don't belong among the society of human beings.

Mr. Lucero (Defendant's Attorney): Your Honor, I don't think I can sit here and listen to that sort of thing.

The Court: You are going to have to listen to it because I consider this a very vulgar, rotten human being.

Mr. Lucero: The court is indicting the whole Mexican group.

The Court: When they are 10 or 12 years of age, going out and having intercourse with anybody without any moral training — they don't even understand the Ten Commandments. That's all. Apparently they don't want to.

So if you want to act like that, the county has a system of taking care of them. They don't care about that. They have no personal self-respect.

Mr. Lucero: The court ought to look at this youngster and deal with this youngster's case.

The Court: All right. That's what I am going to do. The family should be able to control this boy and the young girl.

Mr. Lucero: What appalls me is that the court is saying that Hitler was right in genocide.

The Court: What are we going to do with the mad dogs of our society? Either we have to kill them or send them to an institution or place them out of the hands of good people because that's the theory — one of the theories of punishment is if they get to the position that they want to act like mad dogs, then, we have to separate them from our society.

Well, I will go along with the recommendation. You will learn in time or else you will have to pay for the penalty with the law because the law grinds slowly but exceedingly well. If you are going to be a law violator — you have to make up your mind whether you are going to observe the law or not. If you can't observe the law, you have to be put away.[23]

When this judicial atrocity became public, hundreds of Mexican Americans (including Forumeers) picketed the Superior Court building and a formal complaint was lodged with the Commission on Judicial Qualifications. Chargin requested a reassignment to another department other than juvenile court but would not resign.[24]

Chicano organizations across the country immediately called for massive protest in California and requested their members to lodge formal complaints with the California legislature and judicial officers. The American G.I. Forum was particularly responsive to this request with protests coming in from many state and local units. Hector Garcia, acting as the national chairman of the Forum and as a U.S. commissioner of civil rights joined in a demonstration against the irresponsible and vicious attack by Chargin on the Mexican American community. Dr. Garcia made the salient point that when "militant" Mexicano youth groups such as MAYO cried "Kill the Gringo", practically every Southwestern newpaper, radio, and television station carried the story, and political leaders demanded investigations of MAYO. When an Anglo judge called for suicide and condoned genocide for Mexican Americans, a sudden "loud" silence was heard from those who could do something about it. The U.S. Commission on Civil Rights, including Dr. Garcia, commented that this particular case was the sort of incident that has brought about profound mistrust of the system of criminal justice within the Mexican American community. No statements were forthcoming from Governor Ronald Reagan or the judiciary branch of the California state system.[25] The president of La Confederacion de la Raza Unida demanded an investigation into possible criminal charges against Judge Chargin on the grounds of violating Section 401 of the Penal Code which states, "Every person who deliberately aids, or advises, or encourages another to commit suicide, is guilty of a felony." The California attorney general's office refused because the judge "lacked" the necessary criminal intent to actually encourage suicide.[26]

Judge Gerald S. Chargin did not go entirely unscathed; the California Commission on Judicial Qualifications publicly censured him in the summer of 1970, but he remained on the bench. On Tuesday, June 6, 1972, the people of Santa Clara Valley re-elected this eloquent official to another term.[27] Chargin's views may have been extreme, but they were not unimportant. The national G.I. Forum newspaper constantly reminded its readers of the Chargin incident and still will not allow the memory to fade.

Vietnam

The Chargin affair underlined a basic contention of the Chicano movement. Mexican Americans could not and should not expect equal opportunity of fair play within the traditional American society. Radical solutions posed the only viable answer. Mexican Americans must cease their attempts to penetrate the established system by its terms and develop Chicano systems by Chicano definition. (For example, the emphasis on the Indian heritage and the use of the word "Chicano" were ethnic initiatives apart from Anglo stereotypes.) From the early perspective of the Chicano ideology, groups such as LULAC and the G.I. Forum pursued naive and even cooptative programs.

This criticism stung. By denouncing the results of a protracted and debilitating struggle, Chicano leaders alienated many of the established

Mexican American organizations. By identifying LULAC and the G.I. Forum as identical in their nature and activities, the Chicano analysis displayed its own misconception of history and added to the discontent of both factions. However, the Chicano movement was way ahead on a very important issue - Vietnam.

As mentioned, the national G.I. Forum endorsed the foreign policy of post-war America. The righteousness of the holy crusade and its child, the Cold War, were not challenged. Most Mexican Americans of that era did not relate to or accept the idea that social revolution did not have to embrace the American way. As more nations chose other alternatives, so did the options of American policy lessen precisely because the original analysis of communist or Soviet Union goals never changed. The ultimate flow and results of this attitude were revealed in Southeast Asia.

As "good" Americans and loyal democrats, Forumeers supported the Vietnam policy through the late sixties. Those who called themselves Chicanos, did not. In repudiating the values of the dominant culture, they could also question the extension of those views to other people. In defining their own identity and by focusing on the denial of such by American institutions, recognition of that right for others was a logical step. Exploitation and oppression of Chicanos was linked to similar results for the Third World.

As dissent and protest against the war increased, most of the Forum leadership did not participate. They did not ignore the alarming death rate of Spanish-surnamed soldiers nor the overrepresentation of Mexican American draftees in the service and in Vietnam. However, the same situation existed during World War II, but the leap in understanding necessary to separate the conflict in Vietnam from a war against Hitler was not made. The lack of such experience by young Chicanos eliminated that problem. Their widespread participation in the demonstrations only widened the gap between the Forum and themselves.

The opinion within the G.I. Forum did alter. In June 1970, the California organization reversed its own endorsement and passed a unanimous resolution opposing the "immoral and undeclared war in Vietnam".[28]

The Forum newspaper, *The Forumeer*, edged away from the national position and published other views, including outright opposition. This change reflected the overall frustration experienced by most Americans as Nixon violated his campaign promise and failed to end the conflict. Nixon expanded the war to Cambodia, and the subsequent outrage expressed by many groups who had not questioned previous policy included Forum chapters. In addition, many Forumeers saw the Vietnam debate undermining social programs.

The anti-Vietnam sentiment also demonstrated the influence of the Chicano movement. Again the Forum newspaper and particularly its editor, David Sierra, promoted the new emphasis on ethnic identity and reassessment of the Mexican American in the society. The editorials of the late 1960s and 1970s incorporated the "language" of Chicanismo. Many Forumeers began calling themselves "Chicanos". As evidenced by the support of Forum chapters for the school boycotts, the anti-media campaign, and the Chargin indictment, Forumeers and "Chicanos" could walk together. More of the antagonism was removed as the two groups began talking the same language.[29] As with many traditional attitudes, the trauma of Vietnam produced evolvement in social perspective. The American G.I. Forum shared that experience.

Part 3 - "The New Nixon"

The G.I. Forum continued to press for economic, political, and other civil rights, and its relationship with the executive branch of the federal government changed dramatically. While Madison Avenue, corporations, or even some federal courts could be moved by boycotts, publicity, or facts, Richard M. Nixon, the occupant of the White House from 1969 to August 1974, was unmoved by any pressure other than his own perceived necessity to be re-elected. Consequently, the communication between the Forum and the White House, which at least remained operative from 1961 through 1968, did not flourish with the Republican executive.

President Nixon replaced Vicente Ximenes as Director of the Inter-Agency Committee with Martin G. Castillo and did not reconfirm Dr. Garcia's appointment to the Civil Rights Commission; Nixon did tell Castillo that he expected results from the Committee for the Spanish-speaking. The chairman seemed to take the President at his word when he blasted federal disregard of Mexican American problems, pointing out that after the 1965 Watts riots, the government spent $400 million, yet East Los Angeles, possibly the worst economically depressed barrio in the nation, received only $7.5 million. Castillo also helped process desegregation suits on behalf of Texas Chicanos against twelve state school districts. The Nixon mandate obviously did not include that sort of aid, as Castillo was dismissed from his post.[30] The name of the agency was also changed to the Cabinet Committee on Opportunities for Spanish-Speaking and Henry Ramirez assumed the directorship.[31]

The new name did not signal new policies. In April 1971, a United States Civil Service Commission conference was held ostensibly for improving opportunities of minorities in acquiring civil service jobs. Seventeen Mexican American organizations were not allowed to participate; when the California G.I. Forum treasurer (acting as spokesman for the groups) asked the president to invite them, he was told that the conference was internal, therefore, "outsiders" were not needed — Nixon himself did not reply.

Possibly the president felt uneasy talking with Mexican Americans. In November 1971, he also refused to meet with a delegation of one hundred Chicanos led by California G.I. Forum chairman Antonio Gallegos and LULAC Chairman Frank Galez, who presented a petition to Alexander Butterfield calling for population parity employment of Spanish-speaking Americans in the federal government. Nixon read the petition, ordered it given to Ramirez, and instructed Butterfield to tell the visitors goodbye. Nixon later refused to allow Ramirez to testify on the educational problems of the Spanish-speaking before the Civil Rights Oversight Committee. (Ramirez had been responsible for the report by the U.S. Commission on Civil Rights of Mexican Americans in the Southwest.) But *G.I. Forum News Bulletin* editor, David Sierra, predicted a better reaction from the president around election time.[32]

During the 1972 campaign, Mr. Nixon did indeed make overtures to the Spanish-speaking. He proclaimed National Hispanic Heritage Week on September 16, dispatched his "Hispano" appointees with promises of federal funds for votes and generally irritated most of those Mexican Americans who had been fighting for just such political recognition for twenty-four years. In an interview, Henry Ramirez said that minimal Mexican American support of the president would signal an end to White House concessions.[33]

The Democratic Party, operating with transparent motives, produced its own report, written by a former official of the Southwest Council of La Raza. The Democrats pointed out that the Nixon Administration had, in fact, vetoed federal funds for education, supported the agricultural interests against UFWO, and refused to properly administer the food stamp program to, among others, migrant workers. It also did not fund bilingual education programs already established by Congress. Many rumors (confirmed in the Watergate hearings) circulated that the Nixon campaign fund had given money to the La Raza Unida Party in Texas to undercut the traditional Mexican American support enjoyed by that state's Democratic Party.[34] In one of the most ludicrous moments of the campaign, Anne Armstrong, the wife of a Texas Republican rancher and liaison between Nixon and Spanish-speaking Americans, replied to a question about her qualifications for the position, "You do not have to be 18 to speak for the 18-year-olds."[35] It would certainly help to have been eighteen, and in this euphemistic context, Mexican Americans felt Mrs. Armstrong was lacking.

After Nixon's re-election, he promptly cleaned house of many of the

"Hispano" appointments in his administration. Funds dried up and many Mexican Americans who campaigned for the president were distressed by the cooling of Nixon's attitude toward Latinos.[36] Many people had cooled off to Richard Nixon by the end of the Watergate affair.

Part 4 - Independence

The American G.I. Forum is now active in twenty-eight states and Washington, D.C. The same basic drives and motivations that gave so much momentum to the original 1948 Corpus Christi chapter continue to push the many local, state, and national members to fight for the progress of all Mexican American people. Naturally, many things have changed. The political climate is much more conducive to participation by *Mexicanos* both as office holders and activists; the economic situation is better than in 1948, as is educational attainment. These facts should not obscure the reality of the gap between Anglo progress in these areas and Mexican American status, but neither should any observer fail to notice that status.

An almost incalculable contribution had been made by those men and women who chose to do something in 1948; more and more members have continued those traditions. That tradition has become a reliance on the resources and abilities of Mexican Americans themselves. This learned and developed confidence has not come easy, but it is so obviously present. An article on a local chapter in the February 1975 edition of *The Forumeer* best demonstrates this self-belief and its value. Writing about the Witchita Falls, Texas, G.I. Forum, David Sierra discusses the work of this very active unit in developing information and research in order to successfully obtain federal funds for a very needy area:

> Wichita Falls G.I. Forum has demonstrated that G.I. Forum chapters need not wait for "city fathers" to identify "their" needs. They have taken the bull by the horns, so to speak, done the demographic studies, compiled the facts and figures, identified the needs of their own people, and challenged the perspective city, state, and federal agencies to do their duty. They are encouraging Chicanos to learn to organize themselves, to interpret the laws and guidelines of federally funded programs and to avail themselves of services provided by their government. In the near future the American G.I. Forum of Wichita Falls hopes to involve itself in still more endeavors aiding the disadvantaged and undereducated people of their community.[37]

CHAPTER XII

The American G.I. Forum

Twenty years ago discussion or description of American society focused on the fundamental role of the white middle class. The history of the United States was conceived, in the popular view and by the most well-known historians, as a narrative and analysis of that particular segment. Many topics might be included, such as business history colonial history, Western, diplomatic, political, and so forth. Any inclusion of "other" peoples was either romanticized, as in the depiction of immigrant assimilation, the American Indian, and slavery, or simplistically mentioned "as a passing thought." The suggestion that Mexicans and Mexican Americans might have made some contribution would have received a quizzical and probably patronizing reply. The consensus was intact and the American Dream a reality postured to the world.

This rationalization was shattered by two major events, the black civil rights movement of the late 1950s and the Vietnam debacle, which posed many questions to the "Stars and Stripes" mentality. By the end of the 1960s the consensus had suffered mortal wounds. Those pioneers who had never accepted the "one for all and all for one" vision received new attention. Their work inspired inquiry from a very different perspective. Revisionist histories which not only incorporated other groups but actually focused on American history as a collection of separate but integrated developments involving all of the American people, began to challenge accepted notions. The most obvious results in educational tools were the black history chapters included in the textbooks and a new analysis of the immigrant experience.

Unfortunately, this new direction produced its own limitations. Most of the historians and other researchers who "revealed" these realities did not reach past the black-white axis. They did not proceed with the logic of their own conclusions. Satisfied with a more fair interpretation of (to them) the major racial and cultural components of American society, they did not grasp that other peoples and cultures might have undergone experiences that were as significant and important as the black experience.

The Chicano movement of the 1960s might have altered that perception. When Cesar Chavez and the farm workers' struggle acquired fame and notoriety, here was the opportunity to link that movement with Mexican American history. It did not happen. Chavez and his campaign were not analyzed as a product of Chicano or Mexican American history but as *the* history. As incredible as it sounds, those historians who were able to benefit from the Montgomery to Selma revelations and connect them to Black history could not enact similar hypotheses and methodologies with the Chicano movement. Certainly the fact of slavery, the Civil War, Reconstruction, and twentieth-century developments did create a sense of the black experience, however distorted it might be, and thus make that re-interpretation more possible. But, just as certain, the myopia of the new school, whether the historian was black or white, prevented such revisionism in regard to Mexican Americans. The lack of signposts was not a sufficient excuse.

Fortunately, Chicanos "discovered" their own history. Research stimulated by the events of the 1960's produced many studies on the participation of Americans of Mexican descent in American society and the struggles compelled by the controlling factors. As with black history, there were the pioneers such as George I. Sanchez, Carlos Casteñada, and Ernesto Galarza. There were those who then worked from such material to create a body of Chicano literature. But, again, limitations essentially constructed themselves. The influence of the 1960s, Chicanismo, affected the first studies of that era. Chicanos sought their past from the model of the present; the more popular areas of investigation such as immigration, agriculture, and discrimination and the conclusions drawn from those efforts underlined the dynamic history of Mexican Americans. Cultural heritage described the brilliance of Mexican thought and the constant confrontation with Anglo society. Many Chicano historians, or at least writers, compared "Chicanos" with Mexican Americans and concluded that the second generation of the twentieth-century immigration demonstrated lack of initiative and ability to meet the demands of North American life. The most extreme, but also indicative, of the early "Chicano" studies is Manuel Serwin's *An Awakened Minority: The Mexican-Americans.*

> Coming from a culture that did not prize mass education finding it necessary to put even his elementary school-age children to work and perhaps feeling frustrated that an education would not help him overcome the prejudices and disdainful treatment he received throughout the Southwest, the Mexican failed drastically to take advantage of the educational opportunities opened to him.

Serwin summarized his "analysis" of the post-war generation with an unequivocal statement.

Whatever the causes of the lack of achievement may be, the basic fact of nonachievement cannot be denied. Perhaps it has been partially due to racial prejudice, perhaps to a general lessening of acquisitiveness among all North Americans, or to the decline in drive that is generally found among the children of immigrants. There is no doubt in my mind, however, that there was some truth in Hans Zinsser's autobiography (which I read as a twenty-year old) when he stated, "Give the Mexican a good home diet, cheaper beer, and tons of soap and flea powder, and we shall have a great, tranquil, and friendly neighbor". Perhaps this is what happened to the Mexican American. He was happy. He was isolated and insulated. But he is changing. He had seen the Negro advance and surpass him. And he is seeing his blood-brothers in Mexico recognized and respected. Thus he sees that his Mexican-American culture has failed to give him the drive for such recognition and success. He is becoming aware of his status; he is developing leaders, particularly in the labor field; and he is receiving help from his former tormentors—the North Americans.[1]

More astute works of this period have still relegated the political and organizational efforts by the post-war generation as less than significant. While at least identifying the American G.I. Forum as important, they (for example, Rodolfo Acuña's *Occupied America: The Chicano Struggle Toward Liberation* (1972)) still described the Chicano movement and its ideology as an escape from the assimilative, middle-class, and piecemeal road taken by the post-war groups. Consequently, the organizations such as La Raza Unida offered the only viable approach to the needs of Mexican Americans. Acuña's second edition of *Occupied America* (1980) contains much more pertinent information about the Forum and its activities of the 1950s. His source is the *G.I. Forum News Bulletin*.

The political analysis of the later 1970s has recognized the flaws of these conclusions, or more correctly, presumptions.

That history has undergone more concentrated and less emotional scrutiny in the last few years. One of the most thoughtful presentations has been the application of the concept of internal colonialism to explain the Chicano experience. Mario Barrera's thesis that Chicanos have been an internally colonized people points to the frustrating progress and seeming powerlessness of Chicanos. But, in their analysis of Chicano political development, Chris Garcia and Rudolph de la Garza compare the pluralist, elitist, and internal colonism models as applied to Chicanos.[2] They believe that no one theory sufficiently accounts for that development. They most particularly feel that internal colonialism cannot rationalize the accomplishments of Chicano people, although they do promote that thesis as an historical answer to the Chicano position "assigned" by white America. The history of the American G.I. Forum offers its own insights to this debate.

The experience of the American G.I. Forum clearly negates the shallow theory of the non-achieving, post-war generation. If that was the only accomplishment of the Forum, that is to demonstrate a pattern of positive activism, it would still be a valuable contribution. However, the significance is much more. The G.I. Forum represents the growth of Chicano society in the ability to confront and affect the issues most important to Mexican American people. In addition, the values and programs of the Forum were much different than its predecessors, and provided a transition to the Chicano movement of the late 1960s.

If we adopt Alfredo Cuellar's historical model of Chicano political development, the position and role of the G.I. Forum becomes more evident.[3] As the period of conflict (the nineteenth century) ended, conventional political activity began. The pre-World War II era of adoption and assimilation saw LULAC emerge as the most important organization. Operating during a time of hostility and economic crisis (repatriation and depression), the group conducted its programs and articulated its position in as inoffensive a manner as possible (the word "Latin" circumvented the racial and cultural connotations of "Mexican"). As the first organization to attempt a more inclusive representation of Mexican American needs, LULAC was important. On the other hand, LULAC conspiciously identified with and labeled itself as assimiliative, middle-class Americans. It embraced the melting-pot concept, even as Chicanos were being excluded from that design. At the same time, by overtly eliminating most of the Mexican and Mexican American community from membership, the organization formalized the conditions of mainstreaming as defined by Anglo society. "By accepting the Anglo view of themselves, LULAC members perhaps legitimized to both Mexican Americans and Anglos the racist stereotypes used to justify the oppression and discrimination suffered by the majority of Mexican Americans."[4]

The post-war generation introduced a new assertiveness and a more critical awareness of American society. Reflecting their wartime experience and urbanization, Mexican American groups pursued more aggressive strategies. The most important new organization was the G.I. Forum. Rejecting the LULAC philosophy, the membership openly challenged the dominant institutions and their own stereotyped presumptions about Mexican Americans.

The structure of the Forum fulfilled the five basic requirements or characteristics set out in David Tirado's analysis of community political organizations. As a multi-functional group, the Forum provided benefits, social needs, and activist programs that involved all members; at the same time, the Forum leadership depended on family involvement, although to some degree the auxiliary chapters also perpetuated gender separation. Loyalties to the organization and family prevented the clash of priorities that often dissembled the group capacity to operate. The single-issue crisis approach detailed by Tirado explained the genesis of the Forum with a qualification: the issue was veterans' benefits and not the Longoria incident as reported by most Chicano historians. The fact is significant in that the G.I. Forum had already demonstrated organizational success before the more critical Longoria test.

The remaining factors involved in Tirado's assessment of successful community organization were also a part of Forum success. Hector Garcia was "the type of leader best suited for promoting organizational longevity and vitality", as he acted "with a magnetic personality who (recognized) the need for developing a consensus of opinion among the membership before acting."[5] However, the Forum was also able to distribute and decentralize leadership as a mainstay against dictatorial cultism. Finally, the G.I. Forum employed ethnic symbolism at the grass-roots level to attract membership. The Longoria affair, the Colorado flag incident, and the support for migrant workers are only a few examples. As Tirado pointed out:

> The G.I. Forum's period of greatest success promoting political reform and social action benefiting the Mexican American community was during the 1950's, at a time when other groups timidly shrank from adopting an activist posture for fear of being called Communist. This unique role of the G.I. Forum during the 1950's was made possible by its leaders' skillful manipulation of patriotic symbols and their veteran status to combat accusations that the organization was advocating leftist programs. Although the organization is now criticized by some for being too status quo oriented, the G.I. Forum's effective use of opposition to the importation of agricultural laborers assured the existence of at least one organization committed to protecting the rights of Mexican American citizens during these tense years.[6]

In their own struggle, the G.I. Forum went far beyond the external and self-imposed barriers of the LULAC concept. Mexican Americans affirmed their identity - the Forum worked as Mexican Americans for all Mexican Americans. In so doing, it anticipated the fourth phase of Cuellar's model, the radicalization of Chicano politics, more commonly known as the Movement.

The radicalization was, in part, prefaced by the more overtly political groups such as PASSO and MAPA (Mexican American Political Association). Their failure to expand beyond the local or regional locale does not undermine the significance of the shift toward more concrete politicalization. But the Chicano movement truly promoted the ideology of nationalism, ethnic integrity, and the repudiation of the pluralist society. The revolutionary phase of the late sixties and early seventies was a reaction to the societal position of Mexican Americans but also represented the schisms of the Vietnam era. Thus, the movement more easily rejected the notions of the American system as fundamentally

160

open to all Americans if only education and organization sufficiently represented the rightness of that participation. Only by creating a counter-system, that is by constructing a Chicano society and nation independent of the Anglo restraints, could Chicanos be free and able to define their own lives.

Apart from the somewhat facile interpretation, the Movement did pose a valuable and timely challenge to the pluralist idea inherent in Forum strategy. Especially relevant examples included the two-party structure as unresponsive to Chicano needs, their attitude toward undocumented workers as cooptation, and the participation in federal programs as tokenism by paternalist manipulation. Unfortunately, but perhaps inevitably, a clash developed as the two "sides" acted on the same issues, but from different perspectives. The Chicano movement "shocked" many of the more established organizations and acquired much unfair criticism and even condemnation, particularly from Congressman Henry Gonzalez. In turn, Chicanos reacted with all-inclusive damnation of the "establishment"; Tio Taco became a favorite expression and was aimed at groups such as the G.I. Forum.

Acuña addresses that point (perhaps unintentionally) when he describes the 1966 EEOC walkout as significant because "most of the delegates were established professionals and were not accustomed to such assertive action".[7] The leader of that walkout was the national chairman of the American G.I. Forum and had been a member of the Forum for several years. He and the organization certainly thought they were assertive when protesting police brutality, organizing and participating in poll-tax drives against formidable opposition, and generally implementing Forum programs. Indeed, comparing the EEOC affair with the Felix Longoria investigation does not compliment the former if "assertiveness" is the qualitative criterion. But the EEOC walkout was directed toward the federal government and quite new for Mexican American tactics, and that is precisely the difference. The actions of the "established professionals" was a predictable and logical extension of the historic pattern of the organizations in which these individuals were trained and experienced; but they did not see it as radical; the new militants saw it as a step in that direction.

Related to this type of controversy was the perception of leadership. The leaders and ideologies of the movement questioned the nature of "middle-class" leaders in a struggle that, for them, basically concerned the lower economic classes. Their main objection seemed to be with the LULAC-type elitism; the G.I. Forum became identified with that philosophy. Forum leadership and many members had certainly improved their economic condition by the 1960s. But they had not abandoned the original motivations and directions of the 1940s. Confusion and ignorance of organization histories and development obscured the difference between LULAC and Forum policies; economic position was identified with societal views. The ethnic symbolisms of the Movement too often included simplistic rejection of groups which otherwise still directed their efforts for *Mexicanos* as a total ethnic entity. As Ralph Guzaran indicated:

> How can we ask our children to be proud of being terribly poor?. . .
> Unless Mexican Americans themselves clearly distinguish between ethnicity and social class, a Mexican American youngster might well be ostracized by some peers when he tries to live the life of a middle-class Mexican. As matters stand now, far too often the feeling is that any Mexican American individual who tries to be middle-class in his style of life is "not a true Chicano".[8]

As Chicanos faced the conservative retrenchment of the 1970s these types of obstacles and antagonisms became less diverting. The Movement's ideology became less flamboyant and more conservative. For example, the La Raza Unida experiment as a national party could not overcome the very problems that had limited the expansion of MAPA and PASSO. Cultism developed in some of the locales with the more famous personalities such as Corky Gonzales. The lack of population concentration severely undermined the national concept. In turn, post-war groups such as the G.I. Forum recognized the profound contributions of the Movement, particularly in terms of its ethnic advocacy and the enhanced political consciousness produced by its activities. As indicated in Chapter XI, both groups worked together on many fronts. The post-war and 1960s generation began to see their experience as a positive and on-going part of a total Chicano history.

Certainly the members of the G.I. Forum understood what they were up against in 1948 and the succeeding years. They did not envision radical or revolutionary change as a solution, but neither did they underestimate the racist and institutional resistance of Anglo society toward *any* alteration of the status quo. The methodology of the Forum formulated into a pragmatism born out of a period of unrestrained racism and dogmatic refusal to admit the existence of other people with the same rights and abilities white America took for granted.

The American G.I. Forum denied the subordinate status consigned by Anglo America. Its philosophy and values were translated into a militant espousal for equal opportunity, a position not acceptable to the socio-economic status quo of the post-war era. This militancy was qualified by the experiences of the post-war Mexican American generation; that experience moved Mexican American alternatives and options far beyond the general organizational goals of the immigrant societies of the early twentieth century and the LULAC endeavors of the 1930s and 1940s. It was compatible with the "ideal" concept of American society - equal opportunity for all and did not consider the possibility that certain groups, minorities, or classes, by definition, would never receive that equality. But if the Forum saw the American Dream as an attainable goal, it did not surrender its advocacy of Mexican Americans as deserving of that goal by their own cultural integrity. Their real accomplishments cannot be negated as cooptation or colonial concessions.

The synthesis and growth of Chicano and Mexican American society is predicated on its ability to deal with the American structure. That ability must be channeled into the creation of a more meaningful and higher quality life for Chicano people. Many options and ideas have developed from the internal drive toward such a reality. Assimilation to revolution includes a fairly broad spectrum. Improvement in the material conditions coupled with dynamic restructure of the manner in which Chicanos viewed themselves have been more than significant. That progress has come from the determination and will of many individuals and manifested in many organizations. The American G.I. Forum stands as one of the most important. Its members demonstrated an integrity, dignity, and strength that met the challenge and seized an opportunity at a critical moment in Chicano history. Their lives and their experience changed their society; the history of their organization is eloquent testimony that Chicano people will not be denied.

Notes

I. *Land of the Free, Home of the Brave*

[1] Arthur Whitaker, *The Spanish-American Frontier, 1783-1795* (New York: Houghton Mifflin Co., 1927).

[2] Hugh Thomas, *Cuba: The Pursuit of Freedom* (New York: Harper & Row, 1971), p. 104.

[3] Albert Weinberg, *Manifest Destiny* (Chicago: Quandrangle, 1935).

[4] Walt Whitman, "The Mexican War Justified", "Annexation", in *The Mexican War: Crisis for American Diplomacy*, ed. Archie McDonald (Lexington: D.C. Heath & Co., 1969), p. 47.

[5] Julian Samora, José Bernal, and Albert Peña, *Gunpowder Justice: A Reassessment of the Texas Rangers* (Notre Dame: University of Notre Dame Press, 1979), p. 30.

[6] "All the Rights of Citizens", in *Foreigners in Their Native Land: Historical Roots of the Mexican Americans,* ed. David J. Weber (Albuquerque: University of New Mexico Press, 1973), pp. 162-168.

[7] "Occupation of Mexico", *The United States Magazine and Democratic Review* XXI (November 1847): 381-383, 388-390.

[8] Rodolfo Acuña, *Occupied America: The Chicano Struggle for Liberation* (San Francisco: Canfield Press, 1972), Chapters 2-5.

[9] Robert J. Rosenbaum, "Las Gorras Blancas of San Miguel County, 1884-1890", in *Chicano: The Evolution of a People,* ed. Renato Rosaldo, Robert Calvert, and Gustau L. Seligmann (San Francisco: Rinehart Press, 1973), pp. 128-133.

[10] David J. Weber, "Scare More than Apes: Historical Roots of Anglo-American Stereotypes of Mexicans", in *New Spain's Far Northern Frontier: Essays on Spain in the American West, 1540-1821,* ed. David J. Weber (Albuquerque: University of New Mexico Press, 1979), pp. 293-307.

[11] Carey McWilliams, *Factories in the Fields* (Boston: Little, Brown & Co., 1934).

[12] Charles Cumberland, *Mexico: The Struggle for Modernity* (New York: Oxford University Press, 1968), Chapters 8-9.

[13] George Coalson, "Mexican Contract Labor in American Agriculture", *Southwestern Social Science Quarterly* 33 (Dec. 1952): 229. Mexico was also exempted from the 1921, 1924 national immigration acts. O.M. Scruggs, "Texas and the Bracero Program", *Pacific Historical Review* 32 (August 1963): 251-264.

[14] Mark Reisler, *By the Sweat of Their Brow: Mexican Immigrant Labor in the United States, 1900-1940* (Westport: Greenwood Press, 1976), Chapter 2.

[15] Census data of this period are inaccurate in terms of actual numbers, but the trends or patterns of increase are demonstrable.

[16] Mexican and Mexican American workers attempted to copy their successful counterparts in Mexico; they were more successful in isolated occupations such as Western mining. In the agricultural regions of the Southwest opponents used the anti-foreign and anti-socialist argument to break the unions.

164

[17] Ernesto Galarza, *Farm Workers and Agri-business in California, 1947-1960* (Notre Dame: University of Notre Dame Press, 1977). An important analysis of the inner dynamics of agri-business and the effect on farm workers.

[18] This situation also existed for Puerto Rican immigrants on the East Coast.

[19] Irving G. Hendrick, "Early Schooling for Children of Migrant Farmworkers in California: The 1920's, *Aztlan: International Journal of Chicano Studies Research* 8 (Spring and Summer 1977): 11-26.

[20] One textbook used in Texas in the 1930s and 1940s was in the form of drawings and captions. Anglo Americans were clean-cut, tall, and obviously liberty-loving, God-fearing folks. Mexicans were drawn as short, fat, snarling, or cringing villains. "Greaser", "Pepper-belly" permeate the dialog.

[21] Reisler, *By the Sweat of Their Brow.*

[22] Ibid; Acuña, *Occupied America.*

[23] Abraham Hoffman, *Unwanted Mexican Americans in the Great Depression: Repatriation Pressures, 1929-1939,* (Tucson: University of Arizona Press, 1974).

[24] Reisler, *By the Sweat of Their Brow.*

[25] Hoffman, *Unwanted Mexican Americans,* p. 18.

[26] Manuel Gamio, *Mexican Immigration to the United States: A Study of Human Migration and Adjustment* (New York: Dover Pub. Inc., 1971), pp. 111-118.

II. *World War, Texas*

[1] Richard Polenberg, *War and Society: The United States 1941-1945* (New York: J.B. Lippincott Company, 1972).

[2] See The Atlantic Charter.

[3] Polenberg, *War and Society.*

[4] Paul R. Ehrlich, *The Golden Door: International Migration, Mexico, and the United States* (New York: Ballantine Books, 1979), p. 221.

[5] Paul Morin, *Among the Valiant: Mexican Americans in World War II and Korea* (Los Angeles: Bottden Publishing Company, 1963).

[6] Polenberg, *War and Society,* pp. 117-118.

[7] Carey McWilliams, *North From Mexico* (Westport: Greenwood Publishing Company, 1968), Chapters 10-11.

[8] Rex Crawford, "The Latin Americans in Wartime United States", *Annals of the American Academy of Political and Social Science* (Sept. 1942): 127.

[9] Luis Navarro Garcia, "The North of New Spain as a Political Problem in the Eighteenth Century", in *New Spain's Far Northern Frontier: Essays on Spain in the American West, 1540-1821,* ed. Weber, pp. 201-216.

[10] Alexander DeConde, *A History of American Foreign Policy* (New York: Charles Scribner's Sons, 1971), p. 128.

[11] Ibid., pp. 178-179.

[12] Rupert Richardson, *Texas, the Lone Star State* (New Jersey: Prentice Hall, 1963), pp. 50-51.

[13] Ibid., p. 71; DeConde, *American Foreign Policy,* p. 180.

[14] Ibid., p. 181.

[15] Weber, *Foreigners in Their Native Land,* pp. 101-104.

[16] Richardson, *Texas,* p. 98; the author states that the carnage need not be described.

[17] Leo Grebler, Ralph Gusman and Joanne Moore, *The Mexican American People* (New York: Free Press, 1970), p. 43.

[18] Richardson, *Texas.*

[19] John Garraty, *The American Nation,* pp. 470-482.

[20] Lyle Saunders, " The Social History..."; McWilliams, *North From Mexico,* Chapter 8.

[21] John Womack, "The Chicanos", *New York Review,* August 31, 1972, pp. 12-24.

[22] Gamio, *Mexican Immigration,* p. 30; Matt Meir and Feliciano Rivera, *The Chicanos: A History of Mexican Americans* (New York: Hill and Wang, 1972), p. 136.

[23] U.S. Bureau of the Census, *U.S. Census of Population,* 1950, Vol. 2, Part 3, Persons of Spanish Surname and General Characteristics for Selected States (Wash., D.C., 1955).

[24] Ibid.

[25] Ibid, Table 87. Another study of family income showed annual earnings for average Mexican American families of six at less than $2,250, whereas Anglo families of four had an average income of $5,000, *A Comparison of Family Income and Expenditures for Five Principal Budget Items in Twenty Texas Cities* (Austin: University of Texas Bureau of Business Research, 1943).

[26] Walter Fogel, *Mexican Americans in the Southwest Labor Markets. Advance Report No. 10 Mexican American Study Project,* (Los Angeles: University of California, 1967), p. 51.

[27] Harley Browning and Dale Mclemore, *A Statistical Profile of the Spanish Surname Population of Texas,* (Austin: Population Research Center, University of Texas, 1964), Table 19, p. 36.

[28] Fogel, *Southwest Labor,* p. 72.

[29] Arthur Amber, *The Work and Welfare of Children of Agricultural Laborers in Hidalgo County, Texas* (Washington, D.C.: U.S. Department of Labor, 1943), pp. 14-15.

[30] Herbert Northrup, "Race Discrimination in Trade Unions: The Record and Outlook," *Commentary,* Aug. 1946, p. 128; Carlos Casteneda, "Some Facts on Our Racial Minority," *The Pan American,* John Burma, *Spanish-Speaking Groups in the United States (Salem:* Duke University Press, 1945), p. 70.

[31] Harold Shapiro, "The Pecan Shellers of San Antonio, Texas," *Southwestern Social Science Quarterly* 32 (Mar. 1952): 230.

[32] Ibid.

[33] Sheldon Menefee and Orin Cassmore, *The Pecan Shellers of San Antonio* (Washington, D.C.: U.S. Govt. Printing Office, 1940), p. xvii.

[34] Shapiro, "The Pecan Shellers", pp. 232-237.

[35] Ibid.

[36] Forest Crain, "The Occupational Distribution of Spanish-Name People in Austin, Texas", masters thesis, University of Texas, 1948; Frederic Meyers, *Spanish-Name Persons in the Labor Force in Manufacturing Industry in Texas* (Austin: University of Texas, 1951), p. 23.

[37] Herschel Manuel, "The Mexican Population of Texas," *Southwestern Political and Social Science Quarterly* (June 1934): 47.

[38] Wilson Little, *Spanish-Speaking Children in Texas* (Austin: University of Texas, 1944), p. 64.

[39] Ruth Connor, "Same Community, Home and School Problems of Latin American Children in Austin, Texas", master's thesis, University of Texas, 1949, p. 19.

[40] Ruth Ann Fogartie, "Spanish-Name People in Texas with Special Emphasis on Those Who Are Students in Texas Colleges and Universities", master's thesis, University of Texas, 1948, p. 75.

[41] Walter Fogel, *Education and Income of Mexican Americans in the Southwest,* Mexican American Study Project, Advance Report I (Los Angeles: University of California, 1965), Table 5, p. 8; Allan Beegle et al., "Demographic Characteristics of the U.S.-Mexican Border," *Rural Sociology* 25 (March 1960); *U.S. Census of Population 1950,* PE no. 3c Tables 8 and 9, vol. 2, parts 3, 5, 6, 31, 43, Table 42, *County and City Data Book,* Table 2, Item 28 and Table 3, Item 20 in Joan Moore, *Mexican Americans,* (New Jersey: Prentice Hall, 1970).

[42] Pauline Kibbe, *Latin Americans in Texas* (Albuquerque: University of New Mexico Press. 1946), p. 126.

[43] Frances Woods, "Mexican Ethnic Leadership in San Antonio" PH.d. dissertation, Catholic University of America, 1949, p. 29.

[44] Kibbe, *Latin Americans,* pp. 131-132.

[45] Ibid.

[46] Eugene Richards, "Attitudes of White College Students in the Southwest Toward Ethnic Groups in the United States," *Sociology and Social Research,* 35 (September 1950): 22-30; Ozzie G. Simmons, "The Mutual Images and Expectations of Anglo Americans and Mexican Americans", in *Chicanos: Social and Psychological Perspectives* ed. Marsha Hang and Nathaniel Wagner (St. Louis: C.V. Mosby Company, 1971), pp. 63-65; Pat Walters, *The South and the Nation* (New York: Vintage, 1969), p. 24.

[47] Paul Taylor, "Mexicans North of the Rio Grande," *Survey Graphic* 56, no. 3, (May 1, 1931).

[48] Burma, *Spanish-Speaking Groups,* p. 109.

[49] Interview with Dr. Hector Garcia, January 10, 1975; Jack Dodson, "Minority Group Housing in Two Texas Cities, "in *Studies in Housing and Minority Groups: Special Research Paper to the Commission on Race and Housing,* ed. Nathen Glazer and Davis McEntire (Los Angeles: University of California Press, 1960), pp. 95-97; Burma, *Spanish-Speaking Groups* p. 109.

[50] Jorge Rangel and Carlos Alcala, "Project Report: De Jure Segregation of Chicanos in Texas Schools." *Harvard Civil Rights—Civil Liberties Law Review,* Vol. 7, No. 2, (Mar.

1972), p. 312. This essay on de jure segregation is the definitive statement on Chicano school segregation in Texas.

[51] Ibid, pp. 313-314.

[52] Ibid, p. 317. A report of the Texas Educational Survey Commission in 1952 pointed out disproportionate amounts of money were allocated by local officials to "American schools", Ennis Hall Gilbert, "Some Legal Aspects of the Education of Spanish-Speaking Children in Texas", master's thesis, University of Texas, 1947. Another device used by local officials concerned school attendance. In the 1947-1948 school year, the state used census enumeration to allow money to counties. Those with *low* school attendence received more per capita in actual funds. Therefore, those counties with high Mexican American scholastic age registration did not enforce their truancy laws; opinion of the attorney general of Texas (April 18, 1947): "Based solely on language deficiencies and other individual needs and aptitudes, the school district may maintain separate classes in separate buildings, if necessary, for any pupils with such deficiencies ,needs, or aptitudes. . . through the first three grades."

[53] Rangel and Alcala, "De Jure", pp. 314-315.

[54] Kibbe, *Latin Americans,* pp. 227-229, 232.

[55] Paul Taylor, *An American Mexican Frontier, Nueces County* (New York: Russell & Russell, 1934); Patricia Morgan, *Shame of a Nation: A Documented Story of Police-State Terror Against Mexican Americans in the U.S.A.* (Los Angeles: L.A. Committee for Protection of the Foreign Born, 1934); Moore, *Mexican Americans,* pp. 91-92; Armando Flores, *Ando Sangrando: A Study of Mexican American Police Conflict* (LaPuente: Perspective Publishing Company, 1972).

[56] Edgar Shelton, *Political Conditions Among Texas Mexicans Along the Rio Grande* (San Francisco: R and E Research Associates, 1974);Lura Rouse, "A Study of the Education of Spanish-Speaking Children in Dimmit County, Texas", master's thesis, University of Texas, 1948, p. 26. As in Nueces County, Mexican Americans were not allowed to participate in direct primaries.

[57] Kibbe, *Latin Americans,* pp. 227-229.

[58] Taylor, *Frontier,* p. 238.

[59] Gamio, *Mexican Immigration,* p. 50.

[60] Robert Cuellar, "A Social and Political History of the Mexican American Population of Texas, 1929—1966, master's thesis, North Texas State University, 1969, p. 21; Edward Garza, "LULAC", master's thesis, Southwest Texas State Teachers College, pp. 5-6, 21.

[61] Taylor, *Frontier,* p. 235.

[62] Cuellar, "A Social and Political History", pp. 12—21.

[63] Shapiro, "Pecan Shellers", p. 233.

[64] Cuellar, "A Social and Political History", p. 21.

III. *Welcome Home*

[1] David Ross, *Preparing for Ulysses: Politics and Veterans During World War II* (New York: Columbia University Press, 1969), p. 3.

[2] Ibid.

[3] "Biography of Dr. Hector P. Garcia, Founder of the American G.I. Forum of the U.S.",HPG files. Throughout the footnotes, "HPG" refers to the archives of the American G.I. Forum, Dr. Hector P. Garcia, Corpus Christi, Texas.

[4] "Interview of Dr. Hector Garcia by David G. McComb," *LBJ Library,* July 9, 1969, HPG.

[5] Gamio, *Mexican Immigration.*

[6] Interview with Dr. Hector Garcia, January 10, 1975.

[7] Oscar Phillips, article submitted to *Reader's Digest* on Dr. Garcia, HPG.

[8] Grebler, Guzman, and Moore *The Mexican American People,* p. 156; Rangel and Alcala, "De Jure".

[9] Phillips, p. 3, HPG.

[10] Ibid.

[11] "Biography of Dr. Garcia", HPG.

[12] Phillips, p. 4, HPG.

[13] Fogel, *Education and Income,* Table 5, p. 8.

[14] Phillips, p. 5, HPG.

[15] Taylor, "Mexicans North of the Rio Grande"; Gilbert, "Some Legal Aspects of Education of Spanish-Speaking Children in Texas", p. 34.

[16] Phillips, pp. 5-7, HPG. "Interview of Dr. Garcia".

[17] *Corpus Christi Caller-Times,* March 1948.

[18] *The Sentinel,* Jan. 2, 1948; copy of a speech given to PTA on health, HPG.

[19] *The Sentinel,* Jan. 30, 1948. Dr. Garcia criticized the school board for failure to appoint a Mexican American as principal of a predominantly Mexican American elementary school; "Report on Mathis Labor Camps", 1948, HPG; Interview with Dr. Garcia, Jan. 10, 1975.

[20] *The Sentinel,* Feb. 27, 1948.

[21] Interview of Dr. Garcia by David McComb, p. 35; Interview with Dr. Garcia, Jan. 10, 1975; "A Brief History of the American G.I. Forum", HPG.

[22] Ross, *Preparing for Ulysses,* pp. 135-137.

[23] Interview with Dr. Garcia; Phillips, p. 9, HPG.

[24] Dr. Garcia to Corpus Christi Veterans of Foreign Wars, April 16, 1948, HPG; *The Sentinel,* April 2, 1948; Phillips, p. 9, HPG.

[25] *The Sentinel,* March 26, 1948, and April 2, 1948; minutes of first G.I. Forum meeting, March 26, 1948 HPG.

[26] Ibid., p. 2.

[27] Ibid; interview with Dr. Garcia; minutes of G.I. Forum meeting, March 26, 1948, p. 2, HPG.

[28] Joe E. Geiger, Manager of Corpus Christi VA office, to Dr. Garcia, March 29, 1948, HPG.

[29] *The Sentinel,* April 23, 1948; interview with Dr. Garcia; Phillips, article, p. 10, HPG.

[30] *The Sentinel,* May 14, 1948.

[31] "A Brief History of the American G.I. Forum", p. 1, HPG.

[32] Ibid, Interview with Dr. Garcia.

[33] *The Sentinel,* June 4, 1948, p. 1; June 11, 1948, p. 1; June 25, 1948, p. 1; July 9, 1948, p. 1; July 16, 1948, p. 1; July 23, 1948, p. 1; July 30, 1948, p. 1; Aug. 20, 1948, p. 1; Sept. 24, 1948, p. 1; Oct. 1, 1948, p. 1; Nov. 5, 1948, p. 1; Nov. 19, 1948, p. 1; "A Brief History of the American G.I. Forum, HPG.

[34] Dr. Garcia to Frank Chapa, July 2, 1948, HPG; Alfredo Moreno to Dr. Garcia, Aug. 20, 1948, HPG; Dr. Garcia to Miguel Coronado, Nov. 24, 1948, HPG, Dr. Garcia to Frank Morales, Nov. 24, 1948, HPG; Dr. Garcia to Henry Zambrano, June 19, 1948, HPG.

[35] Dr. Garcia to Joe Geiger, V.A. Office, June 23, 1948, HPG; Dr. Garcia to Dr. E.N. Jones, President of Texas A & I College, June 23, 1948, HPG.

[36] An obvious deduction from the Fogel tables and Wilson Little's *Spanish-Speaking Children in Texas* which point out the low amount of education and high drop-out rate of Mexican Americans.

[37] Ibid, Interview of Dr. Garcia.

[38] Ibid.

[39] Dr. Garcia to Joe Trevino, President of American G.I. Forum, Raymondville, Texas, June 23, 1948, HPG; Dr. Garcia to Joe Cueva, Robstown, Texas, G.I. Forum, June 23, 1948, HPG; Dr. Garcia to C.E. Perez, President of G.I. Forum, Alice, Texas, June 23, 1948, HPG; Dr. Garcia to Guadalupe Valdez, President of G.I. Forum, Kingsville, Texas, June 23, 1948, HPG; Dr. Garcia to Antonio Nerias, 1948, HPG; American G.I. Forum to the Mayor of Corpus Christi, June 16, 1948, HPG.

[40] Letter to Mayor of Corpus Christi, June 16, 1948, HPG; Dr. Garcia to Maj. Gen. K.L. Berry, Aug. 4, 1948, HPG; G.I. Forum to Senator Tom Connally, June 16, 1948, HPG; Dr. Garcia to President Harry Truman, June 1948, HPG; President Truman to G.I. Forum, July 1948, HPG; Letter from Joe Geiger, Corpus Christi VA office, March 29, 1948, HPG; Maj. Gen. Berry to Raul Cortez, President of LULAC, Box 350, files of Beauford Jester, Texas State Archives.

[41] State Rep. Rogers Kelley to Governor Jester, Box 350, files of Beauford Jester, Texas State Archives; Congressman John Lyle to Dr. Garcia, HPG; *The Sentinel, July 30, 1948.*

IV. *The Felix Longoria Affair*

[1] William C. Berman, *The Politics of Civil Rights in the Truman Administration,* (Columbus, Ohio State University Press, 1970), p. 55.

[2] President's commission on Civil Rights, *To Secure These Rights* (New York: Simon and Schuster, 1947), p. 59.

[3] William E. Smith, County Service Officer, Live Oak County, George West, Texas, to Department of Army, Ft. Worth Quartermaster, American Graves Registration, Dec. 1, 1948, HPG.

[4] Notarized statement of Mrs. Beatrice Longoria, Feb. 9, 1948, HPG; notarized statement

170

of Nurse Gladys Bucher, Feb. 9, 1948, HPG; notarized statement of Dr. Hector P. Garcia, Feb, 9, 1948, HPG.

[5] Interview of Dr. Garcia by David McComb, p. 5, HPG.

[6] Notarized statement of Dr. Garcia, HPG; notarized statement of Mrs. Beatrice Longoria, HPG.

[7] Notarized statement of Gladys Bucher, HPG; notarized statement of Dr. Garcia, HPG.

[8] Notarized statement of George Groh, Feb. 18, 1948, HPG; notarized statement of Dr. Garcia, HPG.

[9] Interview of Dr. Garcia by David McComb, p. 7, HPG.

[10] Dr. Hector Garcia, President of American G.I. Forum, to Senator Johnson, Jan. 10, 1949, HPG.

[11] Announcement of American G.I. Forum printouts in Spanish, Jan. 1, 1948, HPG; notarized statement of George Groh, HPG; *Corpus Christi Caller-Times,* "Funeral Home Action Draws Forum Protest", Jan. 11, 1948; *Corpus Christi Caller-Times,* "Latin Service Discouraged by Rice Funeral Home", Jan. 11, 1948.

[12] J.K. Montgomery, Mayor of Three Rivers, to Dr. H. Garcia President of AGIF, Jan. 11, 1948, HPG.

[13] Price Daniel, Attorney General of Texas, to Dr. Hector Garcia, President of AGIF, Jan. 11, 1948, HPG; Congressman John Lyle to Dr. H. Garcia, Jan. 11, 1949, HPG; Congressman Lloyd Bentsen, Jr., to Dr. Hector Garcia, Jan. 11, 1949.

[14] Senator Rogers Kelley (27th District) to Dr. Hector P. Garcia, President, AGIF, Jan. 11, 1949, HPG.

[15] Governor Beauford Jester to Dr. Hector T. (sic) Garcia, Jan. 14, 1948, HPG.

[16] Phillips, article submitted to *Reader's Digest*, p. 13, HPG.

[17] Senator Lyndon B. Johnson to Dr. Hector P. Garcia, President of AGIF, Jan. 11, 1949, HPG.

[18] *Corpus Christi Caller-Times,* Jan. 12, 1949; Jan. 16, 1949; Jan. 19, 1949.LULAC President Raul Cortez to Dr. Garcia, Jan. 14, 1949, HPG; interview with Dr. Garcia, Jan. 10, 1975. Dr. Garcia felt compelled to issue radio announcements and circulars to discontinue donations because so much was collected, enough to eventually set up a small fund for Felix and Beatrice Longoria's daughter, Adelita.

[19] T.W. Kennedy to Dr. Garcia and Mrs. Longoria, Jan. 12, 1949, HPG; Minority Report on the Longoria Investigation, April 17, 1948; HPG, an incident occurred in 1947 with the father and brother of Felix Longoria and another man. This was the only "trouble" on record. Townspeople "told" Kennedy of trouble with Longoria. Obviously, this excuse was extremely weak, *Corpus Christi Caller-Times,* Jan. 14, 1949 and Jan. 13, 1949.

[20] Notarized statement of Guadalupe Longoria, Feb. 29, 1949, HPG; notarized statement of Sara Moreno, Feb. 18, 1949, HPG; notarized statement of Carolina Longoria, March 7, 1949, HPG; copy of statement drawn up by Three Rivers Chamber of Commerce (unsigned), Jan. 1949, HPG; interview with Dr. Garcia.

[21] Nellie Ward Kingea, *History of the First Ten Years of the Texas Good Neighbor Commission* (Ft. Worth: Texas Christian University Press, 1954).

[22] R.E. Smith of GNC to Dr. Hector P. Garcia, Jan. 17, 1949, HPG; Dr. Garcia to Thomas

Sutherland, Jan. 31, 1949, HPG.

[23] *Three Rivers News,* Jan. 20, 1949, p. 1.

[24] Ibid.

[25] Interview of Dr. Garcia by McComb, p. 8, HPG; Senator LBJ to Dr. Garcia, Feb. 16, 1949, HPG; Secretary of Defense to Dr. Garcia, Jan. 11, 1949, HPG; Longoria family to Senator LBJ, Jan. 15, 1949, HPG; Department of Army to Dr. Garcia, Jan. 20, 1949, HPG; Dr. Garcia to Guadalupe Longoria, Jan. 27, 1949, HPG; Longoria family to Senator Johnson, Jan. 31, 1949, HPG; Dr. Garcia to Senator Johnson, Feb. 8, 1949, HPG; Senator Johnson to Dr. Garcia, Feb. 10, 1949, HPG; Dr. Garcia to Senator Johnson, Feb. 11, 1949, HPG; Senator Johnson to Dr. Garcia, Feb. 14, 1949, HPG; Senator Johnson to Dr. Garcia, Feb. 16, 1949, HPG.

[26] Resolution of American Legion, Post 121, Waco, Texas, Jan. 12, 1949, HPG.

[27] *Detroit Free Press,* "Bigotry in Texas", Jan. 14, 1949.

[28] Inter-office communiqué, Governor Beauford Jester's office, Jan. 24, 1949, Box 387, files of Beauford Jester, Texas State Archives.

[29] Resolution of Bexar County General Council of American Legion, San Antonio, Jan. 27, 1949, HPG.

[30] *Corpus Christi Caller-Times,* Feb. 6, 1949.

[31] *Corpus Christi Caller-Times,* "Reps Vote Inquiry," Feb. 17, 1949, and "Funeral for Longoria", Feb. 18, 1949.

[32] *Corpus Christi Caller-Times,* "Corpus Christi Forum Welcomes State Inquiry," Feb. 18, 1949; *Corpus Christi Caller-Times,* Good Neighbor Groups Head Offers to Resign Post," Feb. 19, 1949.

[33] Interview with Dr. Garcia; wheel nuts on some G.I. Forum cars were loosened, but were discovered by the owners.

[34] Ibid.

[35] Phillips, p. 15,HPG.

[36] Notarized statement by George Groh, Feb. 18, 1949, HPG; Minority Report of House Committee, H.S.R. 68, April 7, 1949, HPG.

[37] Notarized statement by Guadalupe Longoria, Feb. 29, 1949, HPG.

[38] *Corpus Christi Caller-Times,* "Three Rivers Inspection Made of Area on Feb. 21, 1949," Feb. 21, 1949; *La Verdad* (Corpus Christi), Feb. 25, 1949; notarized statement of Juventino Ponce, March 12, 1949, HPG.

[39] Majority Report of House Committee, H.S.R. 68, April 7, 1949, HPG.

[40] Ibid., p. 7.

[41] Minority Report of House Committee, H.S.R. 68, April 7, 1949, p. 1, HPG.

[42] Ibid.

[43] *Corpus Christi Caller-Times,* "Tragic Blot," April 8, 1949.

[44] *Corpus Christi Caller-Times,* "Rep. Tinsley Asks Report on Longoria Case Be Withdrawn", Second Minority Report of House Committee, H.S.R. 68, April 1949, HPG.

[45] Oscar Caballero to Dr. Garcia, Jan. 13, 1949, HPG; Alonso Perales to Dr. Garcia, March 16, 1949, HPG; Lyle Saunders to Dr. Garcia, March 14, 1949, HPG; David Parker to Dr. Garcia, March 10, 1949, HPG; file of financial donations with names and amount, HPG.

[46] *Corpus Christi Caller-Times* reporting always stressed the ambiguity of "prejudice". These Anglos in Corpus Christi denouncing Kennedy could never admit the deep and profound nature of bigotry. But many *Mexicanos* and a few Anglos had finally learned.

V. *Texas and Beyond*

[1] *La Verdad; The Sentinel;* "A Brief History of the American G.I. Forum", memo by Dr. Hector Garcia, HPG.

[2] "The Constitution of the American G.I. Forum", State of Texas, Sept. 1949.

[3] Ibid.

[4] Resolution by State Convention, 1949, on Ladies Auxiliaries, HPG.

[5] Ibid.

[6] Ibid.

[7] Ibid.

[8] Ibid.

[9] Ibid.

[10] Ibid.

[11] Ibid.

[12] "Chart of Regional and State Structures of the American G.I. Forum," 1958, HPG; interview with Dr. Hector Garcia, Jan. 10, 1975; "Charter for American G.I. Forum," Dec. 8, 1949, HPG.

[13] Telegram to Senator Lyndon Johnson, Senator Tom Connally, Rep. John Lyle, Rep. Lloyd Bentsen, Carl Gary, Oct. 1949, HPG; resolution of American G.I. Forum, State Convention, Sept. 1949, P.L. 266, HPG; telegram to Rep. Sam Rayburn, Oct. 15, 1949, HPG; Senator Lyndon Johnson to Dr. Hector Garcia, Oct. 5, 1949, HPG; Rep. John Lyle to Dr. Hector Garcia, Oct. 8, 1949, HPG.

[14] Dr. Garcia to Marcos Navaez, Sinto, Texas, Oct. 24, 1949, HPG; Dr. Garcia to Mrs. Arrendondo and Mr. Valles, Oct. 24, 1950, HPG; Dr. Garcia to Jose Tamez, San Benito, Texas, Oct. 24, 1950, HPG; Dr. Garcia to Mateo Perez, Cuero, Texas, Oct. 24, 1950, HPG; Dr. Garcia to Cedaric Martinez, Sonora, Texas, Oct. 25, 1950, HPG; memo to all G.I. Forums, *Draft Board Notices,* July 10, 1950, HPG; resolution of AGIF State Convention, 1950, on draft board representation, August 23, 1950, HPG; *McAllen Newspaper,* "Draft Boards Asked to Name Latin Americans," Oct. 1, 1950; *Las Noticias* (Del Rio), *Insistimos En Que Debemos Tener un Latino en el* Draft Board," Sept. 10, 1950.

[15] Dr. Garcia to Rep. John Lyle, Feb. 1, 1951, HPG; Dr. Garcia to Rep. John Lyle, March 14, 1951, HPG; Lt. R.J. Patterson to Rep. John Lyle, March 7, 1951, HPG; Alberto Garcia to Dr. Hector Garcia, March 1, 1951, HPG; Rep. John Lyle to Dr. Garcia, March 2, 1951, HPG; Rep. John Lyle to Dr. Garcia, March 12, 1951, HPG; Rep. John Lyle to Dr. Garcia, Feb. 7, 1951, HPG; Dr. Garcia to Senator Lyndon B. Johnson, March 14, 1951,

HPG; Dr. Garcia to Evelyn Rice, Aug. 29, 1951, HPG; file on Jose de la Cruz Saenz; a series of letters with charges and counter-charges by Dr. Garcia in regard to VA treatment of a veteran; a typical example of many cases in which the G.I. Forum aided veterans, HPG; Jose Saenz from Adjudication Officer, Jan. 25, 1951; Jose Saenz from Adjudication Officer, March 2, 1951; VA from Jose Saenz, March 10, 1951; Jose Saenz from Adjudication Officer, March 14, 1951; Jose Saenz from Chief of Medical Records and Reports Division, March 15, 1951, HPG; Dr. Garcia to Senator Lyndon Johnson, March 14, 1951, HPG; Senator Johnson to Dr. Hector Garcia, Sept. 13, 1951, HPG; Dr. Garcia to Senator Lyndon Johnson, Aug. 10, 1954, HPG; Senator Johnson to Dr. Hector Garcia, Aug. 13, 1954, HPG; Mrs. Stanley Pace, Commissioner, Foreign Claims Settlement Commission of the U.S., to Senator Lyndon Johnson, Aug. 19, 1954, HPG.

[16] *Border Trends, A Monthly Summary of Significant Events Pertaining to Anglo-Latin Relations in the Southwest,* "The American G.I. Forum", pp. 1-2, Sept. 1948; Ross, *Preparing for Ulysses,* p. 138.

[17] "Important Notice: Mass Protest Against Termination. . . . ," Feb. 21, 1950, HPG; Rep. Bentsen to Dr. Hector Garcia, March 1950, HPG.

[18] Testimony by Dr. Hector Garcia before Special Congressional Subcommittee, March 22, 1950, HPG; Sens. Tom Connally and Lyndon Johnson to Dr. Garcia, May 5, 1950, HPG; Senator Johnson to Dr. Hector Garcia, March 1950, HPG.

[19] Form letter to Forumeers, Sept. 29, 1949, HPG.

[20] Dr. Garcia to Senator Lyndon Johnson, March 21, 1951, HPG; Dr. Garcia to Rep. John Lyle, March 21, 1951, HPG; American G.I. Forum to President Harry S. Truman, March 21, 1951, HPG; Dr. Garcia to Lloyd Bentsen, Nov. 26, 1951, HPG.

[21] Rep. Lloyd Bentsen to Dr. Hector Garcia, March 3, 1952, HPG; Rayburn to Dr. Hector Garcia, March 1, 1952, HPG; Rep. Wingate Lucas to Dr. Hector Garcia, March 3, 1952, HPG; Rep. Wright Patman to Dr. Hector Garcia, March 3, 1952, HPG; Rep. J. Frank Wilson to Dr. Hector Garcia, March 3, 1952, HPG; Rep. Homer Thornsberry to Dr. Hector Garcia, March 4, 1952, HPG; Rep. Omar Burleson to Dr. Hector Garcia, March 4, 1952, HPG; Sen. Tom Connally to Dr. Hector Garcia, March 10, 1952, HPG; Sen. Rogers Kelley to Dr. Hector Garcia, HPG.

[22] Joseph Serna to Ed Idar, June 25, 1954, HPG; Ed Idar to Joseph Serna, July 7, 1954, HPG; resolution by the AGIF, Texas Convention 1950, on infant mortality, Aug. 28, 1950, HPG.

[23] "A Brief History of the American G.I. Forum",1958, HPG.

[24] *San Antonio Express News,* "The Minority No One Knows," July 16, 1972.

[25] Ibid.

[26] Interview with Vicente Ximenes , Sept. 1974; *Forum News Bulletin* Jan. 1957.

[27] Interview with Ximenes.

[28] Interview with Dr. Hector Garcia.

[29] *Forum News Bulletin.*

[30] *News Bulletin.*

[31] Interview with Dr. Garcia.

[32] Ibid.

[33] File on "Patriotism", HPG.

VI. *Many Fronts*

[1] Edna Ferber to Dr. Hector Garcia, 1950, HPG; interview with Dr. Garcia, January 10, 1975.

[2] Kingea, *Good Neighbor Commission.*

[3] J. F. Gray to Nelville Penrose of GNC, files of Beauford Jester, Box 387, Feb. 1948, Texas State Archives.

[4] Gov. Allan Shivers from Press Secretary Weldon Hart, Jan. 23, 1949, files of Beauford Jester, Box 387, Texas State Archives.

[5] Dr. Garcia to Tom Sutherland, Dec. 2, 1949, HPG.

[6] Notarized statement by Tito Diaz, Feb. 1949, HPG; Mayor George Seydler of Gonzales to Dr. Hector Garcia, Feb. 21, 1950, HPG; *La Verdad,* Feb. 24, 1950.

[7] Resolution by the Annual Convention, AGIF, Aug. 19, 1950, HPG; printout from Corpus Christi office, "To All G.I. Forums, Ladies Auxiliaries, and Jr. Forums," Feb. 1951, HPG; printout from Corpus Christi office, "To All Presidents, Chairmen, Officers, and Members of G.I. Forums, Auxiliaries and Jr. Forums", Feb. 2, 1951, HPG.

[8] Printout from Corpus Christi, "To All G.I. Forums, Auxiliaries, and Jr. G.I. Forums," Feb. 20, 1951, HPG; resolution of First G.I. Forum Convention, Sept. 26, 1949, HPG.

[9] Dr. Garcia to Gov. Allan Shivers, April 18, 1951, HPG; proposed agenda for Board of Directors meeting by Ed Idar, p. 2, HPG; resolution on civil rights by Second Annual Convention, Feb. 28, 1950, HPG.

[10] Resolution of Second Annual Convention on employment discrimination, Feb. 28, 1950, HPG; resolution on civil rights by Second Annual Convention, Aug. 28, 1950, HPG.

[11] Joe Salazar, President AGIF, Lorenzo, Texas, to Dan Contreras, President AGIF, Lamesa, Texas, Oct. 23, 1950, HPG.

[12] *Forum News Bulletin,* Oct. 15, 1952, p. 2, HPG; *Forum News Bulletin,* Feb. 15, p. 3, 1953, HPG; *Forum News Bulletin,* March 15, 1953, p. 3, HPG; *Forum News Bulletin,* Jan. 1954, p.8, HPG; *Forum News Bulletin,* June 15, 1953, HPG.

[13] *Forum News Bulletin,* "Federal Grand Jury Indicts State Agent for Beating Latin", Oct. 1954, HPG.

[14] Robert Molina to Dr. Hector Garcia, Sept. 20, 1951, HPG; Dr. Garcia to Robert Molina, Oct. 2, 1951, HPG.

[15] Interview with Dr. Hector Garcia, Jan. 10, 1975.

[16] *El Congresso*, HPG; memo on *El Congresso,* HPG.

[17] *Forum News Bulletin,* "Forum-Sponsored Anti-Discrimination Bill Killed by Tie Vote in New Mexico," April 1953, p. 8, HPG.

[18] *Forum News Bulletin,* "Archbishop Byrne, AFL Endorses New Mexico Statute," Feb. 1955, HPG.

[19] *Forum News Bulletin,* "Anti-Discrimination Bill Passes New Mexico Legislature", March 1955, HPG.

[20] *Forum News Bulletin,* "Albuquerue Forum Asks Civil Service for City Workers on Garbage Department," Sept. 1953, HPG; *Forum News Bulletin,* "Albuquerque G.I. Forums Combine Efforts to Press Change in City Merit System", Oct. 1953, HPG; *Forum News Bulletin,* "G.I. Forum Obtains Merit System", Nov. 1953, HPG.

[21] *Forum News Bulletin,* "Albuquerque Forums Get Joe Valencia Back on City Job," Nov. 1953, HPG.

[22] *Forum News Bulletin,* "Albuquerue G.I. Forums Combine Efforts to Press Change in City Merit System", Oct. 1953, HPG; *Forum News Bulletin,* "Organization Pays Off," Feb. 1953, HPG.

[23] *Forum News Bulletin,* "Albuquerque Wins Another Tussle with City Manager on Personnel Board Appeal", July 1955, HPG; *Forum News Bulletin,* "Wrath of New Mexico Forum and LULACs Aroused by Almagordo District Attorney," Feb. 1955, HPG; Vicent Jasso to editor of *Almagordo News,* Dec. 18, 1954, HPG.

[24] *Forum News Bulletin,* "Colorado G.I. Forum News", Sept. 1953, HPG; *Forum News Bulletin,* "Colorado G.I. Forum News", Oct. 1954, HPG.

[25] George Tindall, *The Emergence of the New South, 1913-1945* (Baton Rouge: Louisiana State UniversityPress, 1967), pp. 639-641; Walters, *The South and the Nation* (New York: Vintage, 1969), p. 235.

[26] See Chapter I.

[27] Senator Rogers Kelley to Dr. Hector Garcia, June 14, 1949, HPG; resolution on poll tax repeal of Second Annual Convention, American G.I. Forum, Aug. 28, 1950, HPG.

[28] Information bulletin to "All Officers, District Chairmans (sic) and Members of the American G.I. Forum, Auxiliaries and Jr. G.I. Forums on Poll Tax Drives, Poll Tax Dances, Poll Taxes," May 19, 1951, HPG; bulletin to Rio Grande Valley area on Poll Tax Drive Conference, Oct. 21, 1955, HPG; bulletin to West Texas officers on poll tax drive, Nov. 10, 1955, HPG.

[29] *Forum News Bulletin,* Jan. 1954, p.4; in one Fort Worth region, registration increased from *six* Mexican American voters in 1950 to 1500 in 1955; in New Mexico, voter registration drives were necessary but without the onerous poll tax requirement.

[30] *Forum News Bulletin,* "G.I. Forum Conducts Poll Tax Drive in Valley," Nov.-Dec., 1956.

[31] Ibid.; *Brownsville Herald,* "Forum Blasts Newspapers", Jan. 25, 1956.

[32] *Corpus Christi Caller-Times,* "Kelley Shirts Debate on Poll-Tax Campaign", Dec. 22, 1955.

[33] Oscar Laurel to Ed Idar, Nov. 1955, HPG.

[34] *Corpus Christi Caller-Times,* Dec. 22, 1955.

[35] *Forum News Bulletin,* "G.I. Forum Conducts Poll Tax Drive in Valley," Nov.-Dec. 1956.

[36] *Daily Texan,* editorial on Valley democracy, Nov. 1955.

[37] *Forum News Bulletin,* "Some Merchants 'Resent' Poll Tax Drive but Forum Christmas Party Still Held," Jan. 1956.

[38] *Forum News Bulletin,* "Shivers at It Again," April, May, June, 1956, HPG; *Corpus*

176

Christi Caller-Times, "American G.I. Forum Asking Valley Quiz," May 5, 1956.

[39] *Valley Evening Monitor,* "Probe of Demo Club Poll Tax Drive Awaits Ruling," May 6, 1956.

[40] *Corpus Christi Caller-Times,* "Forum Cleared of Poll Tax Charges," May 1956; *Forum News Bulletin,* April, May, June 1956.

[41] Ruben Mungula, *A Cotton Picker Finds Justice: The Saga of the Hernandez ease,* American G.I. Forum, 1954, p. 1, HPG. This valuable chronology of the Hernandez Case was not extensively distributed due to lack of funds.

[42] See Chapter I; p. 2.

[43] *San Antonio Express,* "Gus Garcia, Legal Genius" by Jose A: Chacon, March 12, 1972.

[44] Interview with Dr. Garcia, Jan. 10, 1975.

[45] Mungula, *A Cotton Picker Finds Justice,* pp. 2-6.

[46] Ibid., p. 4.

[47] American G.I. Forum, *The Hernandez Case,* May 1954, HPG.

[48] Ed Idar to Albert Armendariz, Oct. 27, 1954, HPG; Ed Idar to Albert Armendariz, Nov. 23, 1953, HPG; press release by G.I. Forum on Hernandez expenses, 1954, HPG; *Forum News Bulletin,* "U.S. Supreme Court to Hear Appeal on Jury Sevice Issue," Dec. 1953.

[49] *The Hernandez Case,* HPG.

[50] Ibid.

[51] Ibid.

[52] Ibid.

[53] *Corpus Christi Caller-Times,* "Sam Houston Termed Wetback," May 1954.

[54] *The Hernandez Case,* HPG.

[55] Ibid.

[56] Ibid.

[57] *Forum News Bulletin,* "New Trial for Hernandez," Feb. 1955.

[58] *San Antonio Express,* Chacon.

VII. *Education is Our Freedom*

[1] Resolution of American G.I. Forum, Texas State Convention, 1950, on Mexican American absentees; Corpus Christi Plan for Annual Back-to-School Drives, Aug. 28, 1950, HPG files.

[2] Ibid.

[3] Ibid.; memo to all state and district officers and directors, forums, auxiliaries, and juniors in Texas, *Back to School Drives,* Aug. 12, 1958, HPG.

[4] *Forum News Bulletin.*

[5] memo, "Back to School Drives" HPG; *Forum News Bulletin,* Grady St. Clair to Dr. Hector Garcia, Sept. 22, 1950, HPG; Charles F. Jones to Dr. Hector Garcia, Sept. 13, 1957,

HPG.

[6] Resolution of American G.I. Forum, Texas State Convention, HPG; memo/letter to G.I. Forum members on kindergarten, July 6, 1957, HPG.

[7] *Forum News Bulletin* (on truancy law); *Corpus Christi Caller-Times,* "Texas Schools Attendance Gains 26,000 During Year", Dec. 27, 1950.

[8] *Vernon's Annotated Revised Statutes of the State of Texas,* Revision of 1925, vol. 8, Article 2901, indicates the right of every child to attend the free public school system.

[9] Rangel and Alcala, " De Jure ", p. 312, footnote 32.

[10] Ibid., p. 334; a birth certificate of 1890 in Beeville, Texas, characterizes a Mexican American child as White.

[11] Ibid.

[12] Hoffman, *Unwanted Mexican Americans*, p. 8.

[13] Garza, "LULAC: League of United Latin American Citizens", p. 6.

[14] *Corpus Christi Caller-Times,* "2 School Heads Admit Charges of Segregation," 1947.

[15] Ibid.

[16] Gilbert, "Some Legal Aspects of the Education of Spanish-Speaking Children in Texas"; Rangel and Alcala, p. 336.

[17] George Sanchez and V. Strickland, *Study of the Educational Opportunities Provided Spanish-Named Children in the Texas School Systems, 1947;* Gus Garcia to Price Daniel, Aug. 18, 1947; Price Daniel to Gus Garcia, Aug. 21, 1947. Quoted in Rangel and Alcala, pp. 335-336.

[18] *The Sentinel,* Jan. 16, 1948, and Jan 2, 1948.

[19] *The Sentinel,* Jan. 23, 1948, and Feb. 27, 1948, and March 5, 1948, and March 12, 1948.

[20] *The Sentinel,* Jan. 30, 1948, and March 16, 1948.

[21] Appendix I. No. 338, Civil District Court of the U.S., Western District of Texas, Minerva Delgado, et al. *vs.* Bastrop ISD of Bastrop Court, et al., Final judgement, June 15, 1948, HPG.

[22] Ibid.

[23] Ibid.

[24] *The Sentinel,* May 21, 1948.

[25] Texas State Department of Education, *Standards and Activities of the Division of Supervision and Accreditation of School Systems, Bulletin* 507 at 45-6 (1948-49), HPG.

[26] Ibid.

[27] *Corpus Christi Caller-Times,* "Legal Remedies to Discrimination to be Discussed," June 3, 1949, and "Schools are Still Segregated - Latin Americans", May 1949.

[28] Statement by L.A. Woods, State Superintendent of Public Instruction, April 23, 1949 with letter to L.A. Woods from T.M. Trimble, First Assistant to State Superintendent, Feb. 1, 1949, HPG; *La Verdad,* "Board Appeals Case Hoping to be Allowed Segregation Under Free Choice Disguise", June 10, 1949.

[29] Statement on George West inspection, HPG.

178

[30] School inspection report of fourteen schools, April 1949, HPG; report on Santa Cruz ISD, May 24, 1949, HPG; American G.I. Forum/LULAC to Governor Beauford Jester, 1949, HPG.

[31] Rangel and Alcala, p. 339.

[32] R.E. Smith to Dr. Hector Garcia, June 3, 1949, HPG.

[33] Resolution by American G.I. Forum of Texas, State Convention, 1949, on federal aid to education, Sept. 26, 1949, HPG; resolution by AGIF of Texas, State Convention, 1949, on segregation, Sept. 26, 1949, HPG; resolution by AGIF of Texas, State Convention, 1949, on free choice, Sept. 26, 1949, HPG; "School Restrictions Not in Compliance with Delgado", Sept. 26, 1949, HPG.

[34] Report on J.F. Gray proposed act, Dec. 12, 1949, HPG.

[35] Dr. Garcia to the President of the School Board, Lubbock ISD, Lubbock, Texas, June 2, 1950, HPG.

[36] Texas Education Agency, "Statement of Policy Pertaining to Segregation of Latin-American Children", May 8, 1950, HPG.

[37] J.W. Edgar to Superintendent of Schools, County Superintendents, President of Board of Trustees, June 21, 1950, HPG.

[38] Letter and report by Dr. Hector Garcia to the State Board of Education and the Commissioner of Education, April 13, 1950, HPG.

[39] Isaac Bergas to Dr. Hector Garcia, July 20, 1950, HPG.

[40] Dr. Garcia to Dr. George Cox, Department of Health, Austin, Texas, May 2, 1951, HPG.

[41] Report on schools in Sandia, Texas, by American G.I. Forum, 1952, HPG.

[42] Ibid.

[43] Ed Idar and Frank Pinedo to Ray Whiteley, Superintendent of Schools, Pecos, Texas, Sept. 27, 1952, HPG.

[44] *Forum News Bulletin,* "Edgar Denies Forum Appeal," May 15, 1953; *Forum News Bulletin,* April 1954.

[45] *Forum News Bulletin,* "Segregation Appeal Filed with Edgar," Sept. 1952; *Forum News Bulletin,* July 15, 1953, Rangel and Alcala, p. 340, footnote 197.

[46] *Forum News Bulletin,* "Edgar Holds Hearing on Segregation Case Involving Hondo Tots", Feb. 1953.

[47] Statement of Case, Max Orta et al. *vs.* Board of Trustees of Hondo ISD, Medina County, Sept. 1953, HPG.

[48] *Forum News Bulletin,* Dec. 15, 1952; interview with Dr. Garcia, Jan. 10, 1975.

[49] Complaint to Enjoin Violation of Federal Civil Rights and for Damages, Jose Cortez et al. *vs.* Carrizo Springs ISD et al. by Cristobal Aldrete, 1956, HPG; Ed Idar to Dr. Hector Garcia, Jan. 4, 1955, HPG; *Forum News Bulletin,* May-June 1955; *Forum News Bulletin,* "Forum Committee Visits Carrizo Springs, Reports No Sign of Segregation," March 1956.

[50] *Corpus Christi Caller-Times,* "Lawyer Gives Advice in Kingsville School Fuss", Aug. 8, 1954; *Forum News Bulletin,* "Kingsville Zoning Brings Charges of School Segregation,"

Sept. 1954; Ed Idar to Dr. Hector Garcia, Dec. 21, 1954, HPG.

[51] "Before the Commissioner of Education of Texas", Mrs. T.R. Rocha at Complaintiffs *vs.* Board of Trustees of Kingsville, ISD, HPG; *Forum News Bulletin,* "Edgar Hears Appeal on Kingsville School Segregation," Jan. 1955.

[52] *Forum News Bulletin,* "Edgar Taken to Federal Court on Segregation Case," April 1955.

[53] Complaint to Enjoin Violation of Federal Civil Rights and for Damages by Gus Garcia and Homer Lopez Attorneys for Plaintiffs, April 21, 1955.

[54] *Forum News Bulletin,* "Kingsville Segregation Settled, But No Thanks to Commissioner Edgar", Sept.- Oct. 1955.

[55] "Preliminary Report on Mathis, Texas, by American G.I. Forum Committee", April 11, 1948, HPG.

[56] Carlos Cadena, Albert Pena, Richard Casillas to J.W. Edgar, Nov. 8, 1954, HPG; Carlos Casillas and Albert Pena to Carlos Cadena, Oct. 20, 1954, HPG; James De Anda to Carlos Casillas, Oct. 5, 1955, HPG.

[57] *Forum News Bulletin,* "Edgar Holds Conference on Mathis School Segregation", Dec. 1954; J.W. Edgar to J.W. Harbin, School Superintendent, Dec. 7, 1954, HPG; Albert Pena and Carlos Casillas to J.W. Edgar, Sept. 13, 1955, HPG.

[58] *Corpus Christi Caller-Times,* "State Closes Mathis School", Oct. 23, 1955; *Corpus Christi Caller-Times,"* Mathis Put on School List Again, 'Taken Off"; *Corpus Christi Caller-Times,* "Mathis School Survey Ordered by Dr. Edgar", Nov. 13, 1955; *Forum News Bulletin,* "Segregation Ending in September at Mathis and Carrizo", May-June 1954.

[59] Complaint to Enjoin Violation of Federal Civil Rights and for Damage, Trinidad Villarreal et al. *vs.* Mathis ISD. Civil Action No. 1385, Jan. 1956, HPG.

[60] Deposition of T.A. Harbin, Mathis ISD Superintendent, Civil Action No. 1385, Jan. 1956, HPG; Deposition of Ellias Villarreal, Civil Action No. 1385, HPG.

[61] Civil Action No. 1385, Motion to Dismiss by Defendants, Dec. 21, 1955, HPG; Civil Action No. 1385, Answer to Defendant, HPG.

[62] Civil Action No. 1385, Plaintiffs Pre-Trial Memorandum, HPG.

[63] Administrative Order by Mathis ISD, 1956, HPG; Resolution of Board of Trustees of Mathis ISD, Oct. 1956, HPG; *Corpus Christi Caller-Times,* "Discrimination Suit Against Mathis Ended", May 4, 1957.

[64] *Forum News Bulletin,* Aug. 1955; James De Anda to Wirin, Sept. 6, 1955, HPG; Dr. Garcia to J.W. Edgar, Sept. 6, 1955, HPG.

[65] Driscoll Board of Trustees to J.W. Edgar, Sept. 13, 1955, HPG.

[66] Herminca Hernandez et al. *vs.*Driscoll Consolidated ISD Civil Action No. 1384, Jan. 1957, HPG.

[67] Civil Action 1384 Deposition by Gordon Green, Driscoll ISD Superintendent, May 1956, HPG.

[68] Civil Action 1384, Memorandum by James V. Allred, Jan. 11, 1957, HPG.

[69] Ibid.

[70] Ibid.

180

[71] Civil Action 1384. Final judgement by James V. Allred, 1957, HPG.

[72] Herbert Parmet, *Eisenhower and the American Crusades* (New York: MacMillan Company, 1972), p. 464.

VIII. *Muchos Mojados y Otras Cosas*

[1] *Forum News Bulletin,* "Joe Martinez Elected Colorado's First State Chairman", Oct. 1953; *Forum News Bulletin,* "New Mexico Holds First State Convention", June 1953; *Forum News Bulletin,* "Ohio's First Forum Was Being Organized When We Hit Press", Dec. 1954; *Forum News Bulletin,* "Molly Galvan Organizes in Utah", Aug. 1954; *Forum News Bulletin,* "Nebraska Joins Forum Family", Sept.-Oct. 1955.

[2] "A Brief History of the American G.I. Forum of the U.S.", HPG. Provision was made for a larger non-veteran membership but control remained with ex-servicemen; *Forum News Bulletin,* "Praise, Commendations Rain Upon Founder of G.I. Forum", July 1958.

[3] *Denver Star,* "DAR Cancels Rites at Industrial School", Feb. 1957.

[4] *Denver Star,* "Old Glory and the DAR," Feb. 11, 1957; *Amarillo Globe,* "Racial Issue Halts Lincoln Day Affair", Feb. 11, 1957.

[5] Press release, Feb. 1957, HPG; Dr. Garcia to President Dwight D. Eisenhower, Feb. 11, 1957, HPG.

[6] Mrs. Frederic A. Graves, President General, National DAR, to Dr. Garcia, Feb. 21, 1957; Vicente Ximenes to Mrs. Frederic Graves, Feb. 21, 1957; *Corpus Christi Times,* "DAR's Patriotic Work in Colorado Vindicated", Feb. 18, 1957; Ernestine Ortega, Chairman of Amarillo G.I. Forum, to Mrs. Frederic A. Graves, Feb. 27, 1957.

[7] Mailout to American G.I. Forum members, 1956, HPG.

[8] Dr. Garcia to Sen. Ralph Yarbrough, Dec. 4, 1957, HPG; Vicente Ximenes to C.W. Burrell, Director of New Mexico FEPC," Oct. 1956; American G.I. Forum Memorandum 5, Oct. 1956, HPG; Vicente Ximenes to Frank Martinez, Chairman of G.I. Forum of Roswell, Sept. 29, 1956.

[9] *Forum News Bulletin,* "Senator Chavez Enters Railway Brotherhood Clause Tiff", Nov. 1956; Dr. Garcia to Senator John Sparkman, Nov. 17, 1956, HPG; John Holton, Adm. Assistant, to Senator Sparkman, to Dr. Garcia, Dec. 13, 1957; C.W. Burrell, Director, New Mexico FEPC, to Vicente Ximenes, Dec. 5, 1957, HPG; C.W. Burrell to Summer Canary, Dec. 5, 1957, HPG; Vicente Jasso to Vicente Ximenes, Dec. 5, 1957, HPG.

[10] *Forum News Bulletin,* "New Mexico Forums Win One Fight, File Complaint Against Unions", Jan. 1958; acknowledgement and complaint filed by AGIF against Brotherhood of Locomotive Firemen, Jan. 2, 1958, HPG; Joseph Contreras, Saginaw, Michigan G.I. Forum, to Vicente Ximenes, March 11, 1958, HPG.

[11] Letter from Joseph Contreras, HPG.

[12] Senator Henry Gonzalez to Dr. Hector Garcia, April 1954, HPG; Dr. Garcia to Senator Abraham Kazen, April 5, 1957, HPG; Statement by Richard M. Casillas on House Bill 831 to Committee on State Affairs, April 3, 1957, HPG; Ed Idar to Senator Abraham Kazen, April 17, 1957, HPG; *Houston Post,* "Let Them Join NAACP, Writes E. Castillo," May 9, 1957.

[13] Vicente Ximenes to Joe Castillo, Dec. 20, 1957, HPG; Molly Galvan to Roger Martinez,

Nov. 20, 1957, HPG; *Forum News Bulletin,* "Pueblo G.I. Forum Turns Thumbs Down on Junior High Segregation Experiment", Dec. 1953. In many Texas cities, Forumeers kept a close watch on the integrated schools to prevent regression. Many letters testify to the sense of accomplishment in preventing noncompliance with the Driscoll decision.

[14] Julian Samora, *Los Mojados* (South Bend: University of Notre Dame Press, 1970). A well reasoned, balanced account of the development of the *mojado* problems.

[15] Ibid, 49.

[16] Pauline Kibbe, "Their American Standard for All Americans", in *Common Ground* (New York: Common Council for American Unity, Sept. 1949). The President's Commission on Migratory Labor labeled this legislation as a dominant factor of the Mexican farm labor program; 142,000 illegal aliens were put under contract.

[17] Weldon Hart to Governor Jester, files of Beauford Jester, Box 387, Texas State Archives. The director of El Paso Employment Services wanted border officials to "turn their heads" to allow the crossing of wetbacks. The growers wanted cheap labor and TEC was ready to place 7,000 wetbacks. A similar incident occurred in 1953 when Mexico threated to cancel the *bracero* program.

[18] Kibbe, "Standards for all Americans", pp. 8-9.

[19] President's Commission on Migratory Labor, *Migratory Labor in American Agriculture* (Washington, D.C.: U.S. Government Printing Office, 1951), pp. 69-70, 77; Lyle Saunders, "The Wetback Problem in the Lower Rio Grande Valley" (Austin: University of Texas, 1951), p. 4.

[20] *The Sentinel,* June 11, 1948; *Corpus Christi Caller-Times,* "Valley G.I. Forums to Fight Wetback Immigration Tide," June 5, 1949; *La Verdad,* "Dr. Garcia Testifies Against Low Wage", Sept. 21, 1949, HPG; Dr. Garcia to Senator Lyndon B. Johnson, Oct. 13, 1949, HPG.

[21] *Corpus Christi Caller,* "Border Patrol Increased to Halt Illegal Workers", July 25, 1949; three articles on wetbacks in *San Antonio Evening News* and *Harlingen Monitor,* May 28, 1949.

[22] "Statement on Health and Welfare Condition Among the Underprivileged Migrant Workers of Texas", for President's Commission on Migratory Labor by Dr. Hector P. Garcia, Aug. 1, 1950, p. 7, HPG.

[23] Ibid., pp. 5-6.

[24] President's Commission on Migratory Labor, *Migratory Labor in American Agriculture* (Washington, D.C.: U.S. Government Printing Office, 1951).

[25] *Corpus Christi Caller,* "Mexico Aid to Ease Labor Shortage Asked," Aug. 8, 1951; *Corpus Christi Caller-Times,* "Texans Win Victory in Wetback Smuggling Bill", February 6, 1952; Sheldon Greene, "Immigration law and Rural Poverty - The Problems of the Illegal Entrant", *Duke Law Journal,* vol. 3,(1969), p. 499; *San Antonio Express,* "Wetbacks Said Hurting Labor," December 1951, Gus Garcia told a labor subcommittee that the wetback invasions stopped what progress was being made; all Mexican Americans were characterized as wetbacks in the perjorative sense.

[26] *La Verdad,* "Mexican Wetback in the U.S.," August 27, 1951; *Galveston News,* "Cheap Labor", September 22, 1953; *Corpus Christi Caller,* "House Passes Wetback Bill", February 27, 1950.

[27] "Wetbacks in Middle of Border War", *Business Week,* October 24, 1953, pp. 62-66.

[28] U.S., Congress, Senate, Committee on Appropriations, *Hearings Before the Committee on Appropriations on H.J. 461.* 83rd Congress, 2nd session, 1954; *Corpus Christi Caller,* "Over One Million Wetbacks Caught by Border Patrol", June 15, 1954.

[29] *Corpus Christi Caller,* "G.I. Forum Takes Stand on Griffin," April 22, 1953; *Forum News Bulletin,* "Idar Opposes Griffin Appointment," May 15, 1953; *La Verdad,* "Editor Taboos Jim Griffin for Agriculture, Immigration Posts", April 4, 1953; Dr. Garcia to Herbert Brownell, August 15, 1953, HPG; *Forum News Bulletin,* "Forum, AFL Urge President Eisenhower to Check on Wetbacks During Valley Visit", October 1953.

[30] Ed Idar to Dr. Hector Garcia, November 23, 1953, HPG; Ed Idar to Herbert Brownell, Attorney General, September 16, 1953, HPG.

[31] "Memo to All State Officers, Directors, G.I. Forums, Auxiliaries, and Junior G.I. Forums in the States of Texas, New Mexico, and Colorado", Dec. 11, 1953, HPG.

[32] *Forum News Bulletin,* "Report on Wetback Problem Published by Forum, AFL", December 1953; Ed Idar to Rep. W.R. Poage, March 2, 1954, HPG; *Forum News Bulletin,* Stanford Law Review Wetback Article Discusses Action by State Governments", May 1954.

[33] U.S., Congress, Senate, Committee on the Judiciary, *Hearings Before the Subcommittee on Immigration and Naturalization on S. 3660 and S. 3661,* 83rd Congress, 2nd Session, July 12-14, 1954, pp. 37, 64-69, 78-80; Senator Pat McCarran, author of new immigration legislation in 1952 aimed at Communist infiltration, stated that agricultural employers in the Southwest needed the illegal aliens; the Congress must face facts. Senate Committee of the Judiciary, *Appropriation Hearings Before the Subcommittee of the Senate Committee of the Judiciary on S. 1917, 83rd Congress, 1st Session, 1953,* cited in Samora: *Los Mojados,* p. 101.

[34] In 1947, due to an "oversupply of labor", anticipated recession and public indignation over health and crime, the Border Patrol apprehended 193,657 illegal aliens. U.S. Department of Justice, *Annual Report of the Immigration and Naturalization Service* (Washington, D.C.: U.S. Government Printing Office, 1947), p. 24.

[35] J.W. Holland to Chris Aldrete, President of G.I. Forum, July 7, 1954, HPG; Ed Idar to Joseph Swing, Commissioner of Immigration and Naturalization, August 14, 1954, HPG; *Forum News Bulletin,* "Texas Board Adopts Budget, Resolutions at Galveston Meet," November 1954; the G.I. Forum had always been cognizant of its responsibilities to protect the civil liberties of all citizens, as numerous letters and accounts testify.

[36] *New York Times,* "Wetback Users' Serenade", in *Forum News Bulletin,* September 1954; *Valley Evening Monitor,* "Border Patrol Aiding Unions in our Valley", Nov. 28, 1955.

[37] Samora, *Los Mojados,* p. 53

[38] Ibid.

[39] U.S. Congress, Senate, Committee on the Judiciary, *Hearings Before the Subcommittee on Immigration and Naturalization on S. 3660 and S. 3661,* 83rd Congress, 2nd Session, July 12-14, 1954, p. 39.

IX. *Public Law 78*

[1] Ernesto Galarza, *Merchants of Labor: The Mexican Bracero Story* (Santa Barbara: McNally & Coftin, 1964). An excellent account of *bracero* legislative history; Coalson, "Mexican Contract Labor in American Agriculture", p. 231.

[2] Ibid., p. 234; U.S. Department of Labor, *Information Concerning Entry of Mexican Agriculture Workers to the U.S.*, prepared by the Bureau of Employment Security Form Placement Service (Washington, D.C.: U.S. Government Printing Office, 1951), p. 11.

[3] Ibid.

[4] Samora, *Los Mojados*, p. 55; Galarza, *Merchants of Labor.*

[5] "Before House Labor Committee, Testimony of Austin E. Anson, Executive Manager, Texas Citrus and Vegetable Growers and Shippers, Harlingen, Texas", January and February 1949, HPG.

[6] *Daily Texan,* "Valley Men Reverse Stand", October 5, 1949. When valley wages were twenty to thirty cents per hour, growers claimed they were higher. When the United States Employment Service demanded forty cents minimum, they claimed it was traditionally twenty cents; Coalson, "Mexican Contract Labor". Texas received 46 percent of all *braceros* and raised wages 15 percent; Dr. Garcia to Don Larsen, U.S. Employment Service, October 4, 1949, HPG; American G.I. Forum to Harry Crozier, TEC, October 16, 1949, HPG.

[7] *Fort Worth Telegram,* "Schools in Winter are Dismissed So Boys May Help Harvest Cotton", October 7, 1951; *Corpus Christi Caller,* "Forum Set to Fight Proposal to Let Children Pick Cotton", August 18, 1951; resolution of American G.I. Forum, Texas State Convention 1949, HPG; *Forum News Bulletin,* "Forum, LULACS urge Back-to-School Move," Sept. 1952; memo to all Presidents of Forums, Auxiliaries, and Jr. G.I. Forums, Civic Clubs and Organizations, all Friends of our "School Children", HPG; *Corpus Christi Caller,* article on Texas Farm Bureau Convention, Nov. 11, 1952; Dr. Garcia to Congressman John Lyle, Nov. 13, 1952, HPG.

[8] *Forum News Bulletin,* "Albuquerque, N.M., Migrant Labor Meet Set for March 4-6", Feb. 15, 1953.

[9] *Rocky Mountain News,* "A Shameful and Black Practice", May 11, 1955; *Forum News Bulletin,* "A Shameful and Black Practice", May and June 1955; *Rocky Mountain News,* "Senators Kill Plan to Study Migrant Camps", Feb. 8, 1956.

[10] *Forum News Bulletin,* "Welfare Payments Light Among Agricultural Workers", Jan. 1956; numerous letters on G.I. Forum participation in setting up Migrant Council, Texas Migrant Council folder, April 1956, HPG.

[11] Ed Idar to Ben Abraham Kazen, Jr., Feb. 20, 1957, HPG; Senator Kazen to Dr. Garcia, March 19, 1957, HPG; "Catholic Council for the Spanish-Speaking", *Desk Notes,* March 13, 1957, HPG; Senator Kazen to Dr. Garcia, April 1, 1957, HPG.

[12] Senator Connally to Dr. Garcia, October 15, 1949, HPG; *Forum News Bulletin, "Bracero* Agreement Protest by Lubbock Forum, Legion Post", September 1953; Ed Idar to Attorney General Herbert Brownell, September 16, 1953, HPG; *Corpus Christi Caller,* "U.S. Readies Alternate *Bracero* Plan", Jan. 15, 1954; "American G.I. Forum of Texas", *Emergency Action Bulletin,* Feb. 25, 1954, HPG; *Forum News Bulletin,* "Quo Vadis", Jan. 1955; *Forum News Bulletin,* "Parole—1955 Style", February 1955; *San Antonio Express,* "G.I. Forum Officials Raps White *Bracero's* Appeal", 1954.

[13] *Albuquerque Journal*, "G.I. Forum Action on Migrant Labor Woes", August 8, 1952. Forumeers obtained interviews with workers on wages and housing; American G.I Forum to U.S. Employment Service, HPG; Dr. Garcia to Harry LeBlanc, Chief of Farm Placement Department, December 11,1957, HPG; Ted Le Berthon, "At the Prevailing Rate", reprint by permission from *The Commonwealth*, 1957, HPG; *Forum News Bulletin*, "El Eco, McAllen Forum, Farm Labor Census Started in Valley", April, 1955; Dr. Garcia to Acting Secretary of Labor James Mitchell, August 5, 1956, HPG.

[14] A press release of the U.S. Section, Joint United States - Mexico Trade Union Committee of December 23, 1957, severely criticized censorship by Labor Department officials and the California State Employment Bureau for their lack of cooperation in publicizing jobs available to domestic farm laborers in order to recruit *braceros* who were more easily exploited; Henry LeBlanc to Dr. Garcia, September 11, 1956, HPG; Don Larin, Chief Farm Placement Service to Dr. Garcia, October 21, 1957, HPG; R.G. Murchison to Dr. Garcia, November 18, 1957, HPG; "Farm Labor Bulletin", *TEC*, September 30, 1957, HPG; Robert Goodwin, Director U.S. Department of Labor, to Dr. Garcia, April, 1958, HPG; Robert Goodwin to Dr. Garcia, August 15, 1956, HPG; *Forum News Bulletin*, "Forum Blocks Request for Alien Workers; Local Labor Available", July 1956.

[15] Dr. Garcia to Secretary of Labor James Mitchell, June 4, 1957, HPG; "Memorandum: To Whom It May Concern", by Dr. Garcia, July 31, 1957, HPG; Petition to Price Daniel, HPG.

[16] Dr. Garcia to Secretary of Labor James Mitchell, June 4, 1957, HPG.

[17] Ed McDonald to Dr. Garcia, November 2, 1957, HPG; Dr. Garcia to Oscar Phillips, November 29, 1957, HPG; Dr. Garcia to Frank Pinedo, November 30, 1957, HPG; Dr. Garcia to Congressman Joe Kilgore, September 8, 1958, HPG; Dr. Garcia to Ed McDonald, August 6, 1958, HPG.

[18] Dr. Garcia to Henry LeBlanc, June 25, 1957, HPG; Dr. Garcia to Texas State AFL, July 1, 1957, HPG; Dr. Garcia to Milton Plumb, July 4, 1957, HPG; Dr. Garcia to Senator Ralph Yarborough, November 11, 1957, HPG; Dr. Garcia to Senatory Lyndon Johnson, November 13, 1957, HPG; Arthur Perry, Administration Assistant to LBJ to Dr. Garcia, November 18, 1957, HPG; *Forum News Bulletin,* October 1957; Henry LeBlanc to Dr. Garcia, June 27, 1957, HPG.

[19] Catholic Council for the Spanish-Speaking, *Desk Notes,* March 8, 1957, BC.SS. Regional Office: San Antonio, Texas.

[20] *Dallas Morning News,* editorial, June 25, 1957; U.S., Congress, House, Committee on Interstate and Foreign Commerce, *Hearings Before a Subcommittee on Interstate and Foreign Commerce on H.R. 9836 to Provide for the Regulation of the Interstate Transportation of Migrant Farm Workers,* 84th Congress, 2nd Session, May 18, 1956, pp. 1-33.

[21] C. Read Granbery, Executive Director of Texas Legislative Council, to Dr. Garcia, September 12, 1956, HPG; Frank Pinedo to Dr. Garcia, August 25, 1957, HPG; *Forum News Bulletin,* "Pinedo Bilked of $9 Million on Labor Import", September 1957; *Corpus Christi Caller-Times, "Braceros* Bilked of $9 Million", October 22, 1957; *Arizona Register,* "Mexico Bishops Plan Fight on Emigration", December 6, 1957.

[22] Milton Plumb to Dr. Garcia, July 10, 1957, HPG; *Forum News Bulletin,* "Migrant Problem a Bandwagon", July 1957.

[23] Dr. Garcia to Secretary James Mitchell, May 22, 1957, HPG; Dr. Garcia to Senator Lyndon Johnson, June 1, 1957, HPG; James O'Connell, Acting Secretary of Labor, to Dr.

Garcia, June 12, 1957, HPG.

[24] Resolution by Colorado G.I. Forum Board of Director, February 24, 1957, HPG; Senator Johnson to Dr. Garcia, March 20, 1957, HPG; Dr. Garcia to Joe Ontiveros, March 12, 1957, HPG; Dr. Garcia to Senator Johnson, March 12, 1957, HPG; Dr. Garcia to Senator Dennis Chavez, March 12, 1957, HPG; Dr. Garcia to Secretary James Mitchell, March 13, 1957, HPG; Congressman Young to Dr. Garcia, March 19, 1957, HPG; Newell Brow, U.S. Department of Labor, to Congressman Young, March 22, 1957, HPG; James O'Connell to Dr. Garcia, March 26, 1957, HPG; James Dodson to Senator Dennis Chavez, April 3, 1957, HPG; James O'Connell to Senator Johnson, March 30, 1957, HPG.

[25] *Forum News Bulletin,* "South Texas Forum District Asks Ike to Stop Import of all Foreign Laborers", March 1958; *Forum News Bulletin,* "Texas Groups Call for Halt of *Bracero* Importation Program (Texas Migrant Council)", December 1958; *Forum News Bulletin,* "Forum Requests Labor Department Stop *Braceros*", April 1958; *Forum News Bulletin,* "Secretary of Labor Hits at Prejudice Among Labor -Industry at Meeting", April 1958; Dr. Garcia to Clarence Lundquist, U.S. Department of Labor, March 17, 1958, HPG; Resolution of Censorship of Price Daniel by the 1958 Texas American G.I. Forum Convention, July 5, 1958, HPG; Resolution of California G.I. Forum, 1958, HPG; Dr. Garcia to Jacob Duran of New Mexico, August 5, 1958, HPG; President's Commission on Migratory Labor, *Second Report to the President on Domestic Migratory Labor* (Washington, D.C.: U.S. Government Printing Office, February 1958); Texas Council of Migrant Labor, *Conclusions and Recommendations,* November 8, 1958, Austin, Texas, HPG; Dr. Garcia to Vicente Ximenes, January 12, 1959, HPG; Jacob Duran to Congressman J. Edgar Chenoweth, August 15, 1959, HPG.

[26] U.S. Department of Labor, "Address by Secretary of Labor James Mitchell to the National Advisory Committee on Farm Labor," (USDL 2704), February 5, 1959, p. 3, HPG.

[27] Dr. Garcia to Secretary of Labor Mitchell, February 6, 1959; Dr. Garcia to Vicente Ximenes, February 17, 1959; "Memorandum by the Founder to All Forum Members", 1958; Val Martinez, Indiana G.I. Forum to Secretary Mitchell, March 6, 1959; Andres De Leon, Jr., Texas G.I. Forum to Secretary Mitchell, March 24, 1959; Florentine Cuevas, Ohio G.I. Forum to Secretary Mitchell, March 29, 1959; Ambrosio Gonzales, Arizona G.I. Forum to Congressman Stewart Udall, March 14, 1959; Mrs. Guadalupe Contreras to Senator Patrick McNamara, March 24, 1959; Monica Ledesma, Colorado G.I. Forum to Senator Gordon Allot, March 10, 1959. The last cited letter best expresses the attitudes of the Forum members:

> We in the G.I. Forum have helped many a family to send their children to school, we have helped in getting them decent clothes for their children, we have given them legal counseling, medical aid for their families. But the one thing we cannot give them is a decent wage to which they can better themselves.

Salvador Olade to Senator Frank Lausche, April 2, 1959, HPG; *Forum News Bulletin,* "Forum Lauds Mitchell on Minimum Wage Stand," April 1959.

[28] Steve Allen, "Must They Work Dirt Cheap", *Coronet Magazine,* March 1967, p. 148.

[29] Newell Brown, Assistant Secretary of Labor, to Dr. Garcia, July 15, 1959, HPG; *Forum News Bulletin,* "More *Braceros* than U.S. Workers in New Mexico", May 1959; *Forum News Bulletin,* "Colorado Forum Pushes Bill on Housing; Farm Bill Bottled Up", May 1959; *Forum News Bulletin,* "Progress Made in Plight of Ohio Migrant Workers, Report Shows", May 1959; *Forum News Bulletin,* "Secretary Mitchell Names Group to Investigate *Bracero* Program", July 1959. A typical opponent of minimum wage provisions for domestic farm workers was Austin Anson, Executive Vice-President of the Texas Citrus and Vegetable Growers and Shippers, the same Austin Anson who vehemently opposed the

186

seventy-five cents minimum wage of 1949 (note 5). U.S., Congress, House, Committee of Education and Labor, *Hearings Before the Subcommittee on Labor Standards of the Committee on Education and Labor on Various Bills Regarding Minimum Wage Legislation,* Part 3, 86th Congress, 2nd Session, May 10, 11, 17, 18, 19, 1960, p. 1237.

[30] U.S. Congress, Senate, Committee on Labor and Public Welfare, *Hearings Before the Subcommittee on Migratory Labor of the Committee on Labor and Public Welfare, on S.1085, S.1778, S.2141, S.2498, Bills Relating to Migratory Labor,* 86th Congress, 1st Session, August 7, 26, September 28, 30, October 1, November 30, December 7-8, 1959; *Forum News Bulletin,* "Ike Adm. Requests Law to Curb Abuses of Migrants", September 1959; *Forum News Bulletin,* "Standards for Labor Aid Set by U.S. Department", September 1959.

[31] "Statement of R.P. Sanchez, Chairman, Committee on Migratory Labor, American G.I. Forum of the U.S., on Proposed Amendments to the Code of Federal Regulations on Interstate Recruitment of Migratory Workers and Placement Policy Before the Hearing Examiner of the U.S. Department of Labor", September 10-11, 1959, HPG; *Forum News Bulletin,* "Forum Attorney Testifies at Migratory Hearings", October 1959; *Forum News Bulletin,* "Appoint Senator Williams, Jr., on Senate Subcommittee on Migrant Labor", December 1959; *Forum News Bulletin,* "Steps Planned to Stabilize Labor", January and February 1960. The Mexican Farm Labor Program Consultants Report supported the basic contentions of G.I. Forum experts in U.S., Congress, Senate, Subcommittees on Labor and Public Welfare *Hearings Before the Subcommittee on Labor and Public Welfare on Bills Relating to Migratory Labor,* Part 1, 86th Congress, 2nd Session, 1960, pp. 741-750. U.S., Congress, House, Committee on Education and Labor, *Hearings Before the Subcommittee on General Education of the Committee on Education and Labor on H.R. 9872 and H.R. 10378,* May 2-5, 13, 1960, 86th Congress, 2nd Session, pp. 202, 207.

[32] *Forum News Bulletin,* "Advocate Defeat of Bills Harmful to Migrant Laborer", March-April 1960; *Forum News Bulletin,* "Gathing Bill Hurts Domestic Farm Migrant Labor and the Small Farmer Asks Gathing Sub-Committee on Equipment", 1960; "Statement of R.P. Sanchez on H.R. 11211 Before Gathings Subcommittee on Equipment, Supplies and Manpower", House Agriculture Committee, March 25, 1960; Dr. Garcia to Congressman John Young, April 23, 1960; Dr. Garcia to Senator Lyndon Johnson, March 30, 1960; U.S. Congress, House, Committee on Agriculture, *Hearings Before the Subcommittee on Equipment, Supplies and Manpower of the Committee on Agriculture Extension of Mexican Farm Labor Program,* 86th Congress, 2nd Session, March 22-25, 1960, pp. 152-153.

[33] *Forum News Bulletin,* "Help Set Record Straight on Intent of Farm Labor Bills", June 1960; Dr. Garcia to Senator Dennis Chavez, September 10, 1960, HPG.

[34] *Forum News Bulletin,* "Confirm Secretary of Labor's Authority Over Farm Worker", September 1960; *Forum News Bulletin,* "Farm Lobby Dealt Blow, Forum's Views Favored", September 1960; *Forum News Bulletin,* "Forum Fares OK on Migratory Labor Legislation", October 1960; Senator Paul Douglas to Dr. Garcia, June 9, 1960; Dr. Garcia to Senator Paul Douglas, June 3, 1960, HPG.

[35] Letter to Dr. Garcia, August 28, 1961, HPG; *Forum News Bulletin,* "Forum Attorney Reports Action on Congressional Migratory Bill", October 1961.

[36] *Forum News Bulletin,* "All Not Lost—New. P.L. 78 Reveals Gains for Migrant Labor", November 1961.

[37] U.S. Department of Labor, *President's Commission on Migratory Labor (Washington,*

D.C.: *U.S. Government Printing Office, 1961), HPG;* Thomas O'Hennad, "Door Opened at Last to Relieving Plight of Migrant Farm Workers and Families", *St. Louis Dispatch,* September 10, 1961; Testimony of G.I. Forum at U.S., Department of Labor Hearing on Public Law 78, HPG; *Forum News Bulletin,* "Urge Support of Migrant Bills Now Before House of Representatives", June 1962; *Forum News Bulletin,* "Law 78, Hit TEC", January 1962; Frank Jaime to U.S. Department of Labor, August 7, 1962, HPG; *Forum News Bulletin,* "Ohio G.I. Forum Provides Funeral", December 1963; John Henning, Under-Secretary of Labor, to Dr. Garcia, June 4, 1963, HPG; Testimony by Felix Salinas on the *Bracero* Program in New Mexico, 1961, HPG; Robert Sanchez to Dr. Garcia, January 13, 1961, HPG.

[38] *Forum News Bulletin,* "Laredo Forum Appeals to President for Solution to Commuter Problem", May 1963, letters to Congress from Laredo G.I. Forum 1963, HPG; *Forum News Bulletin,* editorial, November 1964.

[39] U.S. Congress, Senate, Committee on Labor and Public Welfare, *Hearings Before the Subcommittee on Migratory Labor of the Committee on Labor and Public Welfare, on Bills Relating to Various Migratory Labor Programs,* 88th Congress, 1st Session, April 10, 23, 24, 1963, pp. 51, 116, 716-725; *Los Angeles Times,* "Four Farm Groups Sue Wirtz Over Mexicans", December 11, 1963; *Forum News Bulletin* (Special 1965 Ladies Auxiliary Issue), "A Statement on Farm Labor", February 1965.

[40] *Los Angeles Times* article by Viva Johnson Club, DNC, October 16, 1964, HPG.

X. *The New Frontier, The Great Society*

[1] Governor Allan Shivers to Dr. Hector Garcia, May 8, 1950, HPG; Press Memorandum, Office of the Governor, "Governor Shivers Today. . . ," May 5, 1950, HPG; letter to Dr. Hector Garcia from R.E. Smith, May 5, 1950, HPG.

[2] *Forum News Bulletin,* "Texas Spanish-Speaking Voters Showed Loyalty to Demo Party on November 4", November 1952; file on Adlai Stevenson, HPG.

[3] *Forum News Bulletin,* "Words of Praise to Colorado Convention Sent By Senator Chavez", October 1953; *Forum News Bulletin,* "San Angelo Meeting Gets Great West Texas Turnout", March 1954, *Forum News Bulletin,* "Letter to Ed Idar from Ralph Yarborough", October 1954; *Forum News Bulletin,* Ximenes Reports Only Republican to Win in Bernadillo County Relied on Latin Help", December 1954; *Forum News Bulletin,* "New Mexico Convention News", May and June 1955, *Forum News Bulletin,* "Senator Phillips to Address Texas Convention", May and June 1955; *Forum News Bulletin,* "Governor Johnson Adds Luster to Colorado Convention," July 1955; *Forum News Bulletin,* "Don Politico Points Out Rising Influence of Independent Mexican American Voters", July 1955; *Forum News Bulletin,* "New Mexico Officials Get G.I. Forum Praise for Keeping Pledges," July 1955; *Forum News Bulletin,* "Santa Fe GIs Push Law Through", January 1959; *Forum News Bulletin,* "Governor Docking Declares Founder's Week — Praises Founder and Forum", October 1959; *Forum News Bulletin,* "Forum Lauded by Arizona Solon", July 1958.

[4] *Forum News Bulletin,* "Mexican Americans Win in Asherton", April 1955; *Forum News Bulletin,* "Bay City Sponsors Political Rally in Political Education Program", July 1956; *Forum News Bulletin,* "Forum Places Carlos Teran in Judge's Post in Los Angeles — 1st in History", January 1958; *Forum News Bulletin,* "Kansas Pete Esquivel Named to U.S. Civil Rights Advisor Group-Farmers on Spot", April 1959; *Forum News Bulletin,* "San Antonio G.I. Forum Presses for FEPC Bill", November 1958; *Forum News Bulletin,* "Ap-

point Forumeer - Judge C. Teran to Superior Court", January-February 1960; *Forum News Bulletin,* "Los Angeles Forumeers Lead Protest, Councilman Roybal Gains Stature", March-April 1960; *Forum News Bulletin,* "Forumeers Defeats a Governor Brown Picked Candidate", June 1960; *Forum News Bulletin,* "Democratic Party Recognition Accorded to Mexican American Demos in Texas", February-March 1956; the file of "Ralph Yarborough" in the G.I. Forum archives contains hundreds of letters pertaining to the increasing Forum strength.

[5] *Forum News Bulletin,* "Senator Kennedy Sends Warm Message to G.I. Forum in Los Angeles", September 1959; Dr. Garcia to J. Carlos McCormick, May 18, 1960, HPG.

[6] *Forum News Bulletin,* "Senator Kennedy Joins G.I. Forum", June 1960.

[7] Many Southwestern *Mexicanos* favored Senator Lyndon Johnson as the Democratic nominee, but Dr. Garcia had concluded privately that Johnson had little chance. Also see *Forum News Bulletin,* "Senator L.B. Johnson Greets Forumeers with 'Hi Compadres'", July 1960.

[8] *Forum News Bulletin,* "Dr. Garcia's Statement to the Democratic National Committee", July 1960; Dr. Garcia to Manuel Avila, August 3, 1960, HPG; James Harvey, *Civil Rights During the Kennedy Administration* (Hattiesburg: University & College Press of Mississippi, 1971), pp. 6-20; *Forum News Bulletin,* " Demos Pledge Aid to Farm Workers", September 1960; *Forum News Bulletin,* "Mexican Americans to Ambassador Posts If Elected—Kennedy", September, 1960.

[9] *Forum News Bulletin,* "McCormick Named Coordinator of Viva Kennedy", August 1960; *Forum News Bulletin,* "Forumeers Participate as Individuals in 'Viva Clubs'", October 1960; Ed Idar to Senator John Kennedy, August 31, 1960.

[10] *Forum News Bulletin,* "Forumeers Participate as Individuals in 'Viva' Clubs," August 1960.

[11] *Chicago Sun Times,* "Plan Organization of Kennedy Clubs", September 30, 1960; *Time,* October 10, 1960; *Dallas Morning News,* "Latin Americans Organize Viva Kennedy Committee," October 5, 1960; *Arizona Sun,* "New Mexico Dems Head Drive to Corral the Spanish Vote", October 12, 1960; *The Reporter* (California), October 27, 1960, in *Forum News Bulletin,* November-December 1962.

[12] *Kansas City Star,* "Mexicans Pleased by Election of Kennedy", November 21, 1960; 4,800 votes in Illinois and 28,000 votes in Texas would have made Richard Nixon President. Both states were areas of heavy Viva Kennedy activity; F. Chris Garcia, Rudolph O. de la Garza, *The Chicano Political Experience: Three Perspectives* (North Scituate, Duxbury Press, 1977) p. 101.

[13] Manuel Avila to Jose Alvarado, November 28, 1960, HPG; Dr. Garcia to Carlos McCormick, February 18, 1961, HPG; *Corpus Christi Caller-Times,* "High Job Offered Latin American", February 8, 1961; *Forum News Bulletin,* "Senator Chavez Changes Spanish-American Brings Some Appointments, " March 1961.

[14] Dr. Garcia to Judge Ted Butler, January 27, 1960; Dr. Garcia to Attorney General William Rogers, March 3, 1960; Dr. Garcia to Secretary of Treasury Robert Anderson, March 3, 1960; Dr. Garcia to President Dwight D. Eisenhower, March 4, 1960; Ed Idar to Dr. Hector Garcia, July 26, 1960; Dr. Garcia to Senator John Kennedy, December 1960, HPG.

[15] *Corpus Christi Caller,* "Battle Boils Over Latin America as U.S. Judge", January 14, 1961; statement of national coordinator of NAPA, April 1961; Dr. Garcia to Manuel Avila, March 25, 1961; Ed Idar to Dr. George I. Sanchez, HPG.

[16] Narrative Report of National Political Leadership Conference, March 26, 1961, HPG; *Forum News Bulletin*, "Dr. Garcia to Head 1st National Political Association of Spanish Speaking", May 1961; *Valley Morning Star*, "Viva Kennedy Leaders in Revolt", June 28, 1961.

[17] *Forum News Bulletin*, "Forumeer Henry B. Gonzalez Wins Congressional Seat for Texas Demos", November 1961; *Forum News Bulletin*, "Mexican American Voter Role as a Balance of Power Factor Dramatically Illustrated", June 1961.

[18] *Dallas Morning News*, "Crystal City Gave PASO Pilot Project It Needed", May 7, 1962; Dr. Garcia to Danny Aguirre, December 13, 1962; Dr. Garcia to Manuel Avila, February 24, 1962, HPG; *Valley Evening Monitor*, PASO Officials Accuse Anglos of Injecting Race Issue in Valley", May 24, 1962; Dr. Garcia to Dr. George I. Sanchez, May 25, 1962, HPG.

[19] Dr. Garcia to Director of Urban Renewal, September, 1, 1961; letter to Burke Marshal, Asst. Attorney General, Civil Rights Division, September 30, 1961; memo to Hector Garcia on Failure of Department of Labor to investigate discrimination, October3, 1951; Vice-President Johnson to Hector Garcia, October 1, 1962.

[20] *Forum News Bulletin*, "Labor Secretary Goldberg Addresses GI Forums in Founder's City", September 1961; *American G.I. Forum*, "Information for Progress", and "The Battle for Latin Americans is On", August 1962, HPG; *Forum News Bulletin*, "Latin Ambassador A Hit--What We'ev Been Saying", September 1961; PASO press release, "The October 22 Proclamation...", October 24, 1962, HPG; Lee White, Asst. Special Council to the President, to Dr. Garcia, March 15, 1962, HPG; *Forum News Bulletin*, "Drs. Hector and Cleo Garcia at Important LBJ Gathering of Latin Ambassadors", October 1962; *Forum News Bulletin*, "Forum & Nation Mourns Senator Chavez' Death; LBJ and Dr. Garcia Fly to Funeral", November 1962.

[21] Dr. Garcia to Robert Kennedy, May 15, 1963; Dr. Garcia to Robert Kennedy, June 13, 1963; James De Anda to Jose Alvarado, June 7, 1963, HPG; *Forum News Bulletin*, "Hail 15th Confab, Fortells Big Year, Bob Kennedy Lauds Spanish Speaking", December 1963.

[22] Theodore Sorensen, *Kennedy* (New York: Harper & Row, 1955), pp. 470—472.

[23] Ibid, p. 477; James Harvey,*Civil Rights During the Kennedy Administration;* Henry Fairlie, *The Kennedy Promise: The Politics of Expectation* (New York: Doubleday & Company, Inc., 1973), pp. 249—256; William O'Neil, *Coming Apart* (Chicago: Quadrangle, 1971), p. 73—75.

[24] Attorney General Robert Kennedy desegregated several Southern schools by personal coersion as well as securing voting rights for many citizens by "personal persuasion". See O'Niel, *Coming Apart*, p. 89.

[25] Hugh Sidney, *A Very Personal Presidency: Lyndon Johnson in the White House* (New York: Atheneum, 1968), pp. 239—240; address by Senator Lyndon B. Johnson before the annual banquet of the American G.I. Forum, August 1, 1953, HPG; *Forum News Bulletin*, letters to editor, February 1954; see "Important Persons, LBJ" for several hundred letters from LBJ to various Forumeers in HPG files; Rowland Evans and Robert Novak describe Mexican American support of LBJ as "Boss-led, like any segregatd minority". Evans and Novak illustrate their own ignorance; Rowland Evans and Robert Novak, *Lyndon B. Johnson: The Exercise of Power* (New York: New American Library, 1966), p. 132.

[26] Dr. Garcia to President Johnson, December 1963, HPG; *Forum News Bulletin*, "Forum at Equal Opportunity Parley, LBJ Fete Has Guacamole and Refritos", May 1962;

American G.I. Forum "Resolution to the Senate...of the 1963 Convention of the American G.I. Forum", June 12, 1964, HPG.

[27] *Forum News Bulletin,* "Forum Opens D.C. Office", May 1964; the Forum chapter in Washington, D.C. had been very effective in disseminating information on employment opportunity progress and other federal programs. Information for Progress had begun in 1961, but the official G.I. Forum lobby opened in 1964. *Forum News Bulletin,* "Washington, D.C. Forum Offers Information on Government Jobs", April 1963; also see file on Information for Progress, HPG.

[28] Many writers of the Johnson presidency have alluded to LBJ's experiences as a young school teacher of very poor Mexican American children in Cotulla, Texas. This association provides an educational and emotional experience that John Kennedy never had. Johnson often described this period as an example of the meaning of poverty and bigotry. After his presidential message on behave of the 1964 Civil Rights Act, Johnson told Dr. Garcia that during that Speech his thoughts lingered on his Cotulla students; in his Congressional speech on the 1965 Voting Rights Act, LBJ did mention Mexican Americans. See Hugh Sidney, *A Very Personal Presidency,* pp. 14, 36; William White, *The Professional: Lyndon B. Johnson* (Boston: Houghton Mifflin Company, 1964), p. 100; interview with Dr. Garcia, January 10, 1975; and Particularly O'Niel, *Coming Apart,* pp. 129 and 118.

[29] Telegram from the White House to Dr. Garcia, July 10, 1964; *Forum News Bulletin,* "Forumeers on Civil Rights Committee", September 1964.

[30] *Forum News Bulletin,* "Mrs Lyndon Johnson to Address Delegates", July 1964; *Forum News Bulletin,* "Ximenes, Ramos Lead Viva Johnson Clubs", November 1964.

[31] American G.I. Forum, Washington, D.C., office, "Testimony on the Office of Economic Opportunity Submitted by Rudy Ramos, Director of the Washington, D.C., Office of the American G.I. Forum", April 26, 1965, HPG; *The Forumeer,* "Forum Members Prominent at Great Society Conference", July 1965.

[32] *The Forumeer,* "White House Conference on EEO", and "Dr. Hector Garcia Presents Statements to the President", October 1965; *The Forumeer,* "Top Posts for Spanish-Speaking Americans Asked on Anti-Poverty Program", September 1965; *The Forumeer,* "Regional Coordinator Post Accepted by Del Rio's Chris Alderete", "Rudolph Gonzalez Heads Denver War on Poverty", and "Freemont Forumeer on Board of Economic Opportunity Agency", November 1965; Dr. Garcia to Franklin Roosevelt, Jr., April 22, 1966 HPG; *Corpus Christi Caller,* "Head of EEOC in Corpus Christi", December 15, 1965.

[33] *The Forumeer,* "War on Poverty Battle in San Jose", January 1966.

[34] American G.I. Forum, Washington, D.C., Report, "Anatomy of a Presidential Statement on Equal Employment Opportunity and Civil Rights for Mexican Americans", 1966, HPG; *The Forumeer,* editorial, April 1966.

[35] *The Forumeer,* "Forum Delegates Walk Out", April 1966; *The Forumeer,* "EEOC Charged—Discrimination", June 1966.

[36] *Washington Post,* May 22,1966; *The Forumeer,* "Corky Gonzalez Ousted as Denver Youth Corp Director", June 1966; *The Forumeer,* "M-A Walkout Leaders Honored", June 1966.

[37] *The Forumeer,* editorial, July 1967; *The Forumeer,* "Forum Approves Operation SER", December 1967; *The Forumeer,* "Que Vamos A Ser", February 1967; *The Forumeer,* "SER Begins Working Agreement With California", February 1967.

[38] *The Forumeer,* "Forum Rejects Rioting as Means to Civil Rights", August 1967; Forumeers did desist in peaceful protests as exampled by El Paso members in El Paso protesting slums, *The Forumeer,* "El Paso Forum Protests Slums", February 1967.

[39] *The Forumeer,* "Cabinet Committee Hears M-A in El Paso, October 27-28"; *The Forumeer,* "1,000 at M-A Hearing in El Paso", November 1967; Acuña, *Occupied America.*

[40] *The Forumeer,* "1,000 at M-A Hearing in El Paso", November 1967.

[41] *The Forumeer,* "Dr. Garcia Gets U.N. Post", October 1967; *The Forumeer,* "Dr. Garcia on Civil Rights Board", November 1968.

[42] Sidney's account of LBJ in *A Very Personal Presidency* is probably the most balanced assessment of President Lyndon Johnson.

[43] Although scholarly analyses of the Great Society vary in their view of the effect of the Johnson programs (*Coming Apart vs. The Making of a President, 1972*), a personal experience may add to a better perspective. Many Mexican Americans in Austin, Texas, benefitted from the "Great Society", particularly Medicare and Model Cities—having been a part of that community, the author can testify to the success of these programs.

XI. *New Allies, Old Veterans*

[1] *The Forumeer,* "L.A. High School Students Protest Sub-Standard School", April 1968; *El Paso Times,* "Mexican American Resentment Grows", October 14, 1965.

[2] *El Sol,* "Mexican Americans Boycotting Students at Elsa Suspended", November 22, 1968; Ester Sepulveda, Texas Auxiliary Chairwoman, to A.E. Wells, Superintendent of Abilene Public Schools, November 13, 1969; A.E. Wells to Ester Sepulveda, November 15, 1969; Jr. G.I. Forum President, Mathis, Texas, to Dr. Garcia, April 15, 1970, HPG.

[3] *Corpus Christi Caller-Times,* "Bexar Official, MAYO Leader Nearly Have Fight", April 12, 1969; *Corpus Christi Caller* "Gonzalez Says MAYO Quiz Waste of Time," April 29, 1969.

[4] *Forum News Bulletin,* "Dr. Garcia at Del Rio", May 1969; Dr. Garcia to Assistant Secretary of Defense, Roger Kelley, April 30, 1969; American G.I. Forum, "Table of Contents VISTA Incident" Del Rio, Texas, March 25, 1969, HPG; Dr. Hector Garcia, "Statement of Dr. Hector Garcia of Immediate Press Release", March 25, 1969, HPG; *Corpus Christi Caller* "92 Del Rio Prostester Set Free", March 21, 1969.

[5] Resolution adopted by the American G.I. Forum of the U.S. Convention, "Support, Commend and Congratulate Cesar Chavez", August 27, 1966; *The Forumeer,* "U.F.W.O.C. Family Mistreated at Holiday Inn", October 1970; Dr. Hector P. Garcia, Amador Garcia, and C. Rudolph Garza, Jr., to Speaker Carl Albert demanding investigation of alleged assasination plot against Cesar Chavez, January 4, 1972; *The Forumeer,* "Forum Asked to Continue Support", March 1969; Washington, D.C., Huelga Committee, "An Appeal for Help", American G.I. Forum & LULAC ask for support of Texas farm worker strike, August 1966, HPG; *The Forumeer,* letter of thanks to G.I. Forum from UFWOC, January 1971.

[6] *The Forumeer,* "Ramos Testifies on Immigration", May 1965; Henry B. Gonzales to Rudy Ramos, July 12, 1967, HPG; Dr. Garcia to Senator Harrison Williams, April 19, 1966, HPG; Senator Yarborough to Senator Joseph Clark, July 31, 1967, HPG; Rudy Ramos to Zeke Duran, August 15, 1967, HPG; Congressman M. Udall to Congressman

Emmanuel Cellar, March 7, 1967, HPG; Ed Idar to Texas Lt. Governor Preston Smith, April 25, 1967, HPG; Dr. Garcia to Robert Allen, Texas OEO, July 26, 1968, HPG; R.P. Sanchez to Congressman Joseph Montoya, April 13, 1969, HPG; statement by Dr. Hector Garcia, Founder of American G.I. Forum of the U.S. at hearing held by OSHA of the U.S. Department of Labor, January 30, 1975, HPG.

[7] Gerald Shanklin to George Alvarez, January 7, 1960; Martha Reyna, President, Slaton G.I. Forum Auxiliary to Dr. Garcia, March 7, 1960; Rodrigo Lozano to Dr. Garcia, March 29, 1962; Vicente Ximenes to Alfonso Sanchez, February 22, 1962; copy of statement from Lockney, Texas G.I. Forum warning of potential segregation, September 12, 1962; Ed Idar to Glenn Garret, September 24, 1962; Anguinaldo Zamora to EEC, Austin, Texas, May 3, 1968; statement/letter concerning New Mexico-Texas school segregation and quality education by Dr. Garcia to Eliot Richardson, Secretary of HEW, September 25, 1970; Dr. Garcia to J. Stanley Pottinger, Justice Department on Texas School Districts, October 2, 1970; "List of School Districts Which Have Segregated Schools that are Vestiges of a Former De Jure System Operating for Mexican Americans", HPG.

[8] U.S., Congress, House, *Congressional Record,* 91st Congress, 2nd Session, June 23, 1970, p. E.5824. Answering a complaint of Sonora, Texas, Mexican Americans over *de facto* segregation and improper facilities, Congressman O.C. Fisher maintained, "Why isolated? If the community may be so described, any fool would know it happened simply because Mexican Americans chose to live there".

[9] Dr. Hector Garcia, "Statistics in the Corpus Christi Public Schools", on the lack of education attainment and the absence of Mexican American Staff in a 53 percent Mexican American population plurality; memorandum to school district from J. Stanley Pottinger, May 25, 1970, HPG.

[10] Jose Cisneros *vs.* Corpus Christi Independent School District, Civil Action Number GB-C-95, Southern District of Texas, Corpus Christi Division, p.4, HPG. This was the first application of the *Brown* decision to Mexican American issues.

[11] *Corpus Christi Caller,* "Local School Case Highlights", June 27, 1973; *The Forumeer,* "Dr. Garcia and Sit-in", October 1972; *Corpus Christi Caller,* "Cox Proposal Relies Heavily on Student Transfer", December 6, 1973, and "Order of March 10, 1975, and May 7, 1975, plus Response", HPG.

[12] File of "Concerned Neighbors", HPG.

[13] "Statement of Dr. Hector Garcia before Honorable John Dent, Chairman General Subcommittee on Labor Committee on Education and Labor", December 2, 1969; Clement Aguilar, Nebraska G.I. Forum Chairman, to William Brown, Chairman EEOC, August 23, 1969; Vicente Jimenez to Dr. Garcia, memorandum to all national and state officers on Senate Bill 2453, October 8, 1970, HPG; *The Forumeer,* "G.I. Forum, NAACP joins Forces to Block Lockheed Welfare", June 1971; *The Forumeer,* "G.I. Forum Backs Farah Boycott, Asks More Jobs for View Vets", October 1973.

[14] Matt Hernandez to Arnold Espinosa, April 8 and April 20, 1969; memorandum to all national, state officers, and local chairmen, "Boycott of Coors", April 22, 1969, HPG; *The Forumeer,* "G.I. Forum Continues National Coors Boycott", May 1973; statement by Antonio Morales of the 1975 Texas G.I. Forum Convention.

[15] *The Forumeer,* "G.I. Forum V.O.P. Project Did the Job" (Special Edition), May 1974; Budget Proposal by American G.I. Forum in Pueblo, Colorado, HPG. The G.I. Forum constantly represented Mexican American veterans before Vietnam hearings on the Selective Service.

[16] *San Antonio Express*, "Ethnic Groups Teach Advertising", July 13, 1970; "American G.I. Forum memorandum" by Daniel Campos, 1969.

[17] *The Forumeer*, "Frito-Lay Letters Get No Action", April 1969; *The Forumeer*, "Frito-Lay is Still Around", February 1971.

[18] *The Forumeer*, "Frito Bandito is Still Around", February 1971; *The Wichita Eagle*, "Datelines of the Day", February 18, 1970; letter to Dr. Garcia from John McCarty, April 14, 1970, HPG; Dr. Garcia to John McCarty, September 8, 1970, HPG; *The Forumeer*, Fito-Lay to Dr. Garcia, December 1970; Ezequiel Duran to Dr. Garcia, December 12, 1970, HPG; *El Sol*, "La Campaña del Frito Bandito un Insulto a Mexicanos", January 1971; *Pensacola Journal*, "Angry Mexican Americans Take Aim at Frito Bandito in Suit", January 1, 1971; *Hutchinson News*, "Attack Frito Bandito", February 14, 1971; telegram to Dr. Garcia from Gilbert Herrera and Brownie Treviño, April 1, 1971, HPG.

[19] *New York Times*, "Mexican Americans Take on New Military in Struggle for Identity", April 20, 1969.

[20] *Los Angeles Times*, "Thirty-six Foundations Refuse Bids to Meetings on Mexican Americans", April 1969.

[21] *Washington Post*, "Ford Fund to Aid Minorities", March 26, 1969; Vicente Ximenez to Ed Roybal, October 29, 1969, HPG.

[22] Interview with Vicente Ximenez, August 23, 1974.

[23] *The Forumeer*, transcript by court reporter Susan K. Strahm, October 1969.

[24] *The Forumeer*, "Judge Seeks Temporary Assignment as Chicanos Demonstrate", October 1969.

[25] George Darrah, Michigan G.I. Forum, to California Chief Justice Roger Traynor; Dr. Ladislao Lopez, Missouri G.I. Forum, to Attorney General John Mitchell; Ezequiel Duran, National Executive Secretary, to California Governor Reagan; Manuel Avila to *The Forumeer*, Congressman Ed Roybal to California State Judicial Qualification Board; Senator Joseph Montoya to Carlos Naranjo; Sam Lopez, Kansas G.I. Forum, to Jack Frankel; *The Forumeer*, "Garcia Hits Chagrin Conspiracy of Silence", December 1969; *The Forumeer*, "Chagrin Protest Mounts", December 1969.

[26] *The Forumeer*, "California Law Enforcement to Tolerate Racist Chagrin", February 28, 1970.

[27] *The Forumeer*, "Chagrin Publicly Censured", July 1970; *The Forumeer*, "Chagrin Candidacy Insults Chicanos", May 1972; *The Forumeer*, "Chagrin Re-elected", June 1972. A California judge was dismissed because of profane language and sexual improprieties—Chagrin remained on the bench.

[28] *The Forumeer*, "Anti-War Resolution Passed at California Convention", July 1970.

[29] David Sierra to Ezequiel Duran, HPG; numerous editorials in *The Forumeer*.

[30] *The Forumeer*, "The Inter-Agency Committee to be Squeeky Wheel", November 1969; *The Forumeer*, "Castillo Raps D.C.", October 1969; *The Forumeer*, "Castillo Ousted", January 1971.

[31] *The Texas Observer*, comment on Werdel Report: "He's Got a Lovely Bunch of Coconuts", November 3, 1972, pp. 8-10.

[32] *The Forumeer*, "G.I Forum Speaks to Nion", April 1971; *The Forumeer*, "Chicano

Grievances Given to Nixon at San Clemente", December 1971; *The Forumeer*, "Ramirez Won't Testify Says Rep. Don Edwards", August 1972.

[33] *The Texas Observer*, "He's Got a Lovely Bunch of Coconuts", November 3, 1972, pp. 8-10. *The Forumeer*, "Article from the *Wall Street Journal*", April 1972.

[34] Polly Barragan, "Report of the DNC Office of the Spanish-Speaking", January 3, 1972—July 7, 1972, HPG. Despite the obvious nature of Nixon's campaign overtures, the percentage of Mexican Americans voting for the Republican candidate increased from 18 percent in 1968 to 31 percent in 1972. This "desertion" from the Democratic party was part of the total Democratic vote which McGovern lost. Thirty-seven percent of registered Democrats who voted in 1972 did so for Richard Nixon. George McGovern took too much for granted in regard to the ethnic vote.

[35] *Corpus Christi Caller-Times*, "You Don't Have to be 18", November 6, 1972.

[36] *The Forumeer*, "Honeymoon is Over, Fernandez Raps Nixon", February 1973.

[37] *The Forumeer*, "Wichita Falls Active on Many Fronts", February 1975.

XII. *The American G.I. Forum*

[1] Manuel Servin, "The Post-World War II Mexican-Americans, 1925-65: A Nonachieving Minority", in *An Awakened Minority: The Mexican-Americans*, ed. Manuel Servin (Beverly Hills: Glencoe Press, 1974), pp. 167, 171. This essay was originally presented in 1965. Its subsequent inclusion with a number of very competent articles on the Mexican American underlines its own flaws.

[2] Garcia and de la Garza, *The Chicano Political Experience*. This is the first attempt to analyze the political experience of Chicano in a single monograph.

[3] Alfredo Cuellar, "Perspective on Politics", *Mexican Americans*, ed. Moore, Chapter 8.

[4] Garcia and de la Garza, p. 29.

[5] Miguel David Tirado, "Mexican American Community Political Organization: The Key to Chicano Power" in *La Causa Politica: A Chicano Political Reader*, ed. F. Chris Garcia, (Notre Dame: University of Notre Dame Press, 1974), p. 124.

[6] Ibid., pp. 80-81.

[7] Acuna, *Occupied America*, pp. 222-226.

[8] Ellwyn Stoddard, *Mexican Americans* (New York: Random House, 1973) pp. 168-169.

Selected Bibliography

Books

Acuña, Rodolfo. *Occupied America: The Chicanos' Struggle Toward Liberation.* San Francisco, Canfield Press, 1972.

American G.I. Forum and Texas State Federation of Labor. *What Price Wetbacks?* Austin: Texas AF of L, 1953.

Berman, William. *The Politics of Civil Rights in the Truman Administration.* Columbus: Ohio State University Press, 1970.

Browning, Harley, and McLemore, Dale. *A Statistical Profile of the Spanish Surname Population of Texas.* Austin: Population Research Center, University of Texas, 1964.

Burma, John. *Spanish-Speaking Groups in the United States.* Salem: Duke University Press, 1954.

Cassmore, Olin, and Menefee, Seldon. *The Pecan Shellers of San Antonio.* Washington, D.C.: U.S. Government Printing Office, 1940.

Cuellar, Robert. *A Social and Political History of the Mexican American Population of Texas, 1929-1963.* San Francisco: Rand E. Research Associates, 1974.

Cumberland, Charles. *Mexico: The Struggle for Modernity.* New York: Oxford University Press, 1968.

DeConde, Alexander. *A History of American Foreign Policy.* New York: Charles Scribner's Sons, 1971.

Eisenhower, Dwight D. *Mandate for Change: 1953-1956.* Garden City: Doubleday, 1963.

———. *Waging Peace: 1956-1961.* Garden City: Doubleday, 1963.

Ehrlich, Paul. *The Golden Door: International Migration, Mexico, and the United States.* New York: Ballantine Books, 1979.

Evans, Rowland, and Novak, Robert. *Lyndon B. Johnson: The Exercise of Power.* New York: New American Library, 1966.

Fairlie, Henry. *The Kennedy Promise: The Politics of Expectation.* New York: Doubleday & Company, Inc. 1973.

Flores, Armando. *Ando Sangrando: A Study of Mexican American Police Conflict.* La Puente: Perspective Publishing Company, 1972.

Fogel, Walter. *Education and Income of Mexican Americans in the Southwest.* Mexican American Study Project, Advance Report I. Los Angeles: University of California, 1965.

———. *Mexican Americans in the Southwest Labor Markets.* Mexican American Study Project, Advance Report No. 10. Los Angeles: University of California, 1967.

Galarza, Ernesto. *Merchants of Labor: The Mexican Bracero Story.* Santa Barbara: McNally & Loftin, 1964.

————. *Farm Workers and Agri-business in California, 1947-1960.* Notre Dame: University of Notre Dame Press, 1977.

Gamio, Manuel. *Mexican Immigration to the United States.*1930. Reprint New York: Dover Publications, 1971.

Garcia, F. Chris, ed. *La Causa Politica: A Chicano Politics Reader.* Notre Dame: University of Notre Dame Press, 1974.

Garcia, F. Chris, and de la Garza, Rudolph O. *The Chicano Political Experience: Three Perspectives.* North Scituate, Mass: Duxbury Press, 1977.

Gregler, Leo; Guzman, Ralph; and Moore, Joanne. *The Mexican American People.* New York: Free Press, 1970.

Harvey, James. *Civil Rights During the Kennedy Administration.* Hattiesburg: University & College Press of Mississippi, 1971.

Hoffman, Abraham. *Unwanted Mexican Americans in the Great Depression: Repatriation Pressures, 1929-1939.* Tucson: University of Arizona Press, 1970.

Hughes, Emmet. *The Ordeal of Power: A Political Memoir of the Eisenhower Years.* New York: Atheneum, 1963.

Kibbe, Pauline. *Latin Americans in Texas.* Albuquerque: University of New Mexico Press, 1946.

Kingrea, Nellie. *History of the First Ten Years of the Texas Good Neighbor Commission.* Ft. Worth: Texas Christian University Press, 1954.

Little, Wilson. *Spanish-Speaking Children in Texas.* Austin: University of Texas, 1930.

McDonald, Archie P., ed. *The Mexican War: Crisis for American Diplomacy.* Lexington, Mass.: D.C. Heath and Company, 1969.

McWilliams, Carey. *Factories in the Fields.* 1935. Reprint. Archon Books, 1969.

————. *North From Mexico,* 2nd ed. New York: Greenwood Press, 1968.

Manuel, Herschel. *The Education of Mexican and Spanish-Speaking Children in Texas.* Austin: University of Texas, 1930.

Matthiessen, Peter. *Sal Si Puedes: Cesar Chavez and the New American Revolution.* New York: Dell, 1969.

Meir, Matt, and Rivera, Feliciano. *The Chicanos: A History of Mexican Americans.* New York: Hill and Wang, 1972.

Merk, Frederic. *Manifest Destiny and Mission in American History.* New York: Vintage, 1963.

Meyers, Frederic. *Spanish-Name Persons in the Labor Force in Manufacturing Industry in Texas.* Austin: University of Texas Press, 1951.

Moore, Joan. *Mexican Americans.* Englewood Cliffs: Prentice Hall, 1960.

Moquin, Wayne, ed. *A Documentary History of the Mexican American.* New York: Praeger, 1971.

Morgan, Patricia. *Shame of a Nation: A Documented Story of Police-State Terror Against Mexican Americans in the U.S.A.* Los Angeles: L.A. Committee for Protection of the Foreign Born, 1934.

Morin, Raul. *Among the Valiant: Mexican Americans in World War II and Korea.* Los Angeles: Bottden Publishing Company, 1963.

O'Neil, William. *Coming Apart: An Informal History of the Sixties.* Chicago: Quadrangle, 1971.

Parmet, Herbert. *Eisenhower and the American Crusades.* New York: Macmillian Company, 1972.

Pitt, Leonard. *The Decline of the Californias: A Social History of the Spanish-Speaking Californians, 1846-1890.* Berkeley: University of California Press, 1971.

Polenberg, Richard. *War and Society: The United States, 1941-1945.* New York: J.B. Lippincott Company, 1972.

Reisler, Mark. *By the Sweat of Their Brow: Mexican Immigrant Labor in the United States, 1900-1940.* Westport, Conn.: Greenwood Press, 1976.

Rendon, Armando. *Chicano Manifesto.* New York: Collier Books, 1971.

Richardson, Rupert. *Texas, the Lone Star State.* Englewood Cliffs: Prentice Hall, 1963.

Romano V. Octavio, ed. *Voices: Readings from El Grito, a Journal of Contemporary Mexican American Thought, 1967-1973.* Berkeley: Quinto Sol Publications, 1973.

Rosaldo, Renato; Calvert, Robert A.; and Seligmann, Gustau L., eds. *Chicano: The Evolution of a People.* San Francisco: Rinehart Press, 1973.

Ross, Davis. *Preparing for Ulysses: Politics and Veterans During World War II.* New York: Columbia University Press, 1969.

Ross, Irwin. *The Loneliest Campaign.* New York: New American Library, 1968.

Rubel, Arthur J. *Across the Tracks, Mexican Americans in a Texas City.* Austin: University of Texas Press, 1966.

Samora, Julian. *Los Mojados.* South Bend: University of Notre Dame Press, 1970.

———. Bernal, Jose; and Pena, Albert. *Gunpowder Justice: A Reassessment of the Texas Rangers.* Notre Dame: University of Notre Dame Press, 1974.

Schlesinger, Arthur. *A Thousand Days: John F. Kennedy in the White House.* Greenwich: Fawcett Publishers, Inc., 1965.

Servin, Manuel, ed.. *The Mexican Americans, An Awakening Minority.* Beverly Hills: Glencoe Press, 1970.

Schockley, John Staples. *Chicano Revolt in A Texas Town.* Notre Dame: University of Notre Dame Press, 1974.

Shelton, Edgar. *Political Conditions Among Texas Mexicans Along the Rio Grande.* San Francisco: Rand E. Research Associates, 1974.

Sidney, Hugh. *A Very Personal Presidency: Lyndon Johnson in the White House.* New York: Atheneum, 1968.

———. *John F. Kennedy, President.* New York: Atheneum, 1964.

Singletary, Otis A. *The Mexican War.* Chicago: University of Chicago Press, 1960.

Sorensen, Theordore C. *Kennedy*. New York: Harper & Row, 1965.

Stoddard, Ellwyn. *Mexican Americans*. New York: Random House, 1973.

Taylor, Paul. *An American Mexican Frontier, Nueces County*. New York: Russell & Russell, 1934.

Thomas, Hugh. *Cuba: The Persuit of Freedom*. New York: Harper & Row, 1971.

Tindall, George. *The Emergence of the New South, 1913-1945*. Baton Rouge: Louisiana State University Press, 1930.

———. *Mexican Labor in the United States*. Vol. I. Berkeley: University of California Press, 1930.

To Secure These Rights: The Report of the President's Commission on Civil Rights. New York: Simon and Schuster, 1947.

Tuck, Ruth. *Not With the Fist: Mexican Americans in a Southwest City*. New York: Harcourt Brace and Company, 1946.

Wager, Nathaniel N., and Haug, Marsha J., eds. *Chicanos: Social and Psychological Perspectives*. St. Louis: C.V. Mosby Company, 1971.

Walters, Pat. *The South and the Nation*. New York: Vintage, 1969.

Weber, David J., ed. *Foreigners in Their Native Land, Historical Roots of the Mexican Americans*. Albuquerque: University of *New Mexico Press, 1973*.

———. *New Spain's Far Northern Frontier, Essays on Spain in the American West, 1540-1821*. Albuquerque: University of New Mexico Press, 1979.

White, Theodore. *The Making of the President, 1960*. New York: New American Library, 1961.

———. *The Making of the President, 1964*. New York: New American Library, 1965.

———. *The Making of the President, 1968*. New York: Pocket Books, 1969.

———. *The Making of the President, 1972*. New York: Atheneum, 1973.

White, William. *The Professional, Lyndon B. Johnso.i*. Boston' Houghton Mifflin Company, 1964.

Theses and Dissertations

Connor, Ruth. "Some Community, Home, and School Problems of Latin American Children in Austin, Texas." Master's Thesis, University of Texas, 1949.

Crain, Forest. "The Occupational Distribution of Spanish-Name People in Austin, Texas." Master's Thesis, University of Texas, 1948.

Forgartie, Ruth Ann. "Spanish-Name People in Texas with Special Emphasis on Those Who Are Students in Texas Colleges and Universities." Master's Thesis, University of Texas, 1948.

Garza, Edward. "L.U.L.A.C." Master's Thesis, Southwest Texas State Teachers College, 1951.

Gilbert, Ennis Hall. "Some Legal Aspects of the Education of Spanish-Speaking Children in Texas." Master's Thesis, University of Texas, 1947.

Rouse, Lura. "A Study of the Education of Spanish-Speaking Children in Dimmitt

County, Texas." Master's Thesis, University of Texas, 1948.

Woods, Frances. "Mexican Ethnic Leadership in San Antonio." Ph.D. Dissertation, Catholic University of America, 1949.

Articles and Pamphlets

A Comparison of Family Income and Expenditures for Five Principal Budget Items in Twenty Texas Cities. Austin: University of Texas Bureau of Business Research, 1943.

Allen, Steve. "Must They Work Dirt Cheap." *Coronet Magazine,* March 1967.

Border Trends, A Monthly Summary of Significant Events Pertaining to Anglo-Latin Relations in the Southwest. September 1948.

Beegle, Allan et al. "Demographic Characteristics of the U.S. - Mexican Border." *Rural Sociology 25 (March 1960).*

Casteneda, Carlos. "Some Facts on Our Racial Minority." *The Pan American,* October 1944.

Coalson, George. "Mexican Contract Labor in American Agriculture." *Southwestern Social Science Quarterly* 33 (December 1952).

Crawford, Rex. "The Latin Americans in Wartime United States." *Annals of the American Academy of Political and Social Science,* September 1942.

Dodson, Jack. "Minority Group Housing in Two Texas Cities." In *Studies in Housing and Minority Groups: Special Research Report to the Commission on Race and Housing.* Ed. Nathan Glazer and Davis McEntire. Los Angeles: University of California Press, 1960.

Greene, Sheldon. "Immigration Law and Rural Poverty-The Problems of the Illegal Entrant." *Duke Law Journal,* No. 3 (1969).

Hendrick, Irving G. "Early Schooling for Children of Migrant Farmworkers." *Aztlan: International Journal of Chicano Studies Research,* Vol. 8 (Spring, Summer 1977).

Kibbe, Pauline. "The American Standard for All Americans." *Common Ground,* 1949.

Manuel, Herschel. "The Mexican Population of Texas." *Southwestern Political and Social Science Quarterly,* June 1934.

Mungula, Ruben. *A Cotton Picker Finds Justice: The Saga of the Hernandez Case.* American .G.I. Forum, 1954.

Northrup, Herbert. "Race Discrimination in Trade Unions; The Record and Outlook." *Commentary,* August 1946.

Rangel, Jorge, and Alcala, Carlos. "Project Report: De Jure Segregation of Chicanos in Texas Schools." *Harvard Civil Rights-Civil Liberties Law Review.* Vol. 7, No. 2 (March 1972).

Richards, Eugene. "Attitudes of White College Students in the Southwest Toward Ethnic Groups in the United States." *Sociology and Social Research* 35 (September 1950).

Rosales, Francisco A. "Mexicanos in Indiana Harbor During the 1920's: Prosperity and Depression." *Revista Chicano-Riqueña,* Año Cuatro, Numero Cuatro (Otoño 1976).

Sanchez, George. "Concerning Segregation of Spanish-Speaking Children in Public Schools." Inter-American Education Occassional Papers IX. Austin: University of Texas,

1951.

Saunders, Lyle. "The Social History of Spanish-Speaking People in Southwestern U.S. Since 1846." *Summarized Proceedings II.* Southwestern Council on Education of Spanish-Speaking People, 1950.

―――. "The Spanish-Speaking Population of Texas." Austin: University of Texas Press, December 1949.

―――. "The Wetback Problem in the Lower Rio Grande Valley." Austin. University of Texas, 1951.

Scruggs, O.M., "Texas and the Bracero Program." *Pacific Historical Review* 32 (August 1963).

Sepulveda, Ciro. "The Origins of the Urban Colonias in the Midwest, 1910-1930." *Revista Chicano Riqueña.* Año Cuatro, Numero Cuatro (Otoño 1976).

Shapiro, Harold. "The Pecan Shellers of San Antonio, Texas." *Southwestern Social Science Quarterly* 32 (March 1952).

Simmons, Ozzie G. "The Mutual Images and Expectations of Anglo-Americans and Mexican Americans." In *Chicanos: Social and Psychological Perspectives.* ed. Marsha Haug and Nathaniel Wagner , St. Louis: C.V. Mosby Company, 1971.

Taylor, Paul. "Mexicans North of the Rio Grande." *Survey Graphic* 56 (May 1931).

Weeks, O. Douglas. "The Texas-Mexicans and the Politics of South Texas." *American Political Science Review* 24 (August 1930).

"Wetbacks in Middle of Border War," *Business Week,* October 24, 1953.

Womack, John. "The Chicanos—A Special Supplement", *The New York Review,* August 31, 1972.

Public Documents

Amber, Arthur. *The Work and Welfare of Children of Agricultural Laborers in Hidalgo County, Texas.* U.S. Department of Labor, Washington, D.C.: U.S. Government Printing Office, 1943.

President's Commission on Migratory Labor. *Migratory Labor in American Agriculture.* Washington, D.C.: U.S. Government Printing Office, 1951.

President's Commission on Migratory Labor. *Second Report to the President on Domestic Migratory Labor.* Washington, D.C.: U.S. Government Printing Office, 1958.

U.S. Bureau of the Census. *United States Census, 1950: Spanish-Surnamed Population.*

U.S. Bureau of the Census. *United States Census, 1960: Spanish-Surnamed Population.*

U.S. Congress. House. Committee on Agriculture. *Hearings Before the Subcommittee on Equipment, Supplies, and Manpower of the Committee on Agriculture on H.R. 9869, H.R. 9871, H.R.9875, H.R. 10093, H.R.1061, H.R. 11211, H.R. 11225, H.R. 11239, H.R. 11291, H.R. 11296, H.R. 11312, H.R. 11313, H.R. 11367, H.R. 11372, H.R. 11429, and H.R. 1153.* 86th Congress, 2nd Session, March 22-25, 31, 1960.

U.S. Congress. House. Committee on Education and Labor. *Hearings Before the Subcommittee on Education and Labor on Various Bills Regarding Minimum Wage Legislation.* Part I. 82nd Congress, 2nd Session, March 16, 17, 23, 24, 29, 30, 31, April 7, 11, 13,

1960.

U.S. Congress. House. Committee on Education and Labor. *Hearings Before the Sub-committee on Education and Labor on Various Bills Regarding Minimum Wage.* Part 2, 86th Congress, 2nd Session, April 19-21, 26-27, May 3 and 5, 1960.

U.S. Congress. House. On Education and Labor. *Hearings Before the Subcommittee on Labor Standards of the Committee on Education and Labor on Various Bills Regarding Minimum Wage Legislation.* Part 3, 86th Congress, 2nd Session, May 10, 11, 17, 18, 19, 1960.

U.S. Congress. House. Committee on Education and Labor. *Hearings Before the Sub-committee on General Education of the Committee on Education and Labor on H.R. 9872 and H.R 10378.* 86th Congress, 2nd Session, May 2, 3, 5, 13, 1960.

U.S. Congress. House. Committee on Interstate and Foreign Commerce. *Hearings Before the Subcommittee of the Committee on Interstate and Foreign Commerce on H.R. 9836 and S. 3391.* 84th Congress, 2nd Session, May 18, 1956.

U.S. Congress. Senate. Committee on Appropriations. *Hearings on H.J. Res. 461.* 83rd Congress, 2nd Session, 1954.

U.S. Congress. Senate. Committee on the Judiciary. *Hearings Before the Subcommittee on Immigration and Naturalization of the Committee on the Judiciary on S. 3660 and S. 3661.* 3rd Congress, 2nd Session, July 12-14, 1954.

U.S. Congress. Senate. Committee on Labor and Public Welfare. *Hearings Before the Subcommittee on Migratory Labor on S. 1085, S. 1778, S. 2141, and S. 2498, Bills Relating to Migratory Labor.* 86th Congress, 1st Session, August 7, 26, Sept. 28, 30, October 1, November 30, December 7-8, 1959.

U.S. Congress. Senate. Committee on Labor and Public Welfare. *Hearings Before the Subcommittee on Migratory Labor on Bills Relating to Various Migratory Labor Pro-grams.* 88th Congress, 1st Session, April 10, 23, 24, 1963.

U.S. Department of Labor. *Annual Report of the Immigration and Naturalization Service.* Washington, D.C.: U.S. Government Printing Office, 1947, 1954.

U.S. Department of Labor. *Information Concerning Entry of Mexican Agricultural Workers to the United States.* Prepared by the Bureau of Employment Security, Farm Placement Office. Washington, D.C.: U.S. Government Printing Office, 1951.

U.S. Department of Labor. *President's Commission on Migratory Labor. Washington, D.C.: U.S. Government Printing Office, 1961.*

Newspapers

Albuquerque Journal

Amarillo Globe

American G.I. Forum News Bulletin

American G.I. Forum - The Forumeer

Arizona Register

Brownsville Herald

Corpus Christi Caller

Corpus Christi Caller-Times

Daily Texan (University of Texas)

Dallas Morning News

Denver Star

El Paso Times

El Sol (Houston, Texas)

Fort Worth Telegram

Galveston News

Harlingen Monitor

Houston Post

Las Noticias (Del Rio, Texas)

La Verdad (Del Rio, Texas)

Los Angeles Times

New York Times

Rocky Mountain News (Denver)

San Antonio Evening News

San Antonio Express

St. Louis Dispatch

The Sentinel (Corpus Christi)

The Texas Observer (Austin)

Valley Evening Monitor (McAllen, Texas)

Washington Post

Manuscript Collections

Files of the American G.I. Forum. Office of Dr. Hector Garcia, Corpus Christi, Texas.

Beauford Jester File. Texas State Archives.

Interviews

Dr. Hector Garcia

Vicente Ximenes

Rosa Ena Gutierrez

Emma

Bennie Saavedra

Josephine Saavedra

Ignacio Moreno

Leodoro Hernandez